a seaman's guide to the RULE OF THE ROAD

a seaman's guide to the RULE OF THE ROAD

A programmed text on the International Regulations for Preventing Collisions at Sea, 1972

NAVAL INSTITUTE PRESS
Annapolis, Maryland 21402

New Edition, 2nd Impression 1976

Published and distributed in the United States of America by the Naval Institute Press, Annapolis, Maryland 21402. Library of Congress Catalog Card No. 75–6241. ISBN 0–87021–873–5.

This edition was prepared by J. W. W. Ford, M.B.E., in the Training Services Division of ESL BRISTOL and was illustrated in the Art Department of the Company.

The Publishers wish to acknowledge permission given by the Inter-Governmental Maritime Consultative Organization for the reproduction of the 'International Regulations for Preventing Collisions at Sea, 1972' as published by that body in 1973.

The Publishers also acknowledge permission given by Her Majesty's Stationery Office for the reproduction of the Rules from their typesetting in White Paper Shipping, Miscellaneous No. 28 (1973).

Printed in Great Britain by
St Stephen's Bristol Press Ltd.

Foreword by Admiral Sir Edward Ashmore GCB DSC
Chief of Naval Staff and First Sea Lord

The importance of safety at sea has never been greater, and each year that passes increases the need for everyone in charge of a vessel to be able to apply the Seaman's 'Rule of the Road' quickly and correctly in order to navigate safely in the busy waters of our world.

This second edition of 'A Seaman's Guide to the Rule of the Road' is based on the 'International Regulations for Preventing Collisions at Sea, 1972' and, like the first edition, is a programmed learning text.

Only experience can give the seaman the confidence to apply these rules quickly and accurately in all situations but before taking charge of a vessel he must know their substance and meaning. The first edition has proved extremely effective in achieving this latter objective and I am sure this edition will be no less successful.

I commend this book to all who go about their business in ships and to those who spend their leisure time 'messing about in boats'.

ADMIRAL

Preface

This programmed book has been written and validated with the full support and co-operation of the Royal Navy.

Aim of the book

This book is designed to teach Royal Navy and Merchant Navy personnel sufficient theoretical knowledge of the Regulations for Preventing Collisions at Sea to meet the needs of the Officer of the Watch.

Use of the book

Because programmed learning is an extremely concentrated way of absorbing information, we recommend that this text is only studied for periods of about one and a half hours at a time and for a total time of not more than three or four hours in a day.

In order to understand the Rules, it is necessary to see them in the context of sea experience. If the student does not have this experience, then we recommend that an experienced officer should discuss the Rules with him, particularly those of a general nature such as Rules 2, 5, 6 and 8 and Annex IV to the Regulations. This, in our view, would be an essential part of any course on the Rule of the Road.

Previous knowledge assumed

A general knowledge of sea-terms is assumed. A familiarity with the concepts of alteration of course and speed, relative course, true course, relative bearing, true bearing and bearing movements is necessary for the understanding of the programme.

An outline knowledge of the specific functions mentioned in the Rules, such as the duties of a pilot vessel, operating aircraft, cable laying, etc., is also necessary.

Preface (continued)

Conventions of the text

Some special conventions have been used in the illustrations and text of this programme.

In order to make the inclination of the ship and the lights and shapes that she carries readily distinguishable, the drawings are not to scale.

The programme is written so that everything is seen, or heard, from the point of view of the Officer of the Watch of a power-driven vessel or, in Chapter 6, of the helmsman of a sailing vessel.

Except in Chapter 6, all situations are depicted as seen from the bridge of a power-driven vessel. Where the student is supposed to be looking forward, a jackstaff, or small foremast, is used to indicate the direction of his own ship's head. Where the student is supposed to be looking in some other direction, no jackstaff is shown.

Preface (continued)

Acknowledgments

We would like to acknowledge the detailed and constructive help given at all stages in the writing of the programme by Lieutenant Commander P. S. Booth, Royal Navy, and Lieutenant C. Napier, Royal Navy, of H.M.S. Dryad, and Lieutenant J. K. F. Smith, Royal Navy, of the Royal Naval School of Educational and Training Technology.

Our thanks are also due to the Captain, Britannia Royal Naval College, Dartmouth, for making young officers under training available for validation; to Lieutenant Commander E. K. Somerville-Jones, Royal Navy, for his help and co-operation and to the Departments of the Ministry of Defence (Navy) and particularly Commander R. T. King, Royal Navy, who have given their advice and assistance throughout.

Contents

Contents (continued)

Contents (continued)

Contents (continued)

Contents (continued)

Validation

This ESL programme has been tested on four classes of young officers undergoing pre-sea training for the Royal Navy.

Following the test, the results were analyzed and any necessary modifications were made. The **average score** in the post-programme test was 89·1%.

The classes were made up of 68 students with an average age of 21 years. The academic background of the group ranged from 5 'O' level passes to 1–3 'A' level passes per student.

The average study time of the students was approximately 6½ hours.

Further details of the validation results for this programme may be obtained from the Publishers on request.

Notes to the student

This is a programmed book. This means that on each page, the information given is followed by a question and you should answer this question before looking at the next page. You are recommended to write down your answer to each question as some of the questions require fairly complicated answers.

When you have answered the question on any one page you will be able to check it by looking at the correct answer which you will find at the top of the following page. When reading each left-hand page you may find it convenient to cover, with your hand or a piece of paper, the answer which is given on the right-hand page.

Each chapter begins with an introductory page which tells you which Rules are covered by that chapter. In order to become familiar with the language and layout of the Rules, you should turn to the tinted pages at the end of the book and read the appropriate Rules whenever you are instructed to do so.

At the end of every chapter there is a test covering the material taught in that chapter. You are recommended to work through the tests when you come to them, writing down your answer to each question. The correct answers are given immediately after each test, together with page-references for any questions you may have answered wrongly. Thus you can check your own progress immediately after every chapter and then revise any points which you may not have learnt thoroughly the first time

CHAPTER 1. PRELIMINARY AND DEFINITIONS

At the beginning of each chapter and occasionally during the programme, you will be asked to read the relevant part of the International Regulations for Preventing Collisions at Sea, 1972. For the sake of brevity, the programme will refer to these Regulations as the Rules.

Refer to the Rules only when you are specifically asked to do so or when you feel you really need to do so.

Now turn to the Rules and read **once** through Rule 1 (a), (b), (c) and (e).

If the Rule of the Road is to be effective in preventing collisions at sea, it must be made quite clear where these Rules apply and who is bound to follow them. Rule 1 (a), (b) and (c) is designed to make this point clear. In simplified terms it states that:

if you are in charge of any vessel capable of being used for transport on water,

and

if that vessel is on the high seas, or any navigable waters connected with the high seas,

then you **must obey the Rules** except where they are modified by any **Special Rules** made by the Government of any state.

Suppose you were in charge of a motor launch in the tidal waters of the River Thames and you encountered another manned boat. Should you obey the Rules?

Yes. You would be using a vessel for transport on navigable waters connected with the high seas.

Governments are allowed to make modifications to the Rules with respect to:

additional station or signal lights or whistle signals for warships and vessels proceeding under convoy,

and

station or signal lights for vessels engaged in fishing as a fleet.

If you are in charge of any vessel capable of being used for transport on water,

and

if that vessel is on the high seas, or any navigable waters connected with the high seas,

then you must **obey the Rules** except where they are modified by __________ __________ made by Governments.

Special Rules may also be made by Governments of states to cover roadsteads, harbours, rivers, lakes or inland waterways. If you take a vessel on to any of these, you may be on waterways where Governments have imposed Special Rules.

On the high seas and in many estuaries, however, there are no Special Rules so

if you are in charge of any vessel capable of being used for transport on water, and if that vessel is on the high seas, or any navigable waters connected with the high seas,	then you must _____ ____ ________ except where they are modified by Special Rules made by Governments.

Rule 3 (a), (b), (c) and (e) defines the term 'vessel' and the various types of vessel to which the Rules are applicable.

The word 'vessel' includes every description of water craft, including non-displacement craft and seaplanes.

A 'seaplane' includes any aircraft designed to manoeuvre upon water.
Which of the two illustrations represents a vessel for the purpose of the Rules?

Both. In addition to the many different types of conventional vessel, the Rules cover both the craf illustrated.

In Rule 3 (b) there is a definition of a power-driven vessel. In simple terms, the definition is a follows:

> Any vessel propelled by machinery is a power-driven vessel.

If you see an outboard motor dinghy being rowed along, because its motor has broken down, is it a power-driven vessel?

No, because it is not being propelled by machinery.

What sort of Rules the dinghy must follow will depend upon where it is. This is true of any vessel.

<table><tr><td>If you are in charge of any vessel capable of being used for transport on water,

and

if that vessel is on the high seas, or any navigable waters connected with the high seas,</td><td>}</td><td>what Rules must you obey and how might they be modified?</td></tr></table>

The Rules apply to all vessels and nowadays most vessels are power-driven.

However, some vessels are propelled by sails.

An interesting question arises if you see a sailing vessel using sails and an auxiliary engine at the same time.

The only way you can know this is by sighting the black cone, hoisted apex-downwards, in her rigging as required by Rule 25 (e).

The problem is to decide how such a vessel should be classified.

In Rule 3 there is a special paragraph about it but commonsense will tell you if you remember that:

any vessel propelled by machinery is a ______ ________ vessel.

power-driven

A sailing vessel is a vessel propelled by sails and only by sails.

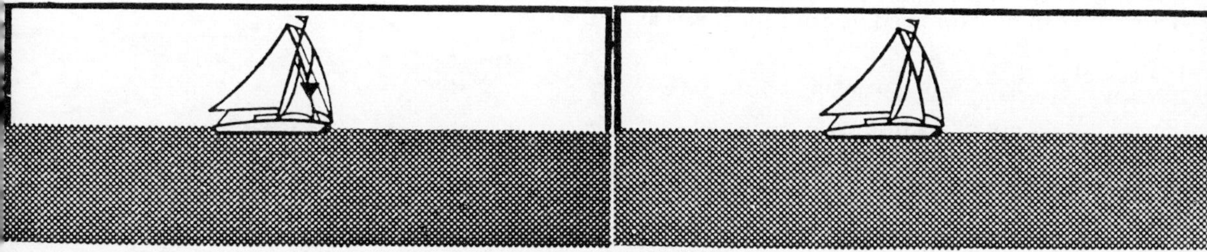

(a) (b)

Which of these two vessels is a sailing vessel?

(b) is the sailing vessel. The inverted cone in (a) indicates that the vessel is power-driven because it has machinery which is in use.

In the Rules, and in this programme, you will frequently come across the term 'under way'. The meaning of the term is not as obvious as it might seem and it is specifically defined in Rule 3 (i). The definition can be expressed, for our purposes as follows:

If a vessel is

not at anchor,
not made fast to the shore, and
not aground,

she is under way.

In order to avoid a collision, especially in fog, you may sometimes have to stop all movement through the water so that your vessel is only drifting.

Is she then under way?

Yes, since she is not at anchor nor made fast nor aground.

It is important to distinguish between the terms ‘making way’ and ‘under way’. Your vessel may be making way (moving) ahead, she may be stopped, or she may be making way astern.

But in all cases, if a vessel is

not at anchor,
not made fast to the shore, and
not aground,

she is __________ .

Note that a vessel need not be moving to be under way.

A vessel might find herself in any of these situations.

(a) Moving ahead through the water.
(b) Engines stopped, but not made fast in any way.
(c) Moving astern through the water.
(d) Riding to a sea anchor.

In which of these situations is the vessel regarded as being under way?

All of them. (She is not at anchor nor made fast nor aground.)

The Rules are designed to ensure the constant application of safe practices in **all conditions.**

The safe practices are based upon the requirement of Rule 6 which, briefly stated, is:

> that every vessel shall **at all times** proceed at a **safe speed** for the **prevailing circumstances and conditions.**

Observance of this Rule will allow the maximum possible________for effective action to be taken to avoid a________.

Observance of this Rule will allow the maximum possible **time** for effective action to be taken to avoid a **collision.**

Throughout this book there are references to safe practices and good seamanship in given situations, but since it is impossible to deal with every circumstance in detail, you should know the factors which must be taken into account **at all times.**

A **proper look-out** by sight and hearing is essential.

You should use all the means available to you e.g., operational radar, to detect the number, location and movement of vessels and other objects in your vicinity.

The efficient use of both look-out and other resources is necessary to **determine** the **prevailing circumstances** and **conditions** in order to establish what a ______ ________ should be. This will allow the **maximum possible time** for **effective action** to be taken to avoid a collision.

A later section of this book refers to 'safe speed' in conditions of restricted visibility but, in fact, there are many situations in which there is a risk of collision even though the visibility is good.

Every vessel shall **at all times** proceed at a **safe speed** for the __________ __________ and __________. This will allow the **maximum possible time** for **effective action** to be taken to avoid a collision.

Every vessel shall at all times proceed at a safe speed for the **prevailing circumstances** and **conditions.**

Rule 6 lists numbers of factors which must be taken into account when determining safe speed. As you read through this book you will recognise where the Rules are being applied in specific situations but:

> every vessel shall __ ___ _____ proceed at a **safe speed** for the **prevailing circumstances and conditions.** This will allow the **maximum possible time** for **effective action** to be taken to avoid a collision.

Every vessel shall **at all times** proceed at a safe speed for the prevailing circumstances and conditions.

The ability to assess safe speed will come with experience and is a matter for individual judgement but a safe speed can only be a speed slow enough to allow the maximum possible ____ for effective action to be taken to ______ ___________ .

time avoid a collision

Now read Rule 7 (d).

Imagine yourself on the bridge of a fair-sized power-driven vessel, under way and moving ahead. You sight another vessel somewhere forward of your beam and several miles away. She may be steaming into your path, or drifting into it, or you may be passing clear of each other.

The only way you can decide whether there is a risk of collision is to take several **compass bearings** of the other vessel at short intervals (usually not more than three minutes).

If the compass bearing of the other ship is steady, or nearly steady, and the range is decreasing, there is a risk of collision.

In your opinion, how small can you allow a change of bearing to be before you must call it nearly steady?

it depends upon how far away the other ship is and on the relative courses and speeds of the two vessels.

Only your own judgement, based on experience at sea, can tell you how much margin to allow. (When taking compass bearings, always aim the azimuth mirror at the part of the vessel which will pass closest to you.)

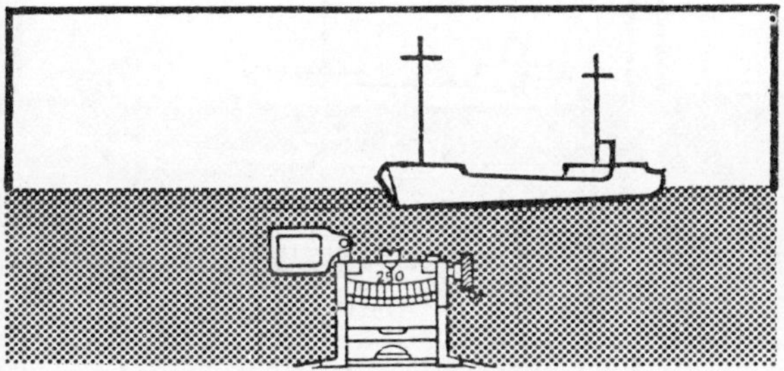

Bearing 250° at 0920

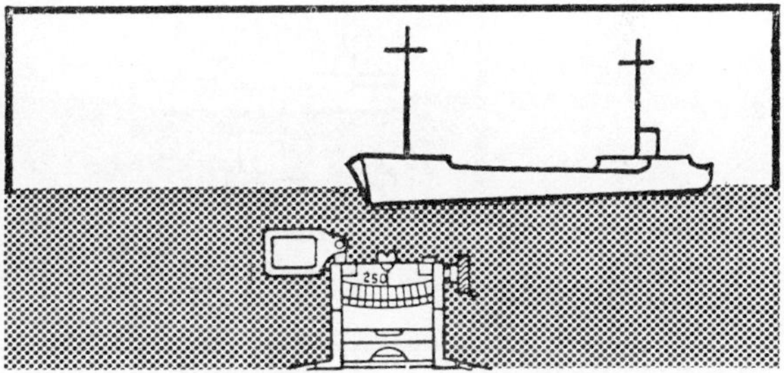

Bearing 252° at 0926

If the compass bearing of the other ship is steady, or nearly steady, and the range is decreasing, there is a ______________________ .

If the compass bearing of the other ship is steady, or nearly steady, and the range is decreasing, there is a **risk of collision.**

Which of these two cases involves a risk of collision between your vessel and the ship you have sighted?

Case A

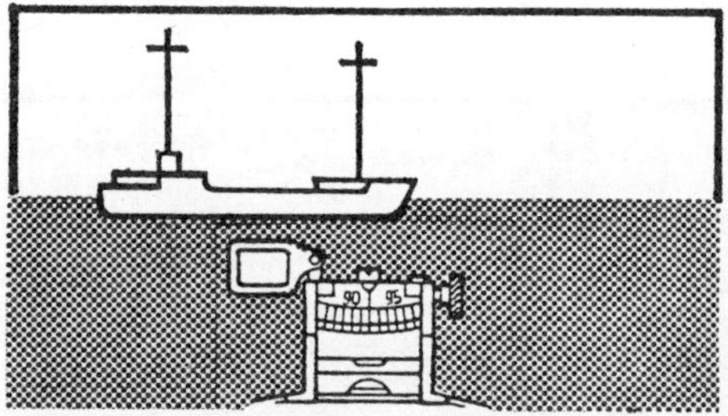

092° at 1142

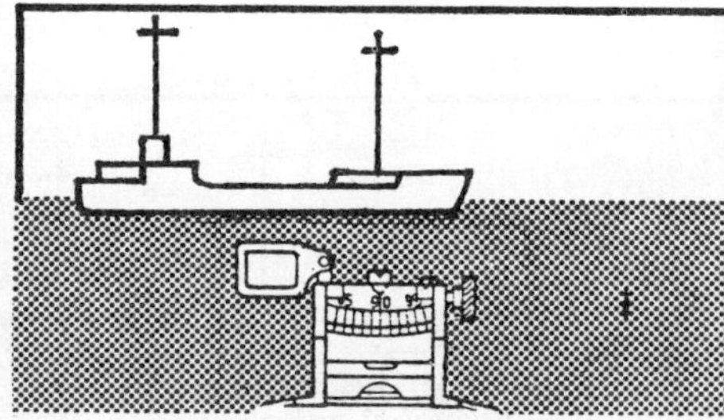

090° at 1147

Case B

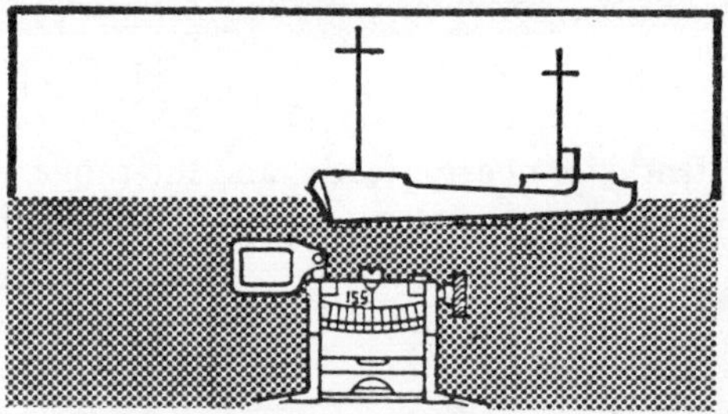

157° at 1429

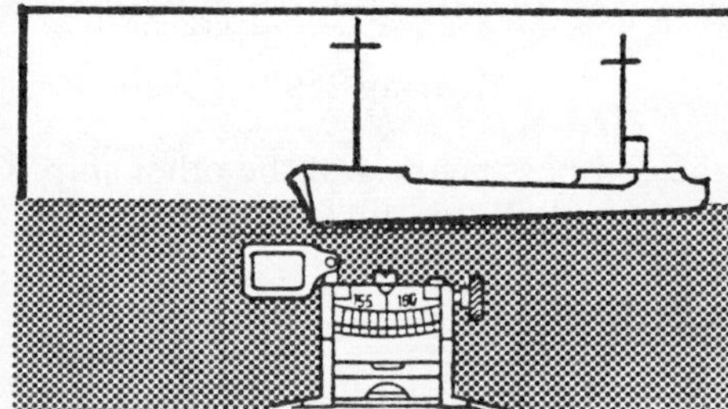

158° at 1434

Both. (Because there are changes of bearing of 2° and 1° which must be regarded as nearly steady. Thus, a risk of collision is involved.)

Test on Chapter 1

1. If a vessel is propelled by machinery, what is it called in the Rules?

2. Which of these statements is true?

   (a) The Rules apply only to vessels on the high seas and tidal waters and they take precedence over any Special Rules made by Governments.
   (b) The Rules apply on all waters navigable by seagoing vessels and connected with the high seas, but they may be modified by Special Rules made by Governments.
   (c) The Rules do not apply to harbours, rivers, lakes or inland waters because these are governed by Special Rules.

3. If a vessel is not at anchor, not made fast to the shore and not aground, how is she described in the Rules?

4. What is a safe speed?

5. If you sight any vessel and the compass bearing remains steady while the range decreases, what does this signify?

Answers to Test

Your answers were in your own words, but you should have included the words in bold type below. If you have given wrong answers, work through the relevant section or sections again.

	Reference
1. A **power-driven vessel.**	pages 6–10
2. (b)	3–4
3. As a **vessel under way.**	10–12
4. A speed which will **allow time** for **effective action** to be taken to **avoid a collision.**	13–17
5. That a **risk of collision** exists.	18–20

CHAPTER 2. THE STEERING RULES. SOUND SIGNALS AND CONDUCT OF VESSELS IN SIGHT OF ONE ANOTHER

Read **once** through Rules 11, 13, 14, 15, 16, 17, 32 and 34.

At this stage of the programme you are asked to imagine yourself as the Officer of the Watch on board a power-driven vessel so you are not yet concerned with encounters between two sailing vessels (Rules 12 & 18).

You are concerned here with the Rules which apply to **vessels in sight of one another.** This means that they apply only when one vessel can be seen by eye from the other.

If you cannot see the other vessel by eye, you are not bound to obey the above Rules.

Of course, this does not relieve you of responsibility if you fail to keep a proper visual look-out, even if you have efficient radar.

These Rules do not apply to vessels in thick fog, nor in any other conditions where it is **impossible** to see the other vessel by eye.

If you cannot see the other vessel by eye, you are __________ to obey the Rules in this chapter.

not bound

In which of these situations are you bound by the Rules which apply to vessels in sight of one another?

(a) Whenever you detect another vessel by radar only.
(b) Whenever you see another vessel by eye.
(c) In fog, when you hear another vessel.

(b) Whenever you see another vessel by eye.

In order to avoid confusion when vessels within sight of one another are manoeuvring, Rule 34 lays down signals which each power-driven vessel **must** give to show her intentions. The signals **must** be given on the ship's whistle and the ship is also allowed to flash a white manoeuvring light in time with the signals. The white light must show all round the horizon and be visible at a minimum range of 5 miles.

The signals are given as one or more **short blasts,** which must last about **1 second** (Rule 32). In this book they are represented by Morse signs.

If you hear these signals definitely coming from a power-driven vessel:

1 short blast of about 1 second (·), the vessel is altering course to **starboard.**
2 short blasts, each about 1 second (··), the vessel is altering course to **port.**
3 short blasts, each about 1 second (···), the vessel is operating **astern propulsion.**

Learn these signals by heart.

You really need to learn these sound signals thoroughly and you must know them from two points of view.

Firstly, if you are **within sight** of another vessel and you:

alter course to **starboard,** sound __ short blast(s).
alter course to **port,** sound __ short blast(s).
operate **astern** propulsion, sound __ short blast(s).

1
2
3

Secondly, you may hear signals from another vessel. In a crowded seaway it could be difficult to tell which vessel is giving them, but you may get a clue from puffs of steam in day-time, or flashing lights at night.

Fit to their correct sound signals the words: port; astern; starboard.

1 short blast (·) means__________.
2 short blasts (··) means_____.
3 short blasts (···) means______.

starboard
port
astern

Just to make sure you know them give the Morse symbols for the sound signals you must make if you are undertaking these manoeuvres **within sight** of another vessel.

If you are altering course to **starboard,** sound (   ).
If you are altering course to **port,** sound (   ).
If you are operating **astern** propulsion, sound (   ).

Finally, how long is a short blast by the definition in the Rules?

Starboard = (·). Port = (··). Astern = (···). About one second.

The manoeuvres of power-driven vessels in sight of one another are governed by Section II of the Rules. You cannot learn all of them at once but it will be convenient to start with Rule 14.

Rule 14 decides the actions of two vessels which meet head-on, or nearly head-on. The Rule can be summarized as follows:

If you sight another power-driven vessel on a **steady bearing, ahead** of your vessel, and head-on or nearly head-on.	alter course to **starboard.**

Learn this by heart before answering the question.

What should the other vessel do? (Imagine yourself on her bridge for a moment.)

She also should alter course to starboard.

Remember the key points:

power-driven vessel
a **steady bearing**
ahead } (or nearly so)
head-on

In this illustration, and elsewhere when appropriate, a simplified foremast has been used to indicate the heading of your vessel.

You have sighted this ship on a bearing of 085°, and it has not changed in the last five minutes.

Notice that her masts are in line with your own foremast:

(a) are you obliged to alter course?
(b) if so, which way should you turn?
(c) what sound signal should you give? (Write in Morse if you wish.)

(a) Yes. (b) To starboard. (c) One short blast (·).

That was a head-on situation. **Crossing** situations are covered by Rules 15, 16 and 17.

If you sight another **power-driven vessel,** with a risk of collision:

(i) **crossing** your course from your **starboard** side.	**give way** (alter course and/or speed) so as to **avoid crossing ahead** of her.
(ii) **crossing** your course from your **port** side	**stand on** (keep your course and speed) while continuing to take bearings of the other vessel.

Learn these by heart before answering the questions below.

This tug is 3 miles away, 45° on your starboard bow, on a steady compass bearing and your speed is about 12 knots.

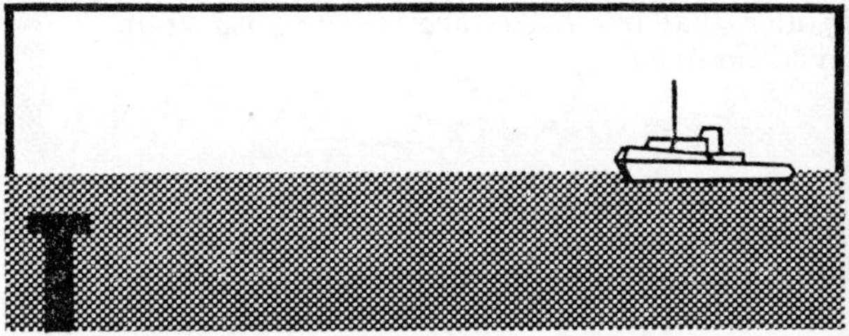

(a) Should you stand on?
(b) Should you alter course? If so, which way?
(c) Should you alter speed?
(d) If a whistle signal is needed, what is the correct Morse symbol?

(a) No.
(b) You could alter course to starboard

or

(c) You could alter course to starboard and reduce speed.
Alternatively, to avoid crossing ahead of the other vessel you could markedly reduce speed without altering course although this action would not be as obvious to the other vessel as an alteration of course to starboard.
(d) If altering course to starboard, 1 short blast (·   ).

Compare these three illustrations.

Bearings: 160°; 160°; 160°. Ahead of your vessel. Present range: 3 miles.

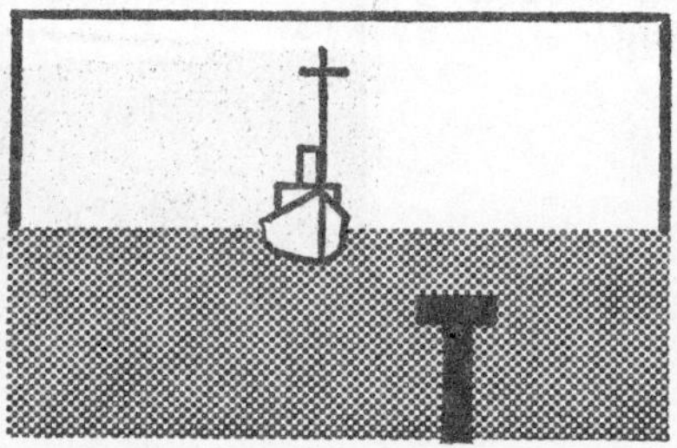

Bearings: 020°; 020·5°; 021°. Fine on your port bow. Present range: 3 miles.

Bearings: 100°; 099·5°; 099°. Fine on your starboard bow. Present range: 3 miles.

Which ones show head-on, or nearly head-on, situations involving a risk of collision?
What action should you take, including any whistle signals required?

All three.
Sound one short blast (·) and alter course to starboard.

If there is a risk of collision with a vessel on your **starboard** side, you should give way.

What must you do if a power-driven vessel is on your **port** side, on a steady bearing?

Stand-on (keep your course and speed), but continue to take bearings of the other vessel.

Before you answer the question at the bottom of the page, take note of these two points.

(i) If possible you must avoid crossing ahead of the vessel in this illustration.
(ii) If you reduce speed without altering course, your action may not be easily apparent to another vessel.

What should you do if a vessel is 30° on your **starboard** bow, on a steady bearing?

Sound one short blast (·   ) and alter course to starboard.

This ship is 45°on your port bow.

She was about 5 miles away when you first sighted her.

You found her last three bearings were 275°, 275·5° and 276°.

What action must you take?

Stand-on (keep your course and speed), but continue to take bearings of the other vessel.

Consider these two entirely separate situations.
(Your own foremast is not shown, so you are not looking right ahead.)

On your port beam, on a steady bearing.

60° on your starboard bow, on a steady bearing.

What would be the correct action in **each case,** including any necessary signals on your ship's whistle?

(A) Stand-on but continue to take bearings.

(B) Sound one short blast (·) and alter course to starboard.

You may be getting the impression that, if you are to give way, you should alter course to starboard, but this is not always the case.

Suppose another ship has emerged from behind a headland on your starboard bow, and her bearing appears to be steady.

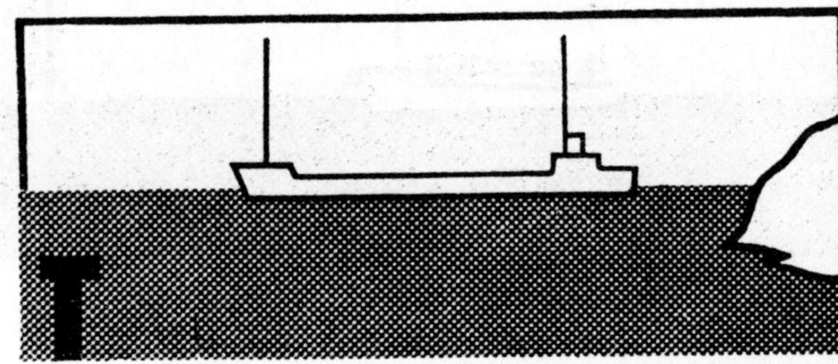

Rule 16 says:

> 'Every vessel which is directed to keep out of the way of another vessel shall, so far as possible, take early and substantial action to keep well clear.'

Your speed is about 8 knots. Should you:

(a) Stand-on?
(b) Make a bold alteration to port?
(c) Make a bold alteration to starboard?
(d) Make a marked reduction in speed, or stop?

What whistle signal should you give, if any?

(d) Make a marked reduction in speed, or stop. (If you operate astern propulsion, sound 3 short blasts (· · ·). Or you might consider (b), Make a bold alteration to port, sounding 2 short blasts (· ·), but remember if you do this you must, if possible, avoid crossing ahead of the other ship (see Rule 15).

Rule 15 says:

> 'When two power-driven vessels are crossing so as to involve risk of collision, the vessel which has the other one on her starboard side shall keep out of the way and shall, if the circumstances of the case admit, avoid crossing ahead of the other vessel.'

So Rules 8 (a), 15 and 16 between them say that your action should be **positive, early, substantial** and **avoid crossing ahead** of the other vessel.

You will have to decide what 'positive', 'early', and 'substantial' mean in each individual case. A good 'rule of thumb' is never to make an initial alteration of course of less than 30°; and if you reduce speed, reduce it to about half your present speed.

What **early action** means will depend, of course, upon the types of vessels involved and the speeds at which they are going but, generally, you should take action as soon as you have determined that you are the give-way vessel.

In any event, if you have to take avoiding action:

it must be **positive** enough and **early** enough to be ______ of avoiding a collision.

certain.

When deciding whether you should alter course or speed, bear in mind that an alteration of course of 30° or more would be easy to see but a reduction of speed would not. Remember, however, that Rule 8 (e) states that if it is necessary, a vessel (in this case the give-way vessel) shall reduce speed, or stop, or operate astern propulsion.

Operating astern propulsion will reduce your speed more quickly and, of course, you must give a sound signal on the ship's whistle.

If you are the give-way vessel, your alteration of course or speed must be **positive** enough and **early** enough to be **certain** of preventing a __________ .

What whistle signal must you give when you operate astern propulsion?

collision 3 short blasts (···)

A large tanker proceeding at her normal passage speed, would probably need a distance of about 2 miles and a time of, perhaps, 15 minutes, to complete a **crash stop.** The same vessel, at the same speed, could carry out a 90° **turn** in 3 minutes and would probably need a distance of only ½ mile in which to make the turn.

Suppose you are the Officer of the Watch of such a ship steaming at full speed. You sight another tanker broad on your starboard bow, approaching you at a fast speed. The compass bearing is steady. You decide (wisely) to take action at a range of 5 miles. If you operate full astern propulsion, the range may be only 1 mile when you stop. If, however, you alter course 60° to starboard, the range will still be about 4 miles by the time you steady on the new course.

Whatever giving-way action you take:

it must be **positive** enough and **early** enough to be **certain** of________ a________.

An alteration of course to starboard would be signalled by________________.

preventing (avoiding) a collision
1 short blast (·)

You have, so far, learned three sound signals.

Rule 34 (d) defines another sound signal, sometimes called the 'Wake-up!' signal:

> 'When vessels in sight of one another are approaching each other and from any cause either vessel fails to understand the intentions or actions of the other, or is in doubt whether sufficient action is being taken by the other to avoid collision, the vessel in doubt shall immediately indicate such doubt by giving at least five short and rapid blasts on the whistle. Such signals may be supplemented by a light signal of at least five short and rapid flashes.'

In Morse, the 'Wake-up!' signal is ________ ( ).

at least (· · · · ·).

Suppose you are in a situation where you should stand-on.

The other vessel is 30° on your port bow, at a range of 3 miles, on a steady bearing. She does not appear to be taking any action to keep out of your way.

What should you do?

(a) Sound at least 5 short blasts and stand-on with caution.
Or (b) Sound at least 5 short blasts and take action to avoid the other vessel.

(a) Sound at least five short blasts and stand-on with caution. (Your duty to stand-on is as binding as the other vessel's duty to give-way in this situation.)

Of course, the situation could be reversed.

This ship is closing fine on your starboard bow.

Suppose that you allow an urgent problem to distract your attention, or that you have been a little careless in taking compass bearings.

You hear seven short blasts (·······) from the other ship.

What do they mean?

'Wake-up!' I do not think you are taking sufficient action to avoid a collision.' (Or words to that effect.)

What is the signal you should use (if you are the standing-on vessel) to indicate doubt about the giving-way vessel's action?

At least 5 short and rapid blasts on the whistle. (At least · · · · ·).

This tanker is 2 miles away, 45° on your starboard bow. In this situation you are the **give-way** vessel.

The bearing has been changing slowly. It has been drawing slowly aft, so you may assume that the tanker will just pass astern of your vessel if you keep your course.

You hear the tanker sound (· · · · ·).

What action should you take? What whistle signal should you make?

Alter course to starboard. Give one short blast (·   ).
(You were about to cross close ahead of the tanker.)

Read Rule 17.

Summarized, it says, in respect of power-driven vessels, that if a collision cannot be avoided by the action of the give-way vessel alone or the give-way vessel has failed to act in accordance with the Rules, then the stand-on vessel should act as necessary to avoid a collision.

Rule 2 states, in effect, that you may have a duty to depart from the Rules if it is the only way to avoid a collision. It warns that you should take every precaution, including any required by the special circumstances of the case.

So, if you are the standing-on vessel, and you are so close that collision cannot be avoided by the action of the giving-way vessel alone. } act as ________ to ________ collision.

necessary avoid

Just what action you should take to get out of immediate danger is difficult to predict. Generally speaking, **it is not wise to turn to port,** because the give-way vessel might turn to starboard at the last moment.

Any action that you take should, obviously, be designed to **avoid** collision but if collision appears to be inevitable, then try to reduce the impact. Operating astern propulsion to reduce the speed as much as possible, will usually soften the blow. But even this depends upon the circumstances of the case.

The only definite statement that can be made is the one we made on the last page.

If you are the standing-on vessel, and you are so close that collision cannot be avoided by the action of the giving-way vessel alone,	act as ________ to ______ a ________.

necessary avoid collision

Suppose that you are the Officer of the Watch on board a large tanker, proceeding at her top speed. At this speed it might take 2 miles to lose all way in a crash stop.

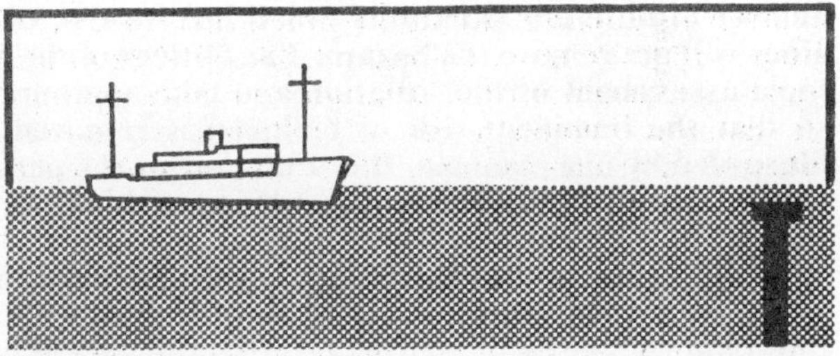

You sight a smaller vessel 50° on your port bow, at a distance of 2 miles. The bearing is steady, but the other vessel does not appear to be giving way.

You sound 5 short blasts and stand-on with caution. Though the other vessel appears to reduce speed a little, the bearing only draws aft about 1°.

Eventually, you are less than 1½ miles apart.

The other vessel might turn to starboard at the last minute.

What should you do now?

Sound (·   ) and alter course to starboard.

This action would be in compliance with Rule 17 (a) (ii) and (c).

Rule 17 (b) should be studied very carefully. Whilst the example just given covers a simple crossing situation in which the give-way vessel is failing to comply with the Rules, **Rule 17 (b) envisages any number of different situations which involve risk of collision where the action of the give-way vessel alone will not remove the hazard. The Officer of the Watch of the stand-on vessel is required to make a rapid assessment of the situation and take appropriate avoiding action at precisely the right moment so that the imminent risk of collision is removed. This is something which cannot be adequately illustrated by one example. It is a matter for the personal judgement of the Officer of the Watch. That judgement will be based upon knowledge of this Rule and experience.**

Whether acting under Rule 17 (a) (ii) where the stand-on vessel may take avoiding action under Rule 17 (b) where the stand-on vessel **shall** take appropriate avoiding action, the Officer of the Watch of the stand-on vessel, in a crossing situation, **should not, when the circumstances admit,** alter course ——— for a vessel on his own portside.

to port

If you were to alter course to port, the vessels may collide or, at the very least, you would place the vessels in a dangerous close-quarters situation.

When you do alter course, for how long would you keep a close check on the effectiveness of your action?

Until the other vessel is finally past and clear.

Rule 17 (d) makes it clear that though the stand-on vessel may find it necessary to take some action of her own to avoid a risk of collision, the give-way vessel is in no way relieved of the obligation to keep________________.

Having dealt with head-on and crossing situations, we are now left with the problem of **overtaking.** This is covered by Rule 13, which can be stated briefly as follows:

While you are in charge of **any vessel** (whether power-driven or not),

if you are (or think you may be) coming up with **any other vessel,** from **any direction** more than 22·5° (2 points) abaft her beam, } **keep out of her way,** until finally **past and clear.**

If you are overtaking a vessel which is fine on your port bow, on a similar course, should you keep your course and speed or should you keep out of her way?

You should keep out of her way.

Rule 13 (a) states:

> 'Notwithstanding anything contained in the Rules of this Section, any vessel overtaking any other shall keep out of the way of the vessel being overtaken.'

If you are (or think you may be) coming up with **any other vessel,** from **any direction** more than 22·5° abaft her beam,	keeep out of her way, until finally —— and ——.

Suppose you are coming up with another vessel, as shown in the illustration.

(a) Make your own approximate estimate of the bearing of your ship relative to the other ship's beam.
(b) Having made your estimate, what must you do?

(a) Your estimate may be any angle abaft her beam. (The point is that, if you are in doubt, you should still keep clear.)
(b) **Keep out of her way,** until finally **past** and **clear.**

Rule 13 explains how to decide whether you are overtaking a vessel at night. The details of lights will be dealt with in another chapter. The important detail to remember at the moment is the angle 22·5°.

This may be important to you if you think you are **being overtaken.** Supposing another power-driven vessel is approaching on your **starboard** side, who should keep clear if she is:

(a) on a steady bearing, 11·25° abaft your starboard beam?
(b) on a steady bearing, 45° abaft your starboard beam?

(a) you (b) the other vessel

These illustrations represent two stages in an overtaking situation.

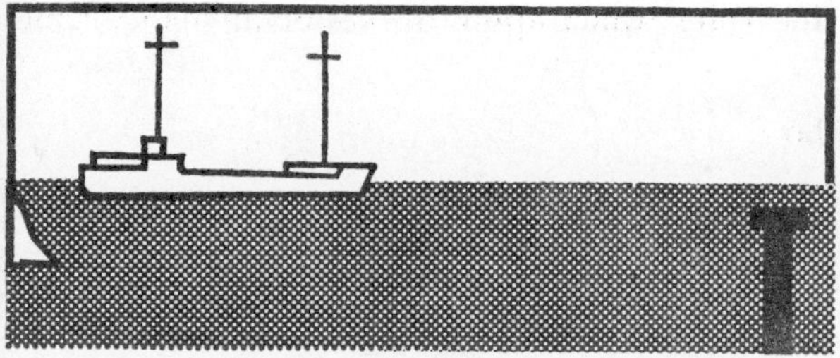

(1) You are gaining rapidly upon another ship on your **port bow,** and her bearing is drawing aft. Your course lies around the headland and you need plenty of sea room.

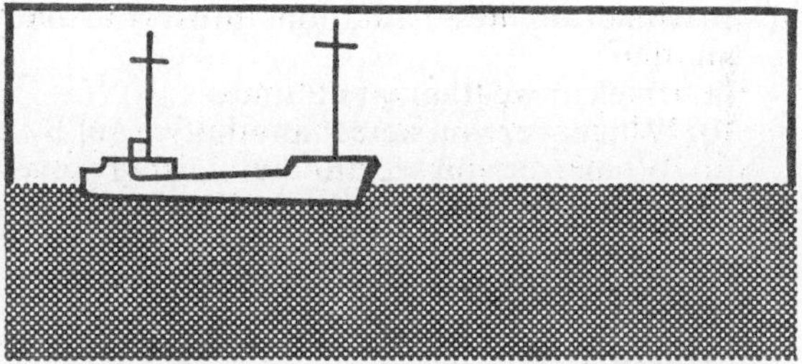

(2) The other ship is now on your **port quarter,** and the headland is well astern. Are you now free to alter course to port?

No. (You must be past and clear of the other vessel first.)

Test on Chapter 2. (Questions marked * are **very important** and must be answered 100% correctly.)

*1. In which of these situations must you obey the Rules which apply to vessels in sight of one another?
   (a) In clear weather, at all times.
   (b) Whenever you detect another vessel by radar.
   (c) Whenever you see another vessel by eye.
   (d) In fog, when you hear another vessel.

*2. If you see another vessel, and she gives any of these signals on her whistle, what does each one signify?
   (a) Three short blasts
   (b) Two short blasts.
   (c) One short blast.
   (d) Five or more short blasts.

*3. If yours is the standing-on vessel, and it appears that the giving-way vessel's action alone will not prevent a collision, what (in general terms) must you do, apart from sounding a warning signal?

*4. What whistle signals should you give to another vessel in sight,
   (a) if you are turning to port?
   (b) if you are operating astern propulsion?

Test (continued)

5. How long should a 'short blast' be?

Bearing has changed ·5° in 5 mins.

6. *(a) What should you do?
   (b) If the other vessel does not appear to be taking sufficient action, how should you indicate your doubt to her?

Bearing steady.

7. *(a) What should you do?
   *(b) What whistle signal should you sound?
   (c) What should the other vessel do?

Test (continued)

8. *(a) Who should give way?
   *(b) What must you avoid doing, if possible?
   (c) What should you do?

Range decreasing, bearing steady.

*9. (a) In general terms, what must you do?
   (b) When does your obligation cease in this situation?

Range decreasing.

Answers to Test

If your answer to any question (or part of a question) marked with an asterisk is wrong, work through the appropriate section again, as indicated.

	Reference
*1 (c) Whenever you see another vessel by eye.	pages 23–25
*2. (a) She is operating **astern propulsion.**	26–30
(b) She is altering course to **port.**	
(c) She is altering course to **starboard.**	
(d) 'Wake-up! I do not think you are taking sufficient action to avoid me.'	42–46
*3. Act as necessary to avoid a collision.	47–48
*4. (a) **Two** short blasts.	26–28
(b) **Three** short blasts.	
5. About **one** second.	26
6. *(a) Keep your course and speed (or stand on) but continue to take bearings.	32–37
(b) By sounding at least **five short and rapid blasts** (or · · · · ·).	42

Answers to Test (continued)

		Reference
7.*(a)	Alter course to **starboard.**	pages 26–30
*(b)	**One** short blast.	
(c)	Alter course to starboard.	
8.*(a)	You should give way.	32–37
*(b)	Avoid **crossing ahead** of the other vessel.	
(c)	Sound **one short** blast (or ·) and alter course to starboard.	
*9. (a)	Keep out of the way,	53–55
(b)	When you are past and clear.	

CHAPTER 3. DAY-TIME RECOGNITION OF VESSELS IN SPECIAL CIRCUMSTANCES

The situations discussed in this chapter are covered by numerous Rules or parts of Rules. The precise sections dealt with are:

Rules: 3 (d), (g), (h); 9 (b), (c); 18; 24 (a); 25 (e); 26; 27 (a) to (f) and (h); 28; 30 (a) and (e).

It may be more convenient for you to copy this list of Rules on a separate piece of paper.

Read **once** through the Rules as listed, paying particular attention to the descriptions of day-time signals.

Rule 18 (a) (iv) can be summed up in the familiar expression, 'steam gives way to sail' although, nowadays, the word 'steam' must be taken to include all power-driven vessels.

Note that Rule 9 (b) does not allow a sailing vessel to impede the passage of a vessel which can safely navigate only within a narrow channel or fairway. Also note that if you are being overtaken by **any** vessel, you have the right of way.

What would you do, in general terms, if you found yourself in the open sea and in the situation shown in the illustration? (You are an Officer of the Watch of a power-driven vessel.)

Keep out of the way of (or, alter course and/or speed to avoid) the sailing vessel, bearing in mind that you should avoid crossing ahead of her.

In keeping clear of a sailing vessel, you should take into account her need for room to manoeuvre according to the direction of the wind. If you pass on her windward side, try to keep well clear so as to avoid taking her wind. If you pass to leeward of a sailing vessel, again allow plenty of room, because of her tendency to make a lot of leeway.

In this situation the wind is blowing from your right.

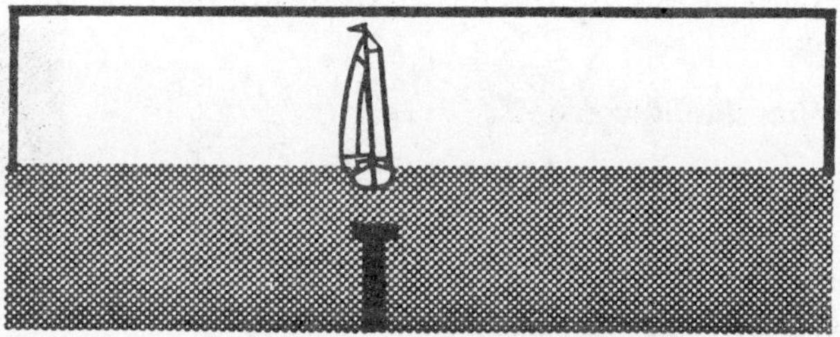

In the situation illustrated above, what avoiding action should you take? What whistle signal should you sound?

Alter course boldly to port (2 short blasts), or to starboard (1 short blast).

As the Officer of the Watch of a power-driven vessel, you sight such a vessel (as shown in the illustration) on a steady bearing.

What should you do?

Stand-on. (Or, keep your course and speed.)

Remember Rule 25 (e).
If there is no triangle hoisted you must assume that the vessel is under sail alone.

You encounter this vessel in the open sea. She is not overtaking you.

Without going into details of your manoeuvres, what must you do?

Keep out of her way.

Note the signal hoisted by the vessel in these two situations.

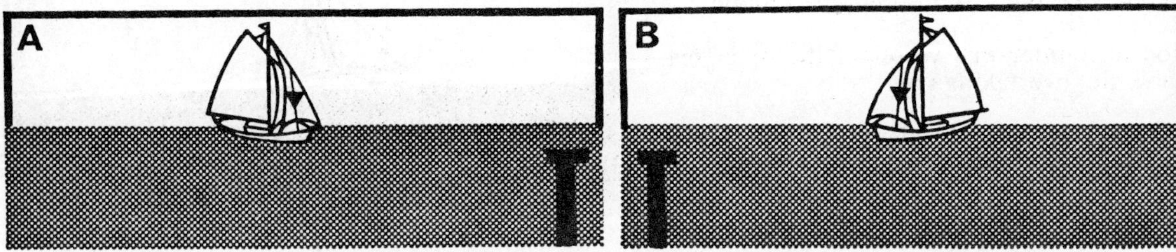

Assuming that you encounter the vessel on a steady bearing in each case, what should you do in situations (A) and (B)? (Remember to state any whistle signals you should make.)

(A) Keep your course and speed (or, stand on).
(B) Sound one short blast (·) and alter course to starboard.

Rule 30 (a) states that by day (that is from sunrise to sunset), a vessel **at anchor** shall exhibit where it can best be seen in the forepart, **one ball.**

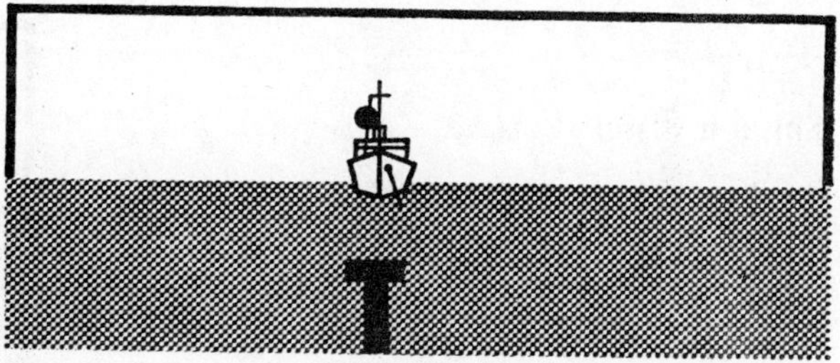

(The Rules in respect of vessels of less than 7 metres in length are included in the section 'specification of lights'.)

Remember that a vessel at anchor is not under way.

In the illustration you are approaching the other vessel.

What should you do?

(a) Alter course to starboard (sound 1 short blast).
(b) Alter course to port (sound 2 short blasts).
(c) Either.

(c) Either.

This is a vessel at ______ .

What must you do, in general terms, if you approach such a vessel?

anchor Keep clear.

This signal is hoisted by a vessel **not under command.**

The black balls (shapes) must again be at least 0·6 metre in diameter and at least 1·5 metres apart in a vertical line.

A vessel **not under command cannot get out of your way.** She may be **stopped,** but she may be **making way.** If stopped, she may be **drifting to leeward.** In the situation illustrated above, what must you do?

(a) Alter course to starboard.
(b) Alter course to port.
(c) Either.

(a) Alter course to starboard, but you must remember to give her a wide berth.

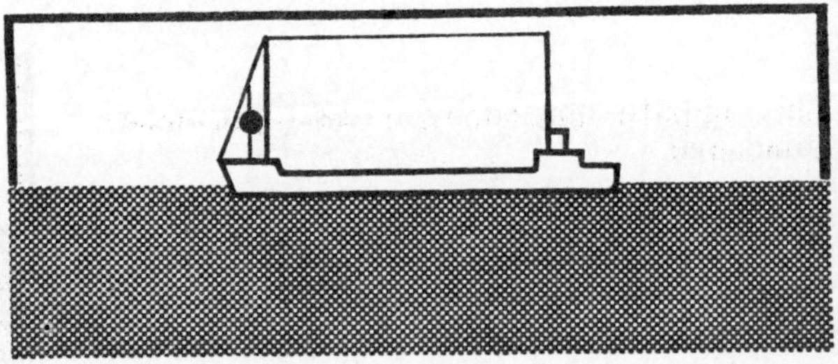

What does this signal indicate?
What, in general terms, should you do if you sight such a signal?

A vessel at anchor.
Keep clear. (Preferably alter course to go round her stern.)

Rule 27 (h) states:

> 'The signals prescribed in this Rule are not signals of vessels in distress and requiring assistance. Such signals are contained in Annex IV to these Regulations.'

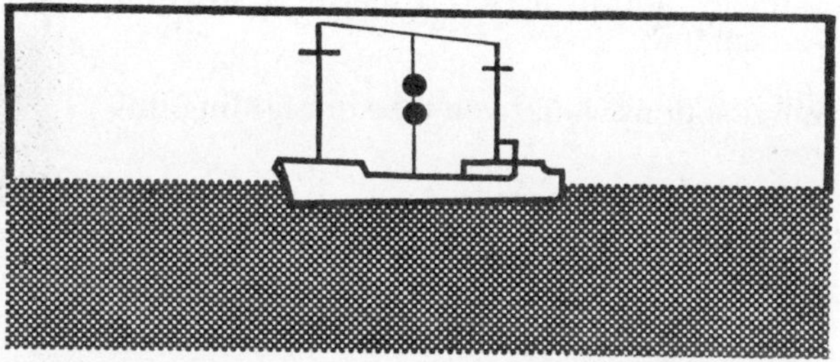

Therefore, you do not go to the assistance of a vessel displaying this signal, unless she shows a distress signal. Instead, you keep clear of her.

This signal indicates a vessel ______________ .

This signal by day indicates a **vessel aground.**

The three black balls are at least 0·6 metre in diameter and at least 1·5 metres apart in a vertical line.

What actions would you take on sighting this vessel?

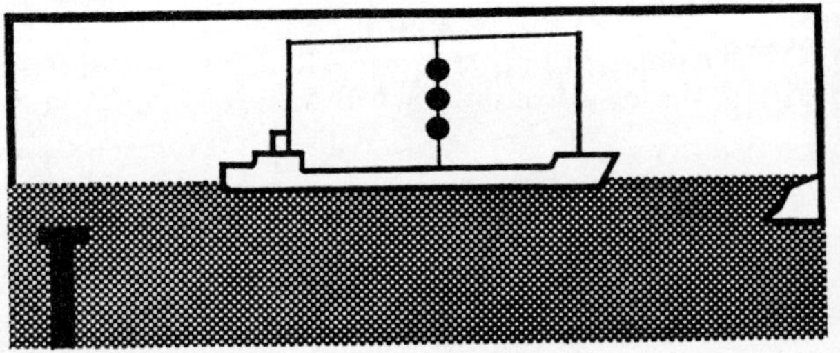

Keep clear of her. (The precise action that you should take would depend upon the navigational circumstances.)

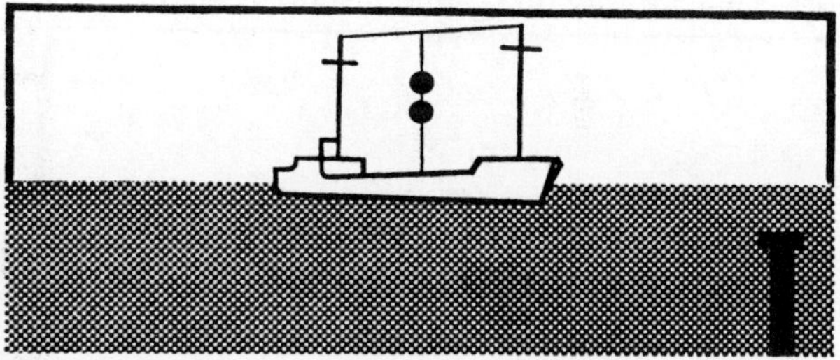

What does this signal indicate?

If the bearing is steady and assuming that the wind is negligible what should you do on approaching this vessel?

(a) Sound 5 short blasts, and await her next manoeuvre.
(b) Go to her assistance?
(c) Sound 2 short blasts and alter course to port keeping well clear.
(d) Alter course to starboard (sound 1 short blast) and keep well clear.
(e) Take all way off (sound 3 short blasts).

A vessel not under command.

(d) Alter course to starboard (sound 1 short blast) and keep well clear.

or

(e) Take all way off (sound 3 short blasts).

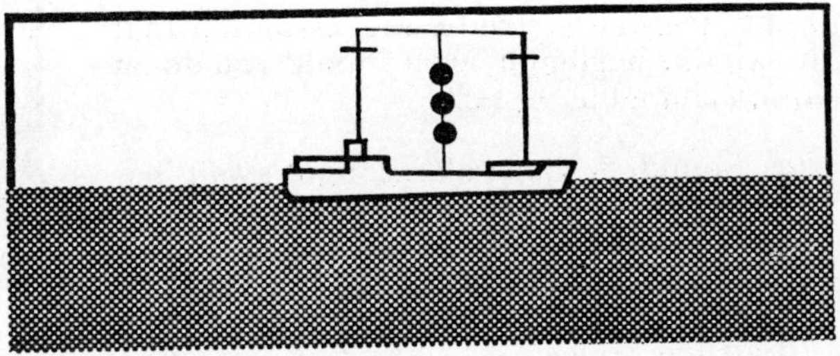

What is this vessel indicating?

In general, what should you do if you encounter a vessel showing this signal?

That she is aground. Keep clear. (The precise action that you should take would depend upon the navigational circumstances.)

Rule 3 (g) defines vessels which are **restricted in their ability to manoeuvre** as required by the Rules and are, therefore, unable to keep out of the way of other vessels. It will be because they are engaged in one of the following:

(a) Laying, servicing or picking up a navigation mark, submarine cable or pipeline. (Sometimes recognisable by the distinctive sheaves in the bows.)
(b) Engaged in dredging, surveying or underwater operations. (Not easily recognisable unless flying flags.)
(c) Engaged in replenishment or transferring persons, provisions or cargo while under way. (Recognisable by two or more vessels side by side or one vessel close astern of another.)
(d) Engaged in the launching or recovery of aircraft. (Distinctive shape of vessel, although sometimes ships other than aircraft carriers can operate helicopters.)
(e) Engaged in minesweeping operations.
(f) Engaged in a towing operation such as **severely restricts the towing vessel and her tow in their ability to deviate from their course.**
(Two or more vessels close together.)

The black shapes illustrated are all at least 0·6 metre in diameter and at least 1·5 metres apart in a vertical line. They are displayed by the vessels listed above except the minesweeper for which there is a special signal. The ship in the illustration should be easy to recognise. In which of the operations is she engaged?

(a) Laying, servicing or picking up a submarine cable or picking up a navigation mark, submarine cable or pipeline or possibly one of the operations in (b).

Here, again, is the list of vessels restricted in their ability to manoeuvre.

(a) Laying, servicing or picking up a navigation mark, submarine cable or pipeline.
(b) Engaged in dredging, surveying or underwater operations.
(c) Engaged in replenishment or transferring persons, provisions or cargo while under way.
(d) Engaged in the launching or recovery of aircraft.
(e) Engaged in minesweeping operations.
(f) Engaged in a towing operation such as severely restricts the towing vessel and her tow in their ability to deviate from their course.

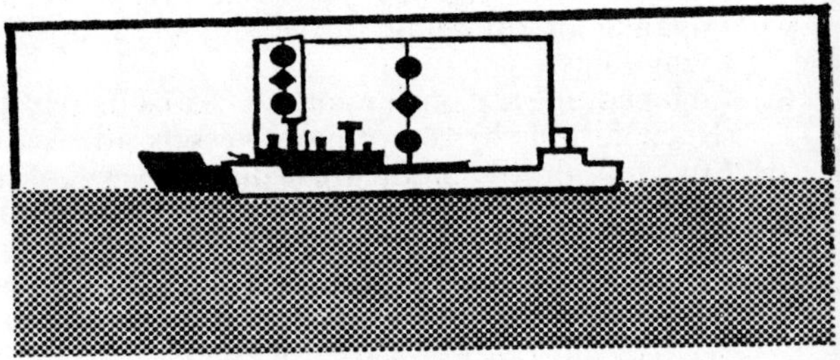

What operation is shown in the illustration?

(c) Replenishment at sea or transferring persons, provisions or cargo while under way.

What is this vessel doing that will restrict its ability to manoeuvre? (It is recognisable by its distinctive shape.)
What must you do if you encounter any vessel showing this signal?

Launching or recovering aircraft.
Keep clear.

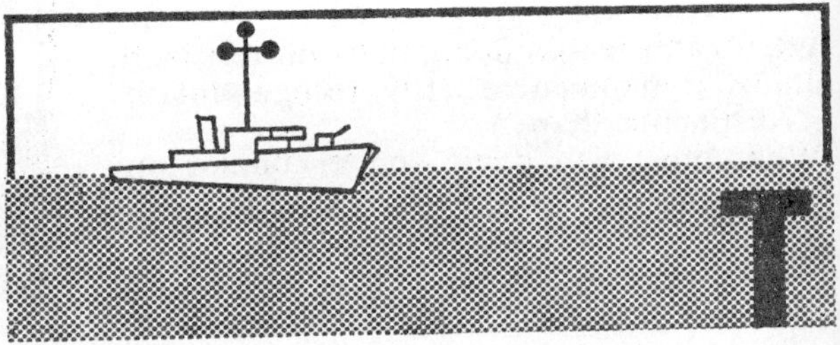

This signal denotes a minesweeper **engaged in minesweeping.** (Rule 27(f)).

Although a vessel engaged in this operation is categorised as a vessel restricted in its ability to manoeuvre, it shows a different signal from that shown by other vessels in the same category because there are additional factors to consider.

The black balls are at least 0·6 metre in diameter.

They indicate that it is dangerous for another vessel to approach closer than 1000 metres astern or 500 metres on either side of the vessel.

If the bearing of the minesweeper in the illustration was steady, what would you do?

Keep well clear (making sure that you do not go closer than 1000 metres astern or 500 metres on either side of the vessel).

Look carefully at this illustration and state **exactly** what the shapes hoisted by this vessel indicate.

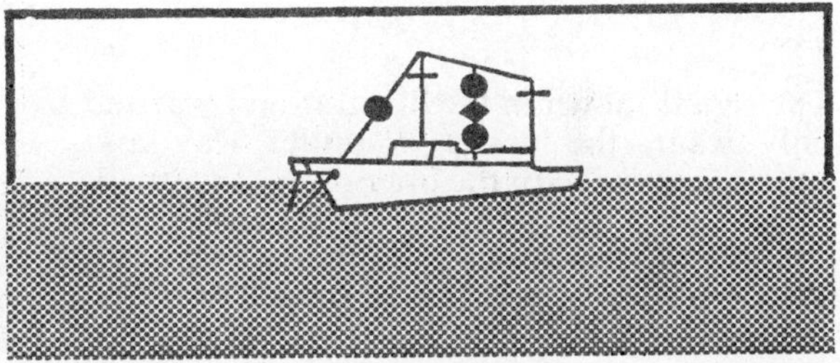

A vessel **at anchor** laying or picking up a submarine cable.

The signal shown in the illustration is carried only when the vessel is under way and actually engaged in the operation concerned.

The operation creates a danger area within 500 metres of the side of the vessel and 1000 metres astern.

(a) What is the vessel doing?
(b) What action should you take if you approach such a vessel from the direction shown?

(a) Minesweeping.
(b) Keep well clear. (Do not forget to sound the appropriate whistle signals.)

Here again, is a vessel engaged in mine-sweeping.

(a) How far does the danger extend sideways?
(b) How far does the danger extend astern?

(a) 500 metres.
(b) 1000 metres.

What does the signal illustrated indicate?

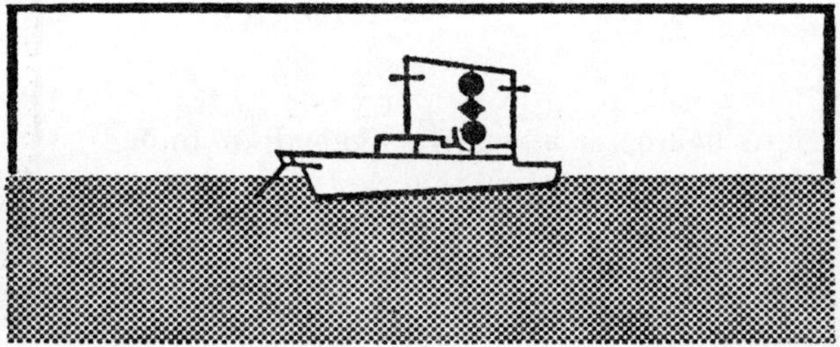

That the vessel is restricted in her ability to manoeuvre.

Rule 27 (d) refers to a vessel engaged in **dredging or underwater operations.**
Briefly, it says that such a vessel will **always** show the signal for a vessel restricted in her ability to manoeuvre but if an obstruction exists, it will display additional signals.

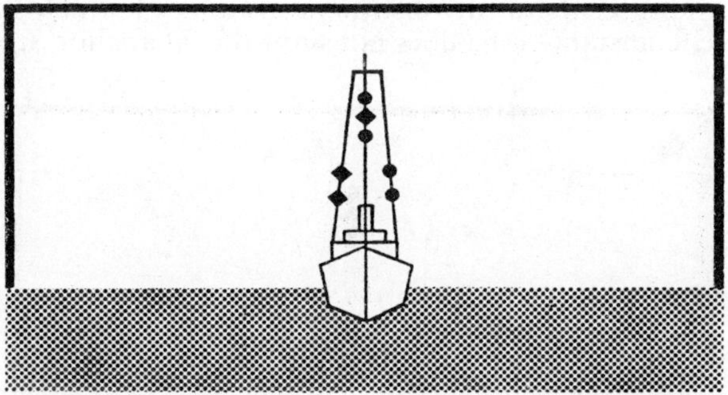

The **two balls** in a vertical line on the port side of this vessel indicate that the obstruction is on that side.

The **two diamonds** in a vertical line on the starboard side indicate that that is the side on which other vessels may pass.

What does the signal in the centre signify?

That the vessel is restricted in her ability to manoeuvre.

When an obstruction **does** exist, whether the vessel is **under way or at anchor,** she shows the signals to indicate where the obstruction is and on which side an approaching vessel may pass. (Under these circumstances she does not show the 'at anchor' signal.)

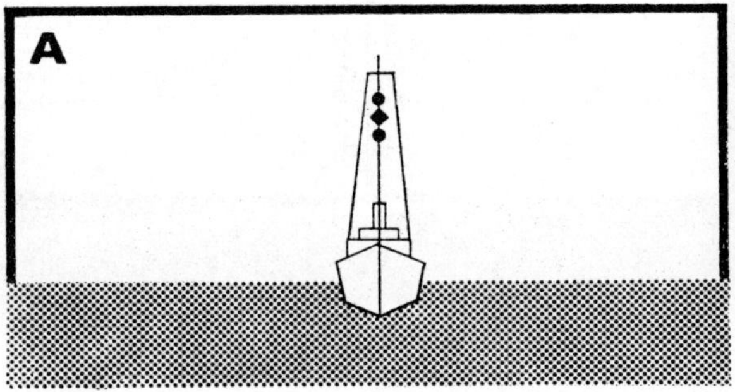

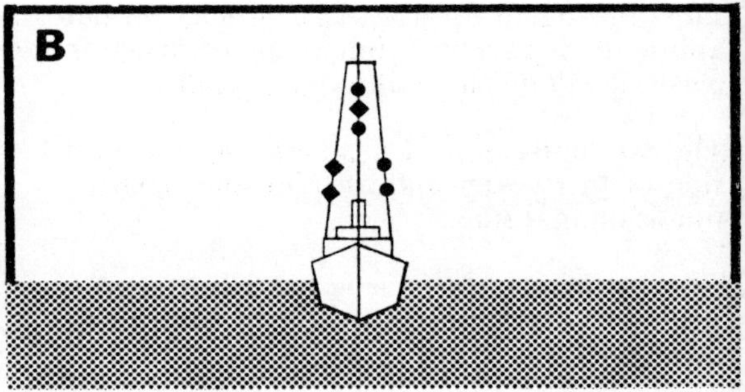

In respect of a vessel designed to engage in dredging or underwater operations, what do the shapes (signals) shown in the illustrations mean?

A The vessel is operating and under way, restricted in her ability to manoeuvre. No obstruction exists.

B The vessel is operating at anchor **or** under way and an obstruction exists. Vessels may pass on the side on which the diamond shapes are displayed.

Rule 27 (e) states:

> 'Whenever the size of a vessel engaged in diving operations makes it impracticable to exhibit the shapes prescribed in Rule 27 (d) (those which relate to the existence of an obstruction) a rigid replica of the International Code Flag 'A' not less than one metre in height shall be exhibited. Measures shall be taken to ensure all-round visibility.'

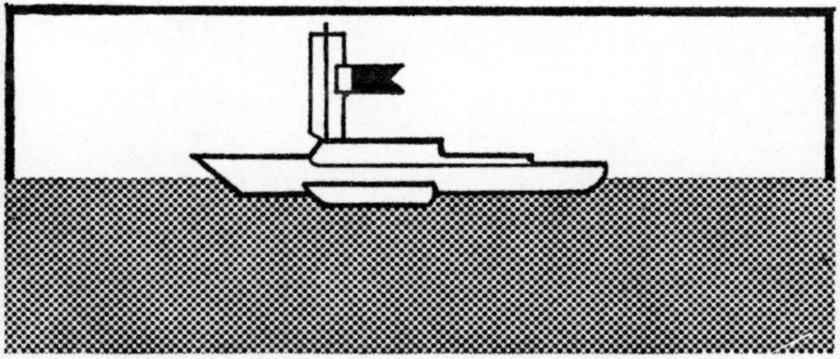

The signal shown here indicates a small vessel engaged in diving operations.

What do the signals illustrated here mean when displayed by a vessel designed for dredging or underwater operations?

That the vessel is operating at anchor.

When the International Code Flag 'A' is exhibited, it must be not less than 1 metre in height and must be visible all-round.

Under what circumstances is it exhibited?

When it is impracticable for a small vessel, engaged in diving operations, to exhibit the shapes normally required by the Rules for a larger vessel.

What should you do, in general, if you encounter this or any other vessel restricted in its ability to manoeuvre?

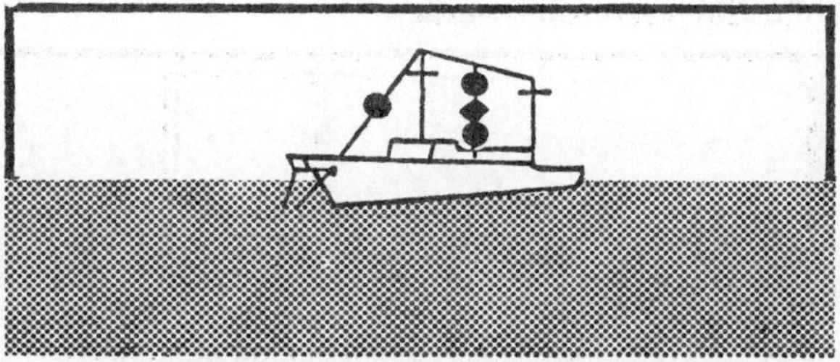

Keep well clear.

Rule 24 covers towing and pushing.
Rule 24 (a) (v) tells us that the following signals shall be displayed **only when** a vessel has a tow more than **200 metres in length.**

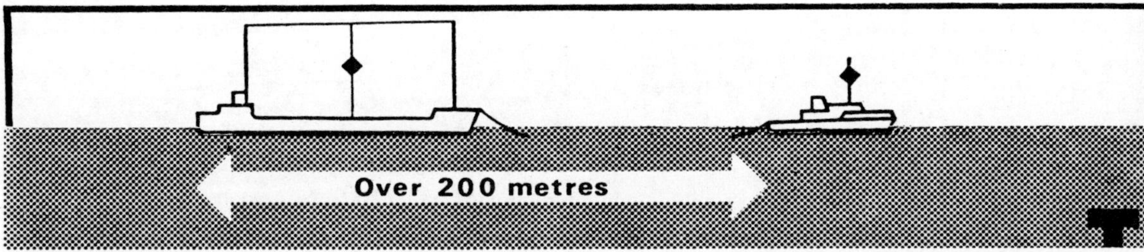

The length of the tow is measured from the **stern** of the towing vessel to the **stern** of the last vessel in the tow. The black diamond shape consists of two cones, base to base and is, therefore, at least 0·2 metres across at its widest point and 1·2 metres in height. It is displayed by all ships in the tow. If the length of the tow is **200 metres or less,** in length, **no signal** is displayed. An important interpretation of the Rules must be considered here. Vessels towing or being towed do not, normally, come under Rule 27 as they **are** under command (unless they are displaying 'not under command' signals).
What should you do if you sighted vessels, such as those illustrated, crossing on your **port side,** 3 miles away, on a steady bearing?

(a) Keep clear.
(b) Stand-on, as for ordinary power-driven vessels.

(b) Stand-on, as for ordinary power-driven vessels.
(But remember your other obligation under Rule 17 and be prepared to take avoiding action earlier than you normally would if the other vessels do not appear to be taking enough action themselves.)

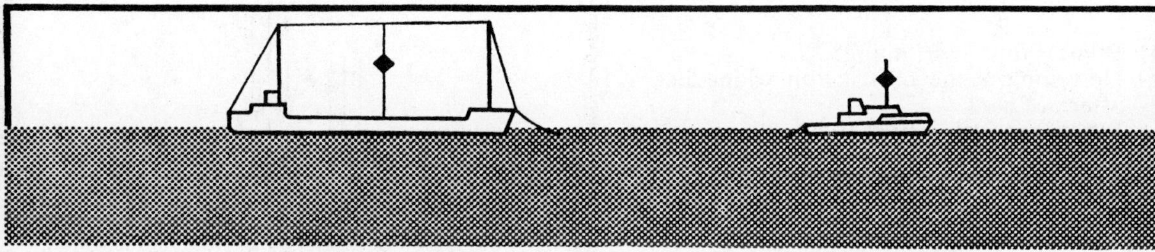

Vessel (B) Vessel (A)

1. The length of the tow is taken from the ______ of vessel (__) to the ______ of vessel (__).

2. Provided that the tow is straightforward and manageable, what signals are displayed when the length of the tow is 200 metres or less?

1. From the **stern** of vessel (A) to the **stern** of vessel (B).
2. None.

(a) What is this vessel doing?
(b) How long is the obstruction which lies astern of her?
(c) What precisely must you do in this situation?

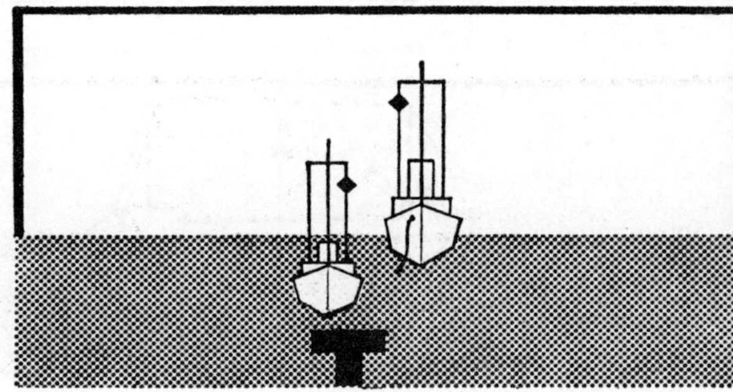

(a) Towing another vessel (or vessels).
(b) More than 200 metres.
(c) Sound 1 short blast (·   ) and alter course to starboard.

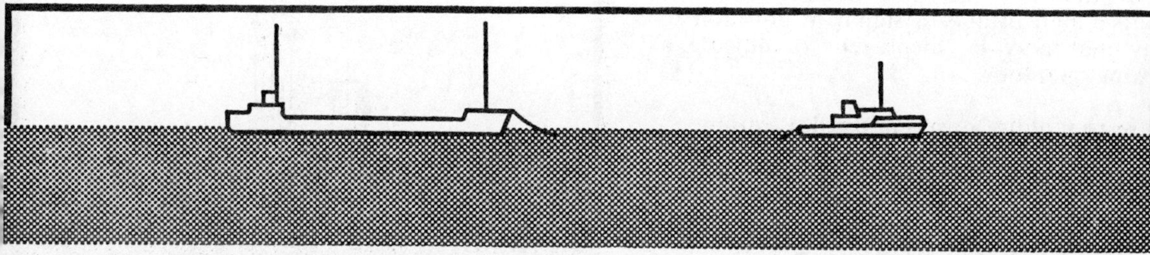

If you see one vessel towing another and neither of them is displaying any signal, what does this indicate?

That the length of the tow is 200 metres or less.

A vessel engaged in a towing operation such as renders her unable to deviate from her course shall display a signal in addition to any that may be displayed to indicate a towing operation.

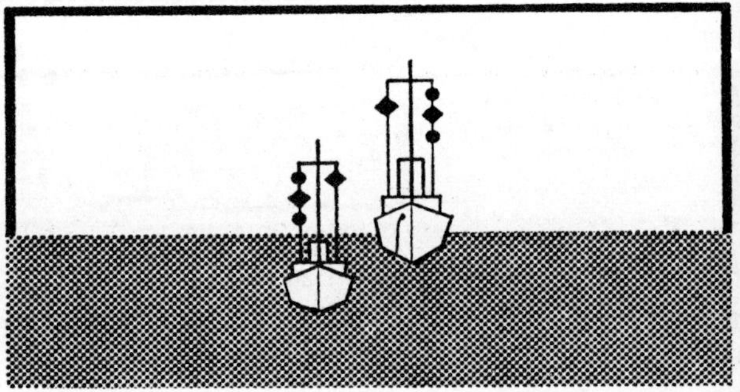

In respect of the vessels in the illustration:

(1) What do the three vertical shapes signify?
(b) What does the single diamond shape signify?

(a) The vessels are restricted in their ability to manoeuvre.
(b) The tow is over 200 metres in length.

What, in general, should you do if you are approaching vessels showing these signals?

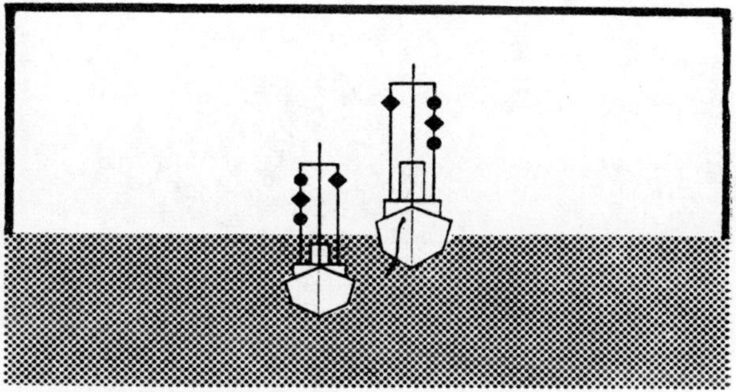

Keep clear.

(a) What circumstances are depicted by this illustration?
(b) What action should you take if you are in charge of an approaching vessel?

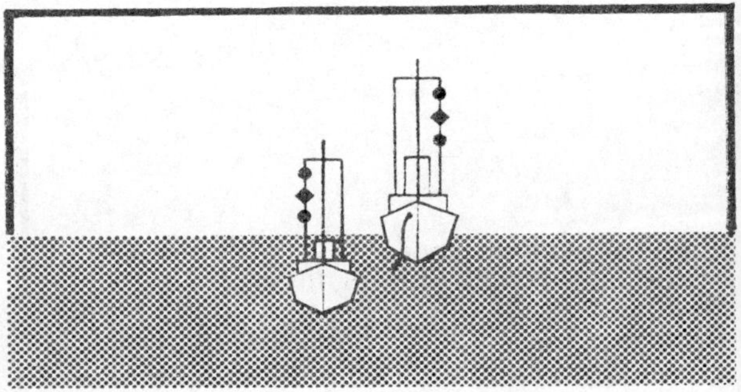

(a) A tow less than 200 metres in length.
    Neither vessel can deviate from her course.
(b) Keep clear.

The term 'vessel constrained by her draught' means a power-driven vessel which because of her draught in relation to the available depth of water is severely restricted in her ability to deviate from the course she is following [Rule 3(h)].

Rule 28 says that, in day-time, **a vessel constrained by her draught** may exhibit a **cylinder** where it can best be seen.

The cylinder must be at least 0·6 metre in diameter and at least 1·2 metres in height.

Rule 18 explains that although a vessel constrained by her draught shall navigate with particular caution having regard to her special condition, all vessels other than those not under command or restricted in their ability to manoeuvre shall **avoid impeding the safe passage of such a vessel.**

What would you do if you were the Officer of the Watch of an approaching vessel in the circumstances illustrated above?

Make an early and considerable alteration of course to starboard and keep clear.

You must recognise that here is a large vessel, moving through a deep water channel.

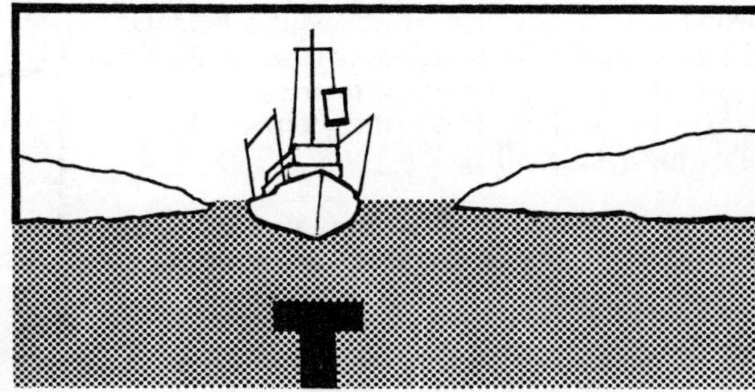

You must **avoid impeding** her **safe passage.**

She is restricted in her ability to manoeuvre because she is ____________ by her ______.

constrained   draught

A vessel constrained by her draught may display a ______ .

When you approach such a vessel you must carry out such actions as will ______ ______ her ______ ______ .

cylinder
avoid impeding   safe passage

Both of the signals illustrated denote vessels engaged in fishing (Rule 26). The black cones are at least 0·6 metre in diameter. Fishing vessels under 20 metres in length may hoist a basket for a signal.

If any vessel has outlying gear extending more than 150 metres, she must display a black cone, point upwards in the direction of the gear.

What must you do if you encounter any vessel engaged in fishing?

Keep clear.

Rule 18 states the Responsibilities between vessels. Summarized, it says that all vessels **not engaged in fishing** (except vessels not under command and vessels restricted in the ability to manoeuvre) shall keep out of the way of vessels that **are** engaged in fishing. However, this Rule does not give a vessel engaged in fishing the right to obstruct a channel or fairway used by other vessels [Rule 9(c)].

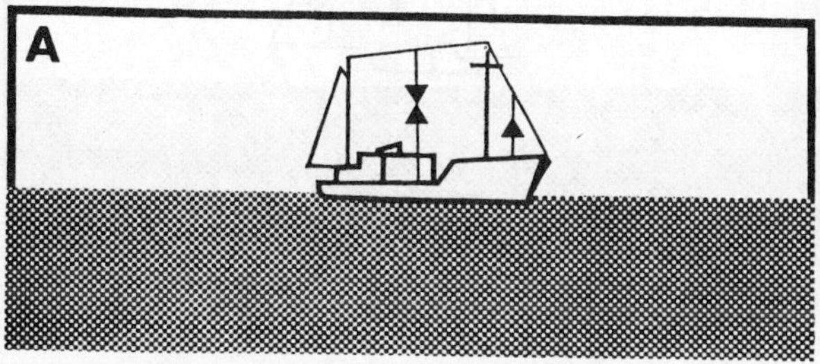

Both of these illustrations show fishing vessels.

What does the single black cone indicate in each case?

The vessels have outlying gear extending more than 150 metres lying ahead.

Imagine that you have sighted this vessel on a steady bearing, at a range of 3 miles.

(a) What does the single black cone indicate?
(b) What actions should you take?

(a) Her outlying gear extends **more than 150 metres** to **port** (or possibly, ahead).
(b) Sound 2 short blasts (· ·) and alter course to port.

---

1. What are the vessels in (A), (B) and (C) doing?
2. What else is indicated by the signals shown by (A), (B) and (C)?

1. Fishing.
2. (A) has outlying gear extending more than 150 metres ahead.
   (B) has outlying gear extending 150 metres or less.
   (C) is less than 20 metres in length, has gear extending 150 metres or less.

Read through Rule 26 (a) (it is only a few lines) before reading the rest of this page.

Earlier in this chapter you learnt that any vessel at anchor displays a black ball in the forepart of the vessel. This is true of all vessels, with one exception.

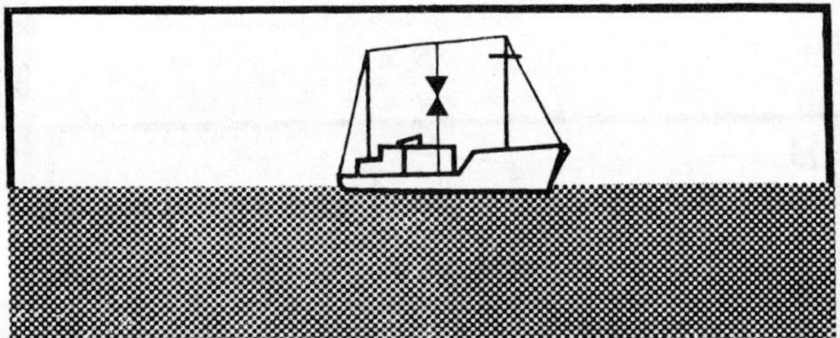

A vessel engaged in fishing displays only the signals prescribed in Rule 26.

Is the vessel in the illustration under way or is she at anchor?

Either may be true: there is no way of knowing.

A vessel engaged in fishing displays only the signals prescribed in Rule 26.

The reasons for this restriction are not stated in the Rules, but vessels fishing may behave in so many different ways, depending upon what they are doing, that it is not possible to identify each type of behaviour.

From your point of view as the Officer of the Watch of an ordinary power-driven vessel, the position is quite straightforward.

If you sight a vessel engaged in fishing, always ——— ————.

(a) What are these vessels actually engaged in doing?
(b) What should you do when you see any one of these vessels?

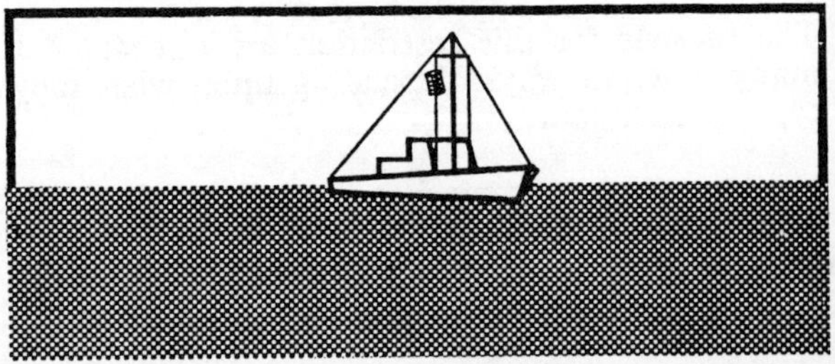

(a) Fishing. (b) Keep clear.

When under way a vessel **engaged in fishing** will **keep out of the way** of those vessels that are excepted from the General Responsibilities of vessels not engaged in fishing. They are:

(a) vessels that are not ______ ________;
(b) vessels that are __________ in their ________ __ __________.

(a) under command
(b) restricted ability to manoeuvre

Test on Chapter 3

All of these questions are marked *. You must get all of them 100% correct before going on to the next chapter.

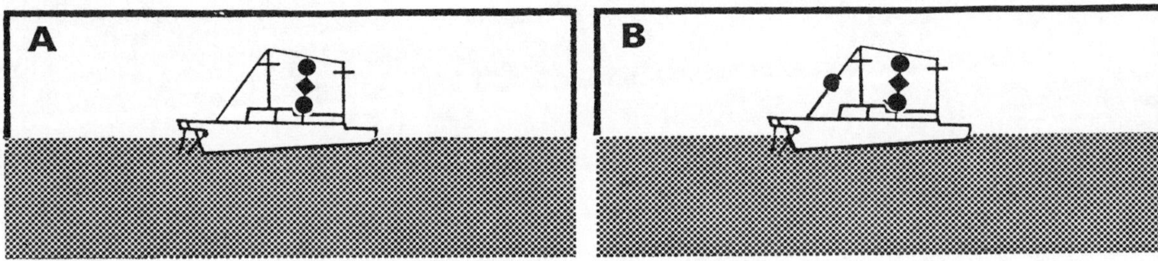

*1. In illustrations (A) and (B), what do the signals mean?

*2. If you approach either of these vessels on a steady bearing in any position, what should you do?

Test (continued)

*3. What are vessels (A), (B) and (C)?

*4. What should you do in each situation shown by (A), (B) and (C)?
(i.e. state whistle signals and alterations of course, if any.)

Test (continued)

*5. What do the signals displayed by vessels (A), (B) and (C) indicate?

*6. What should you do in situation (B)?

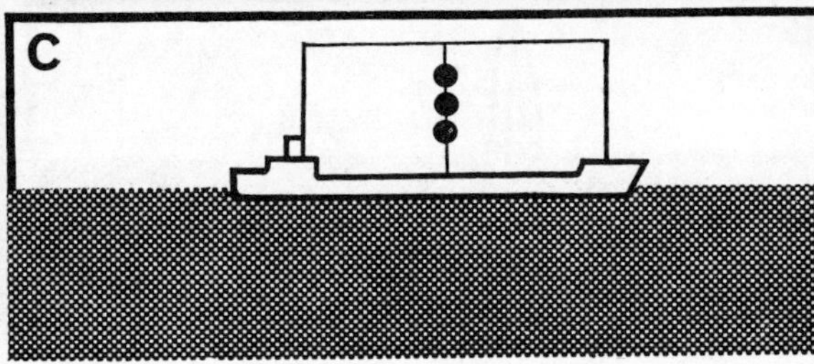

Test (continued)

*7. What exactly do the signals in illustrations (A), (B) and (C) mean, including any distances involved?

*8. What specific action should you take in situation (C)?

Test (continued)

*9. What does the signal displayed in this illustration indicate?

*10. How far does the danger zone extend:
(a) to the side?
(b) astern?

Test (continued)

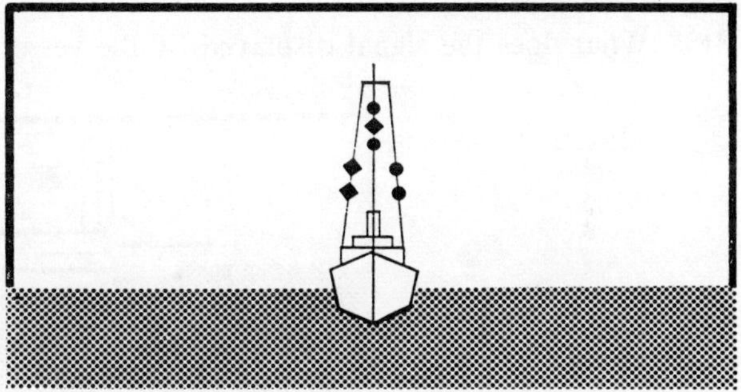

*11. What do the signals displayed in this illustration indicate?

*12. What action must you take if you are approaching a vessel such as that illustrated? (Give any whistle signals.)

*13. What does the signal displayed by the vessel in this illustration denote?

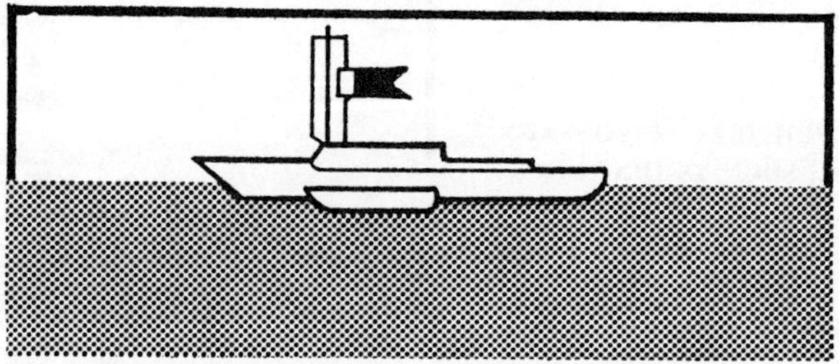

Test (continued)

*14. What is vessel (A) engaged in doing?

*15. What must you do if you see the signal displayed in (A)?

*16. What do the signals in illustration (B) indicate?

*17. How many of the signals mentioned in this chapter are recognised distress signals?

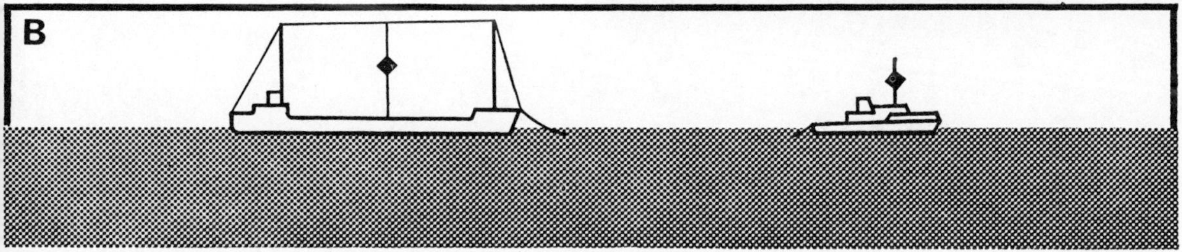

Test (continued)

*18. This illustration shows a tow in progress. What, precisely, do the signals indicate?

*19. What is your responsibility in this situation if you are the Officer of the Watch of an approaching vessel?

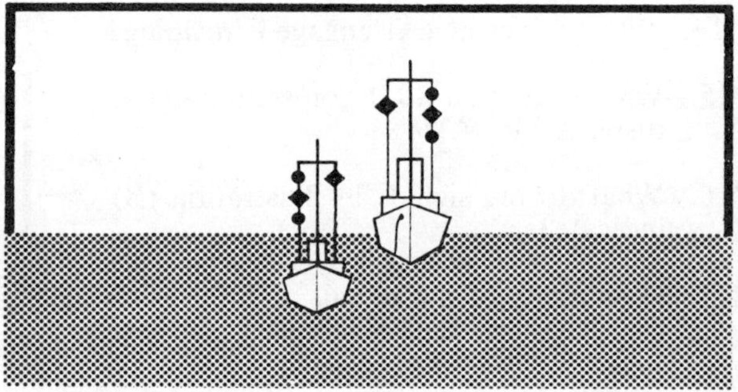

Test (continued)

*20. This large vessel is displaying a cylinder. What does it indicate?

*21. What is your responsibility when approaching such a vessel?

Answers to Test

If all your answers are completely correct, you have a solid foundation for understanding the next chapter, which will take for granted much of the material you learnt in this chapter. If your answer to **any** question (or part of a question) marked with an asterisk is wrong, work through the appropriate section again, as indicated.

		Reference
*1.	(A) Vessel restricted in her ability to manoeuvre, under way. (B) Vessel restricted in her ability to manoeuvre, at anchor.	pages 77–78 81
*2.	**Keep clear** of the other vessel.	79
*3.	(A) and (B) **Sailing vessels.** (C) **Sailing** vessel under **power.**	64–68
*4.	(A) Sound 1 short blast (or ·) and alter course to starboard. (B) Alter course **either way,** sounding one or two short blasts. (C) Keep course and speed (or, stand on).	64–69
*5.	(A) Vessel at anchor. (B) Vessel not under command. (C) Vessel aground.	69–76

Answers to Test (continued)

		Reference
*6.	Alter course to starboard (sound 1 short blast) and keep clear.	pages 71–72
*7.	(A) A vessel **engaged in fishing:** length of vessel **less than 20 metres.** (Outlying gear extending less than 150 metres.) (B) A vessel **engaged in fishing:** outlying **gear** extending **less than 150 metres.** (C) A vessel **engaged in fishing:** outlying **gear** extending **more than 150 metres.**	100–107
*8.	Sound **2 short blasts** (· ·) and alter course to **port.**	103
*9.	A vessel engaged in minesweeping.	80–83
*10.	(a) 500 metres. (b) 1000 metres.	80–83
*11.	A vessel engaged in dredging or underwater operations. Restricted in her ability to manoeuvre. An obstruction exists on her port side. An approaching vessel may pass on her starboard side.	85–86
*12.	Alter course to port (sounding 2 short blasts).	85

Answers to Test (continued)

		Reference
*13.	The vessel is a small vessel engaged in diving operations.	page 87
*14.	Fishing.	100–107
*15.	Keep clear.	100–101
*16.	One vessel towing another. **Length of tow more than 200 metres.**	90– 96
*17.	**None** of them.	
*18.	The vessels are restricted in their ability to manoeuvre and are **severely restricted in their ability to deviate from their course.** The tow is over 200 metres in length.	94–96
*19.	To keep out of the way.	95–96
*20.	The vessel is **constrained by her draught.**	97–99
*21.	To **avoid impeding** her **safe passage.**	97

CHAPTER FOUR—NIGHT-TIME RECOGNITION

This chapter deals with situations covered by Rules 20 to 31. Some of them you read through at the beginning of Chapter 3 but then you were mainly interested in shapes. Now you are concerned with lights.

Read through these Rules once only, before going on to page 122.

Obviously, the proper lights must be shown at night, but it would be wise to learn just when is 'lighting-up time' for vessels.

Summarized, Rule 20 says that the Rules for Lights are applicable in all weathers and shall be complied with **from sunset to sunrise.** During such times, no other lights shall be exhibited except for lights which cannot be mistaken for or interfere with the prescribed lights. Nor must they interfere with the keeping of a proper look-out.

The prescribed lights **shall** also be exhibited between sunrise and sunset during periods of restricted visibility and may be exhibited in all other circumstances when it is deemed necessary.

In other words, you avoid confusing people with extra lights, and you use commonsense about whether to show identification lights outside the hours of darkness.

Whenever else lights **may** be shown, the lights prescribed in the Rules **Must** be shown from ______ to ________.

sunset   sunrise (Make sure you get these words the right way round.)

Because this chapter is concerned with the hours of darkness when silhouettes are hard to see, the Illustrations will show only the lights, the sea and the sky, as in this illustration, for example.

The illustration shows a power-driven vessel under way, less than 50 metres in length, head-on at night.

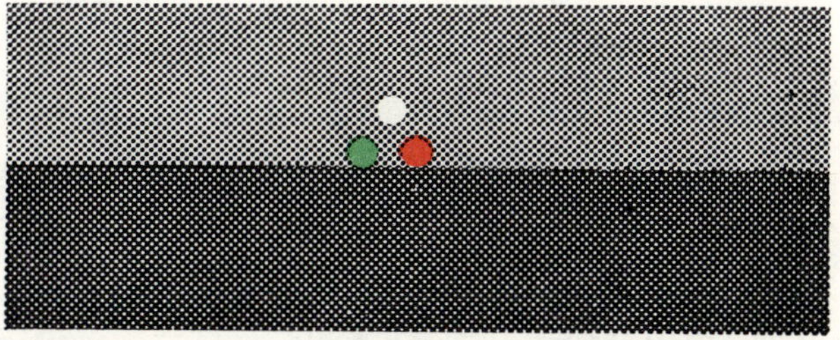

The white light is her masthead light.

The coloured lights are her side lights.

These lights ___ be shown from **sunset** to **sunrise.**

The illustration below shows a plan view of the lights which **must** be shown when under way by a power-driven vessel 50 metres and over in length. Power-driven vessels of under 50 metres need only display one masthead light, although they **may** exhibit two.

Pay particular attention to the arcs of visibility (i.e. the angles) of the lights.

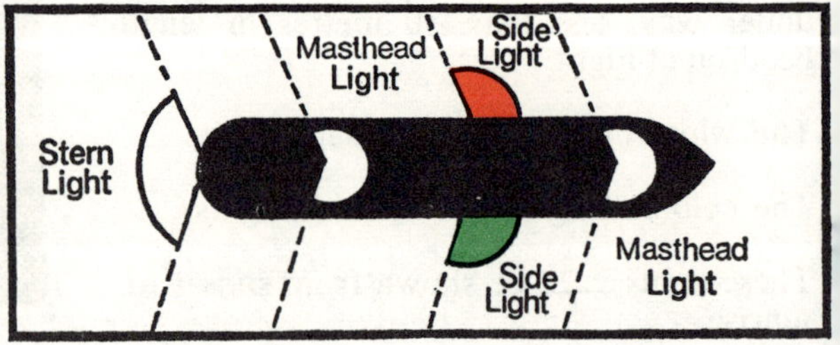

The arc of a masthead light is through the **bows** from 22·5° abaft the beam on **either side.**

The arc of a side light is from **right ahead** to 22·5° abaft the beam on **one side.**

The arc of the stern light is through the **stern** from 22·5° abaft the beam on **either side.**

When must these lights be shown?

From **sunset** to **sunrise.**

Annex I to the Regulations lays down the relative heights of the lights and Rule 22 states how far they must be visible.

The after masthead light must be carried at least 5 metres higher than the forward one.

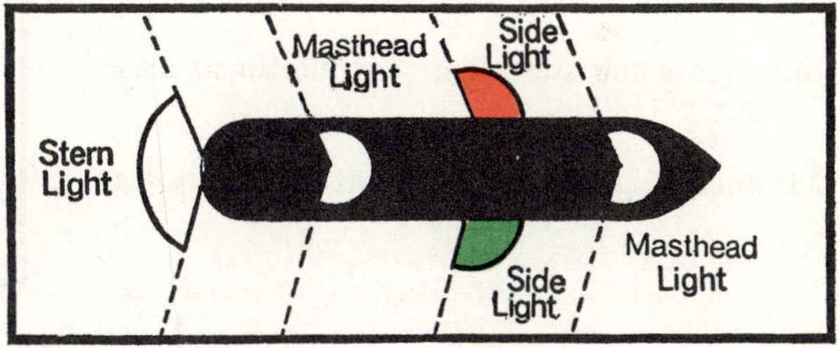

The details of heights and construction of lights are in an appendix to the programme.

What you need to learn here are the arcs of the lights.

If you were overtaking a power-driven vessel at night there would be an arc, astern of her, where you would see only her stern light.

The arc of visibility of the stern light is through the ______ from ____ ° abaft the beam on ______ side.

stern 22·5° either

The distances for which the lights must be visible on a vessel of 50 metres or more in length, are as follows:

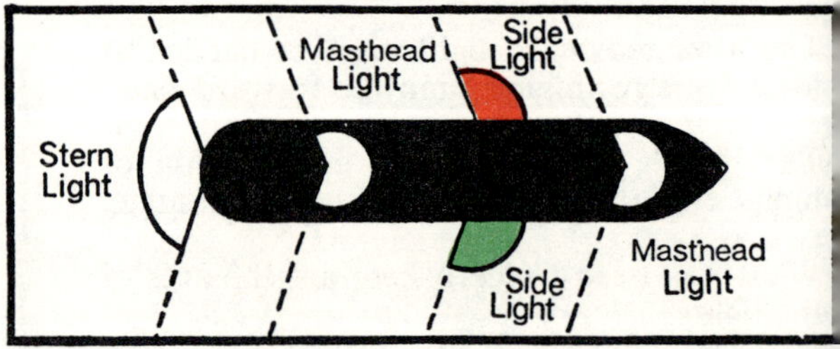

Side lights and stern light: visible for at least 3 miles.

Masthead lights: visible for at least 6 miles.

Thus, if a power-driven vessel is crossing ahead, you would sight her masthead light(s) at least 6 miles away on a clear night, and sight her side lights before she came within 3 miles. If you were overtaking her (i.e. more than 22·5° abaft her beam), you might not sight her until you were 3 miles apart. You can see that the arcs are chosen to help you decide whether you are overtaking.

(a) The arc of visibility of a masthead light is through the ____ from 22·5° **abaft the beam on** ____ ____ side.

(b) The arc of visibility of a side light is from ____ ____ to 22·5° **abaft** the beam on ____ side.

(a) bows either
(b) right ahead one

All the lights prescribed for an ordinary power-driven vessel under way are designed to have a cut-off angle 22·5° abaft the beam, which helps to reduce any doubt about overtaking at night.

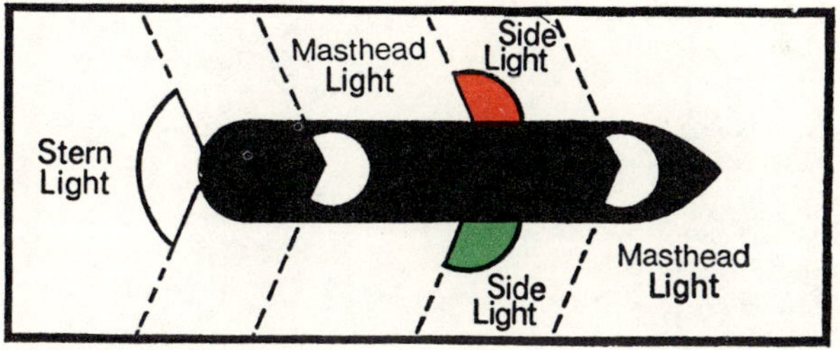

If you are overtaking a vessel at night you will see only her stern light.

As you come up past her you will, of course, see one or other of her side lights and both masthead lights; but you are still the overtaking vessel until you are past and clear.

Complete each of the following statements with about 8 or 9 words.

(a) The arc of a masthead light is through ______________.
(b) The arc of a side light is from ____________
(c) The arc of a stern light is through ____________.

(a) the bow from 22·5° abaft the beam on either side.
(b) right ahead to 22·5° abaft the beam on one side.
(c) the stern from 22·5° abaft the beam on either side.

---

2. Which light **can** only be seen from more than 22·5° abaft the beam?
1. Which lights **cannot** be seen from more than 22·5° abaft the beam?

1. Masthead lights and side lights.
2. Stern light.

What are the arcs of visibility of the following lights?

(a) A masthead light.
(b) A side light.
(c) The stern light.

(a) Through the bows from 22·5° abaft the beam on either side.
(b) From right ahead to 22·5° abaft the beam on one side.
(c) Through the stern from 22·5° abaft the beam on either side.

If you can see one or both of the coloured side lights, it is easy to decide roughly which way a vessel is heading at night. If, however, the other vessel is so far away that her side lights cannot be seen, you have only her masthead lights for a guide. Remember that the **after** masthead light is **higher** than the forward one.

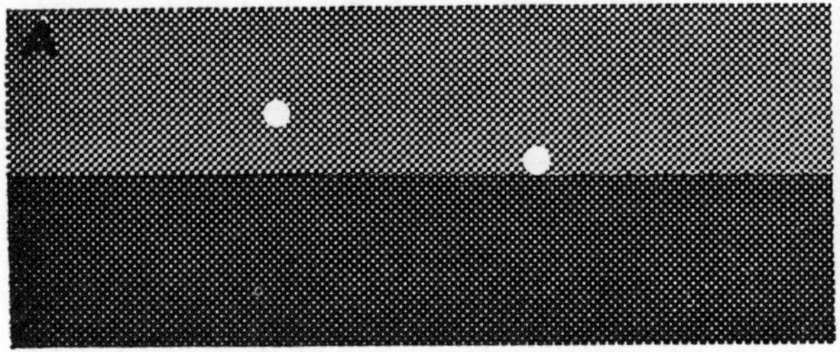

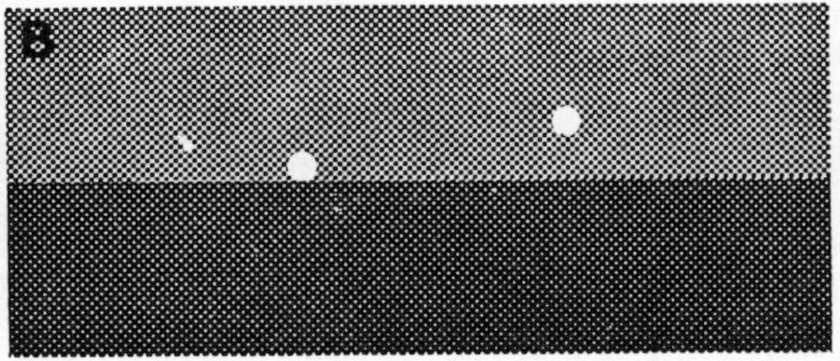

Which of these two vessels is steaming from left to right, as you are looking at them?

(A)

If you see both side lights of a vessel in line with your own foremast, she is head-on to your vessel.

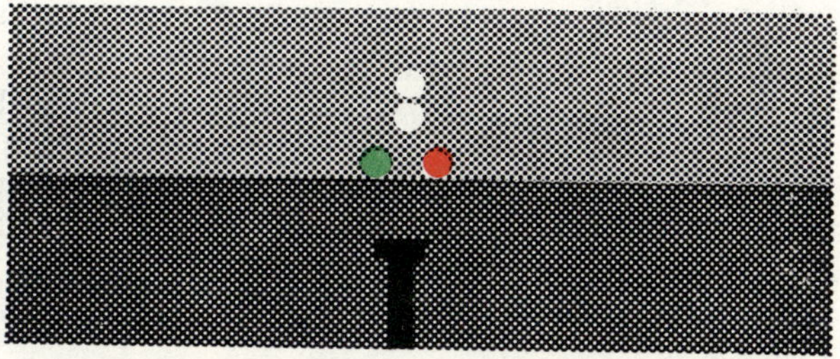

Later on, you will learn that these lights could denote a vessel with a tow, but in any case the lights denote a power-driven vessel.

1. Which way should you alter course?
2. What whistle signal should you sound?

1. To starboard. 2. 1 short blast (·).

These three illustrations are all of the same type of vessel, at a range of about **3 miles.**

1. What type of vessel do they indicate?
2. Is the vessel:
   (i) over 50 metres?
   (ii) 50 metres or under?
   (iii) either?
3. What would you do in situation (A)?

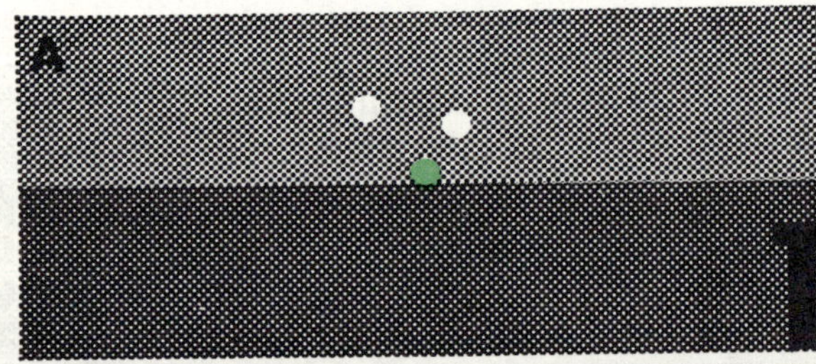

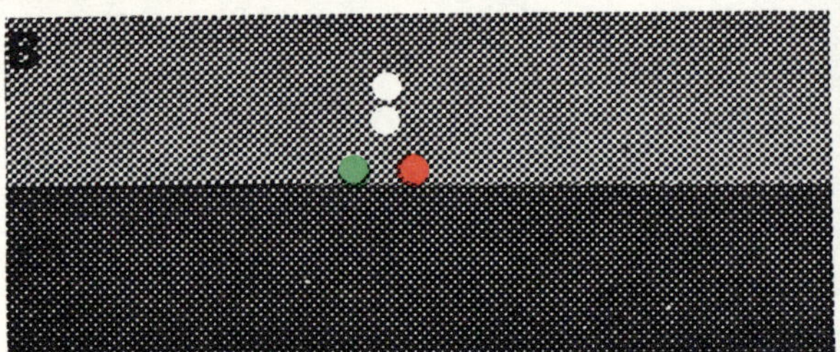

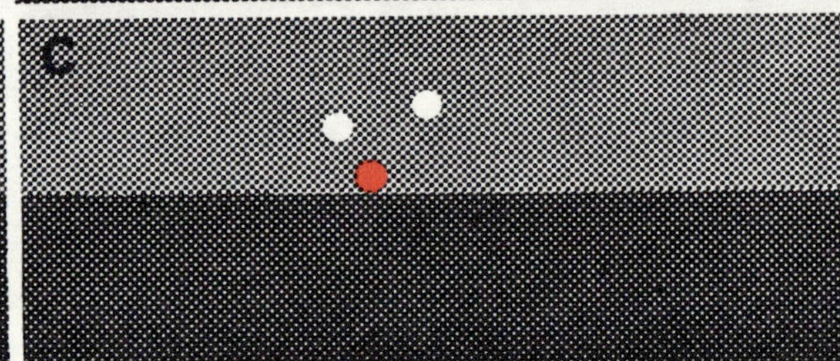

1. A power-driven vessel. 2. (iii) either. 3. Stand-on.

A single white light may not tell you very much, but a group of lights can convey quite a lot of information.

You have sighted these three lights on a steady bearing, at a range of 3 miles.

(a) What type of vessel do they indicate?
(b) Is she under way, or at anchor?
(c) What action should you take?

(a) A power-driven vessel, which may be more (or less) than 50 metres long.
(b) Under way (and **probably making way** as the bearing is steady).
(c) Sound 1 short blast (·   ) and alter course to starboard.

A **single** masthead light indicates a **power-driven** vessel under way, **50 metres** or less in length.

Which of these vessels is heading left to right, as you look at it?

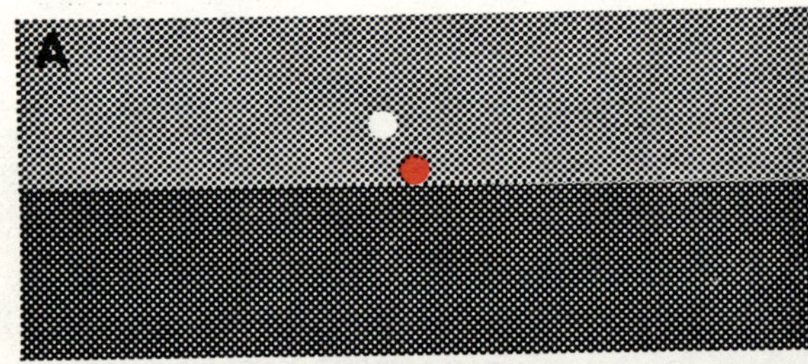

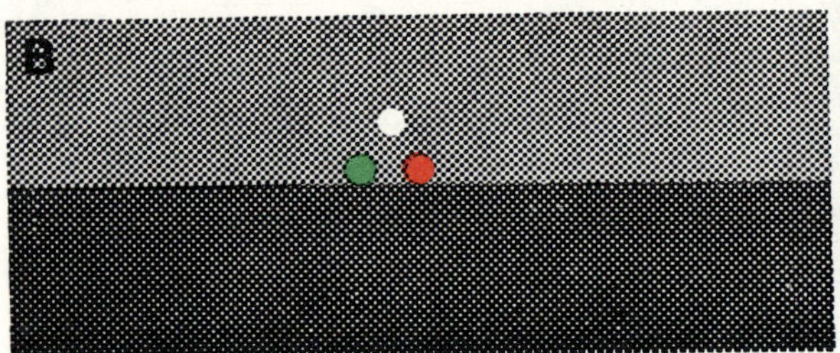

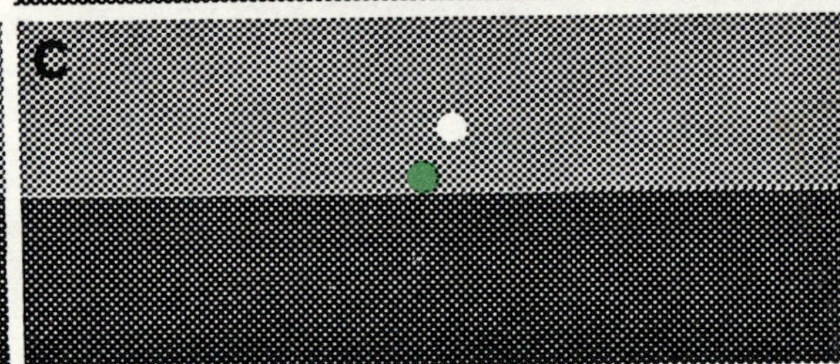

(C)

Whenever you see a vessel's side light you know that she is under way.

(a) What kind of vessel do these lights signify?
(b) What do they indicate about her length?

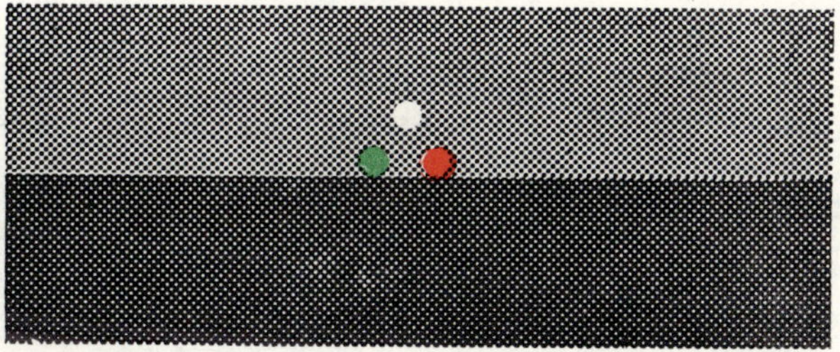

(a) A power-driven vessel under way.
(b) She is less than 50 metres long.

Instead of side lights a **combined lantern** may be displayed by a power-driven vessel **less than 20 metres long.**

If you sight such a vessel in the situation illustrated, at a range of 2 miles, what action must you take?

Sound 1 short blast (·) and alter course to starboard.

---

1. Which of these vessels are 50 metres or less in length?
2. Which one is definitely less than 20 metres in length?

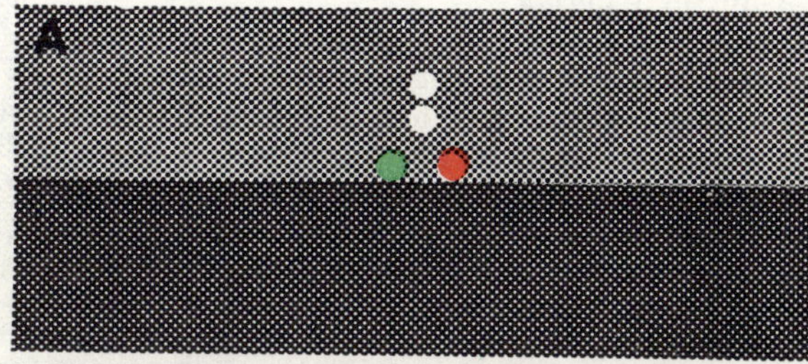

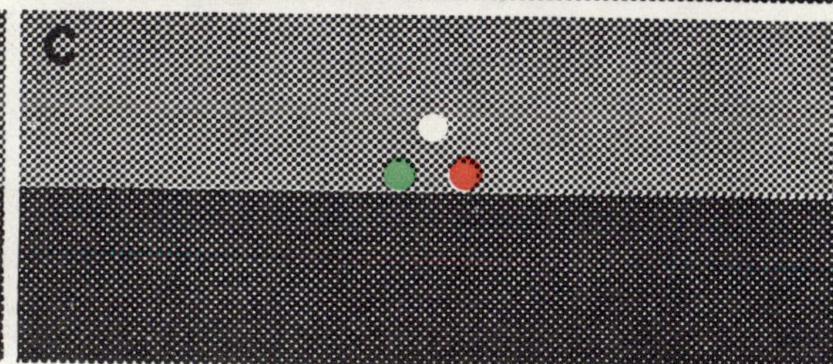

1. (B) and (C) and possibly (A). 2. (B).

The Regulations for towing and pushing are set out in Rule 24.

Power-driven vessels engaged in towing display **extra masthead lights** forward, **side lights, stern light** and a **yellow towing light,** with the same characteristics as a stern light, displayed immediately above the stern light.

A vessel or object being **towed** will not display masthead lights but will display **side lights** and **stern light.**

In both of these illustrations, a power-driven vessel is towing two other vessels. (The stern lights of all the vessels and the towing light of the towing vessel are not visible at this angle.)

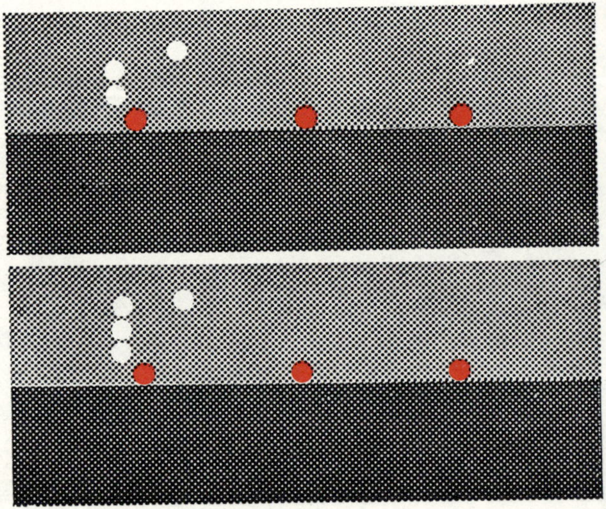

Two forward masthead lights mean that the tow is **200 metres or less.**

Three forward masthead lights mean that the tow is ____ **than 200 metres.**

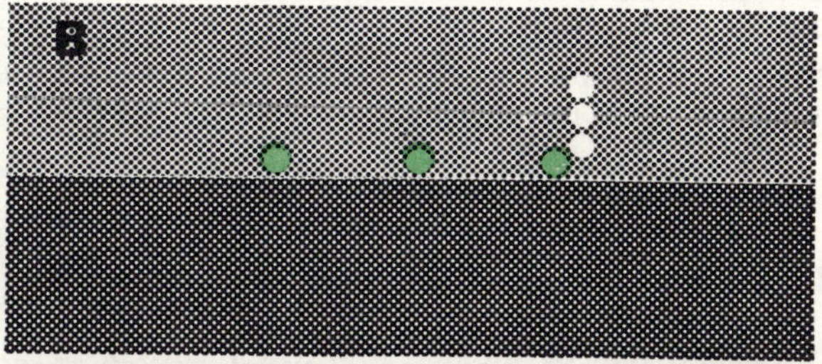

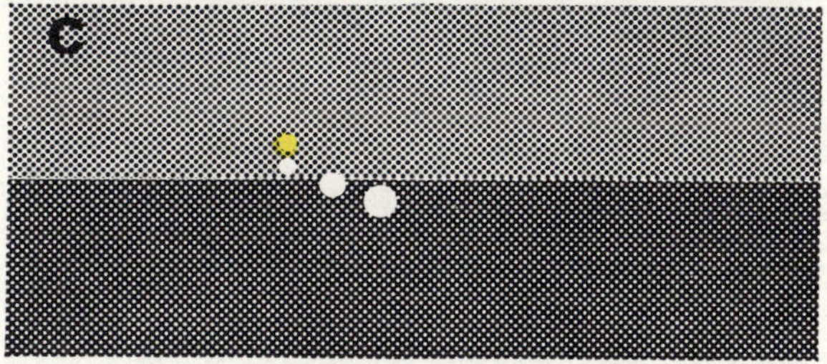

1. What is the length of tow in (A)?
2. What is the length of tow in (B)?
3. In (A) and (B) there are no after masthead lights. This means that the **towing vessel** is less than __ metres long.
4. What do the lights in (C) depict?

1. 200 metres or less. 2. More than 200 metres. 3. 50 metres. 4. One vessel towing two others. Towing light and stern lights visible from the quarter.

When you see both side lights, the other vessel is head-on, or nearly head-on, and the after masthead light tends to merge with the forward ones. In most cases, however, the after masthead light will be seen a little to one side because the vessel is seldom seen exactly head-on.

1. Which of these vessels are engaged in towing?
2. Which one of them is burdened with a tow more than 200 metres in length?

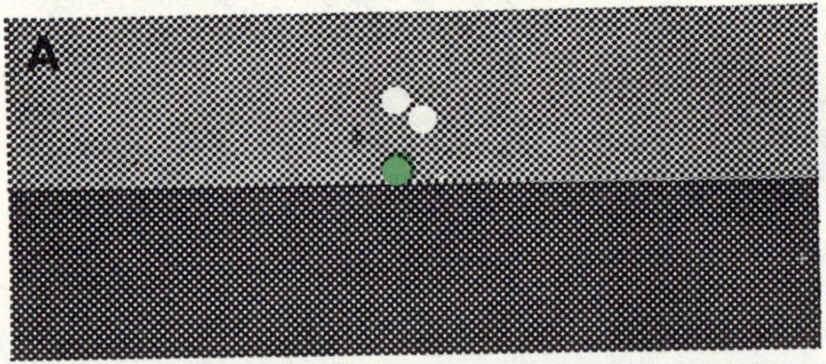

1. (B) and (C).
2. (C).

1. (a) What do the lights in this picture indicate about the length of tow?
   (b) What do the lights indicate about the length of the towing vessel?

2. (a) What is indicated about the length of tow?
   (b) What is indicated about the length of the towing vessel?

1. (a) 200 metres or less.
(b) May be over 50 metres.

2. (a) More than 200 metres.
(b) Less than 50 metres.

Rule 24 (b) says:

'When a pushing vessel and a vessel being pushed ahead are rigidly connected in a **composite unit,** they shall be regarded as a power-driven vessel and exhibit the lights prescribed in Rule 23.'

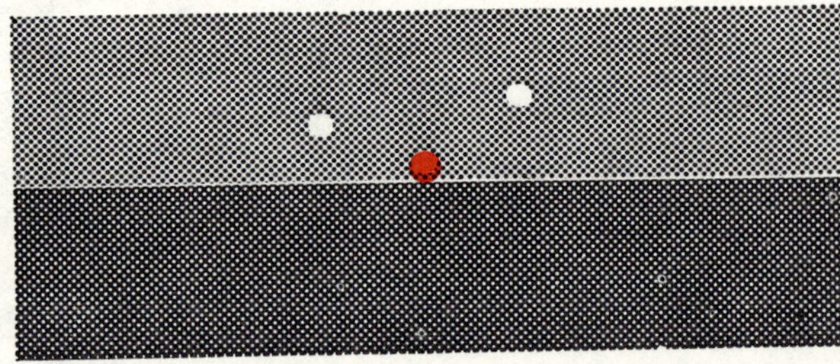

So, what would you assume to be the meaning of the signals in the illustration:

A single vessel
or
one vessel pushing another, the two vessels rigidly connected as a composite unit?

It could be either. (You should take action as you would for a single vessel.)

A vessel engaged in **pushing ahead** (but not as part of a composite unit) or **towing alongside** displays **two masthead lights** forward in a verticle line, **side lights** and **stern light.**

A **vessel being pushed** but not as a part of a composite unit) displays **side lights forward.** If more than one vessel is being pushed, the pushed vessels will be lit as one vessel.

A vessel being **towed alongside** displays a **stern light** and **side lights** at the forward end.

(a) (i) What does illustration (A) represent?
(ii) In what direction is it heading in relation to you?
(b) (i) What does illustration (B) represent?
(ii) In what direction is it heading in relation to you?

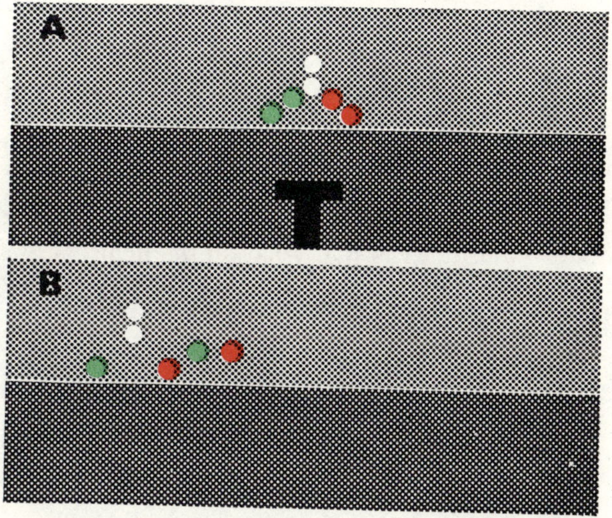

(a) (i) A vessel being pushed (not as part of a composite unit).
(ii) Heading towards you. Head-on.
(b) (i) A vessel being towed alongside. (ii) Heading towards you. End-on.

(a) (i) What situation is illustrated in (A)?
(ii) What action must you take?

(b) (i) What situation is illustrated in (B)?
(ii) What action must you take?

(c) (i) You are coming up on the lights illustrated in (C). What do the lights tell you?
(ii) What action must you take?

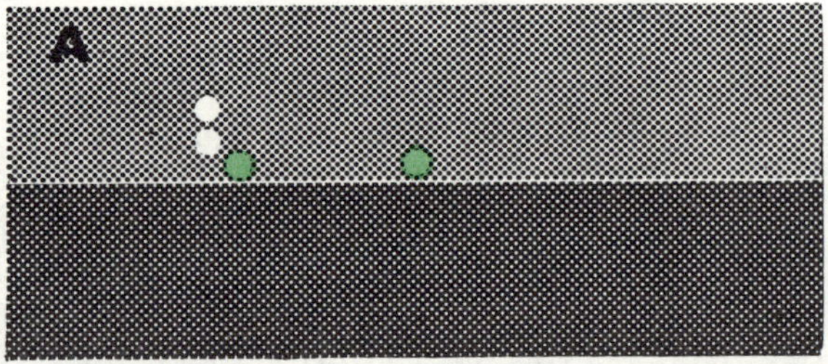

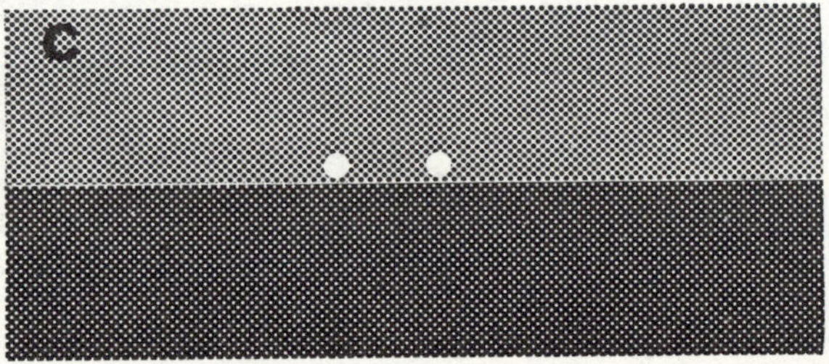

(a) (i) A vessel pushing another from left to right.
(ii) Stand-on.
(b) (i) One vessel pushing another. End-on.
(ii) Alter course to starboard. (Sound one short blast.)
(c) (i) The vessel is towing another alongside on the same heading as you. Stern-on.
(ii) Keep out of the way until past and clear.

One of the vessels in this illustration is displaying two forward masthead lights.

The range is 2 to 3 miles.

(a) What is she engaged in doing?
(b) What should you do?

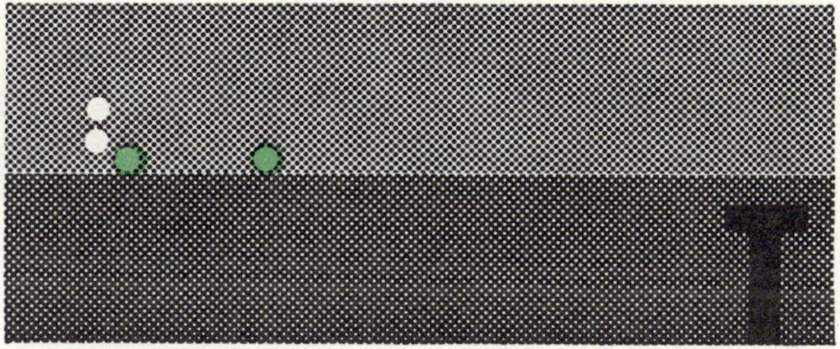

(a) Pushing.
(b) Stand-on with caution.

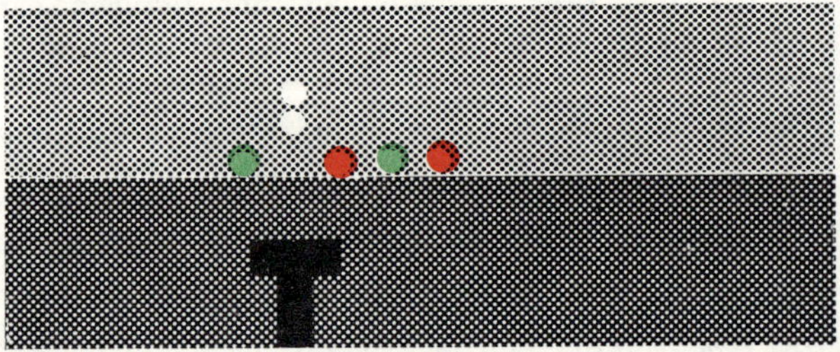

1. What does this illustration represent?
2. What should you do?

1. One vessel towing another alongside, head-on to you.
2. Alter course to starboard (sound one short blast).

To identify vessels towing or pushing at night is probably the most difficult lesson in the whole of this chapter, so do not be discouraged if you have found it heavy going.

If you feel you need a break of five minutes or so, take one now.

When you return to the programme, you will find, on the next few pages, some questions to refresh your memory.

The vessels shown below are exactly head-on and so you cannot tell which masthead lights are forward and which may be aft. This is rare but you should be aware of the problems it raises.

In each of the illustrations (A), (B) and (C)

1. What is each of these vessels doing?
2. Which groups of vessels definitely indicate the lengths involved?
3. What lengths are indicated in your answer to question 2?

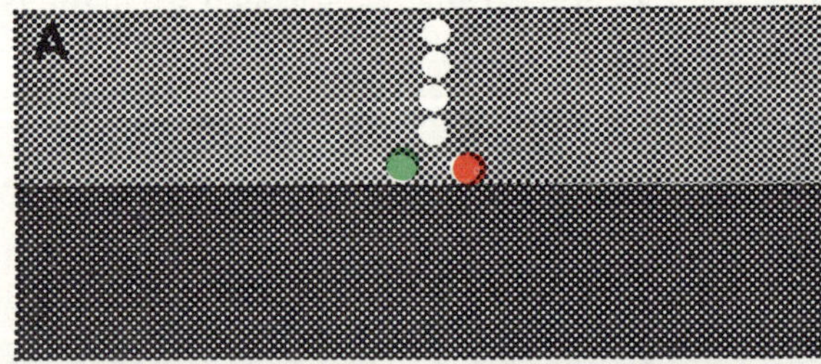

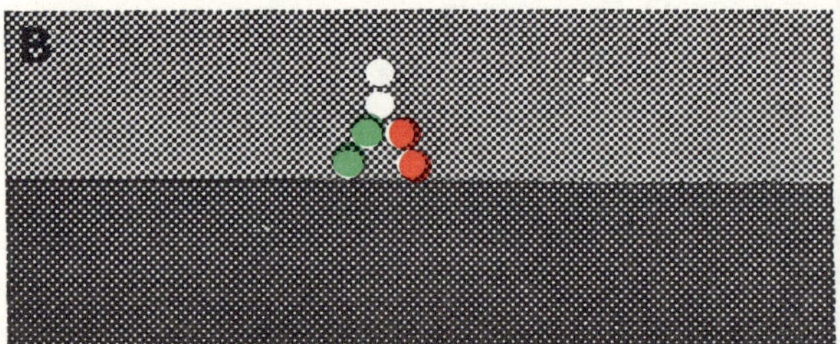

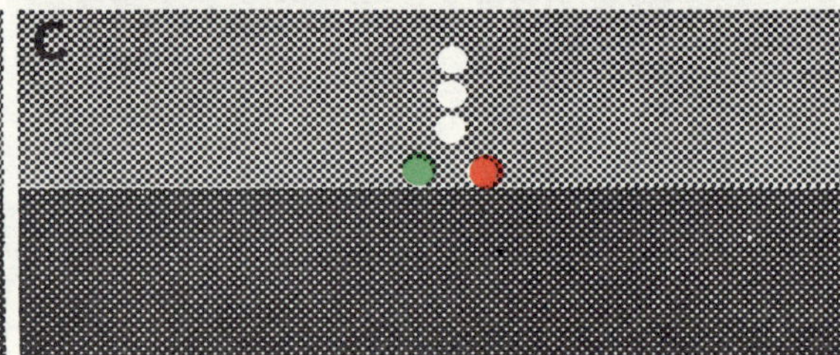

1. (A) Towing.
   (B) Pushing.
   (C) Towing.

2. (A) and (B).

3. (A) Vessel with a tow over 200 metres.
   (B) Vessel of less than 50 metres, pushing.

---

1. What are the vessels in (A), (B) and (C) doing?
2. Which vessel might be more than 50 metres long?
3. What do the lights in (B) indicate?

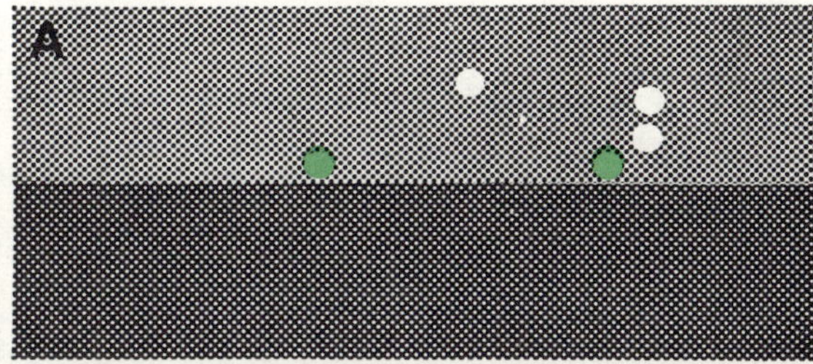

1. (A) Towing.
   (B) Towing.
   (C) Pushing.
2. The towing vessel in (A).
3. Length of tow more than 200 metres and towing vessel under 50 metres.

---

1. What are the vessels in (A) and (B) doing?
2. What is the length of the vessel with masthead lights in (A)?
3. What do the lights in (C) indicate?

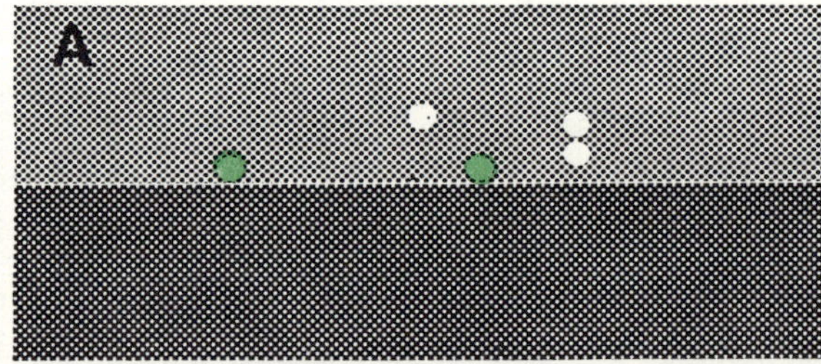

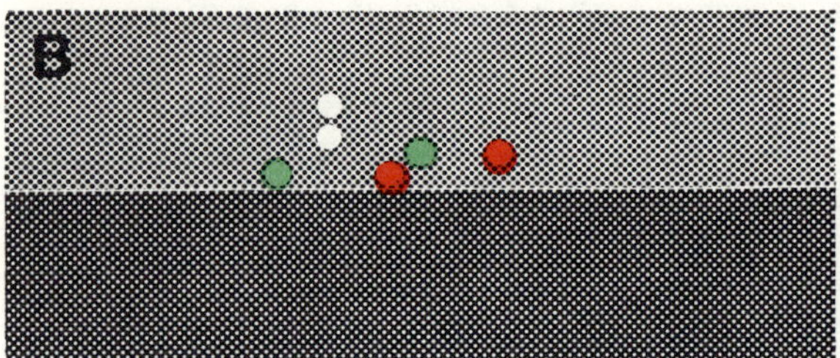

1. (A) Towing.
   (B) Towing alongside.

2. Possibly over 50 metres.

3. One vessel towing another alongside on the same heading as you.

(If you had more than one wrong answer to the questions on pages 148, 149 and 150, you are strongly advised to go back to page 140 and study this section again.)

Rule 25 covers lights which are displayed by **sailing vessels.**

A **sailing vessel under way** is required to display only **side lights** and **stern light.**

A sailing vessel **under 12 metres in length** may **combine those lights in one lantern at or near the masthead.**

However, a sailing vessel may, optionally, exhibit **all-round, coloured sailing lights** at or near the masthead, the upper light being red and the lower green, together with side lights and stern lights in their normal positions.

When coloured 'sailing lights' are displayed, then a combined lantern may not be used.

(Rules in respect of vessels under 7 metres in length are set out in the section 'Specification of Lights'.)

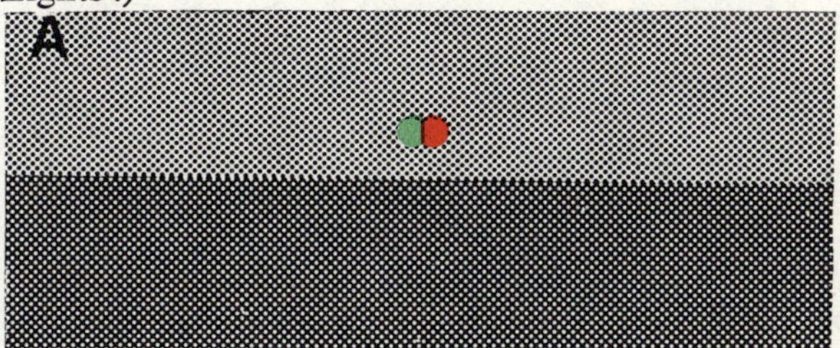

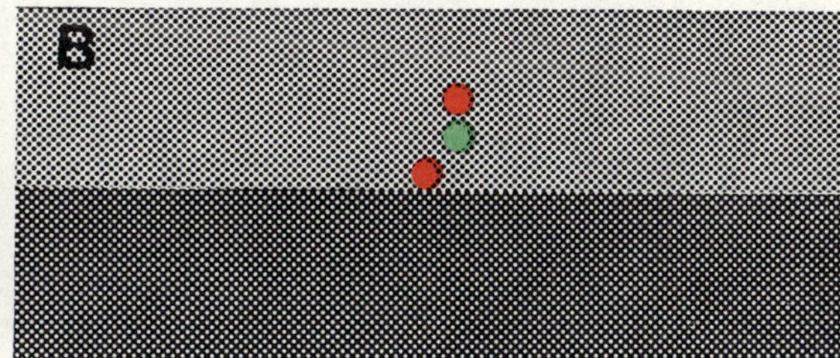

(A) and (B) are different sailing vessels.

1. What do the lights indicate about the vessel in (A)?
2. What is the arc of visibility of the masthead lights in (B)?

1. The sailing vessel is under 12 metres in length.
2. All-round.

The coloured lights on the foremast are optional, so you may often see vessels of this type showing no masthead lights.

What kind of vessel is shown in each of these illustrations?

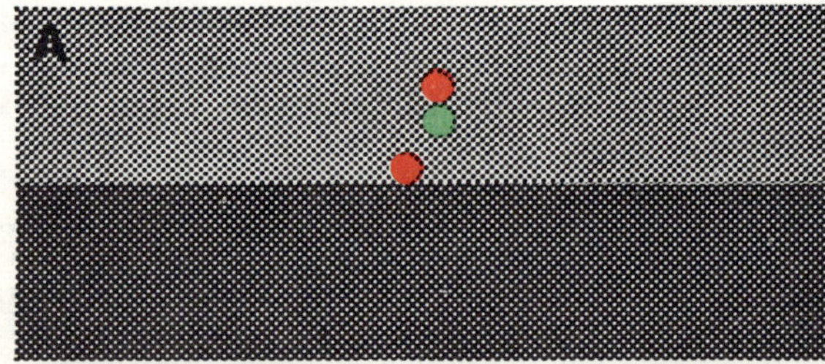

Each of them shows a sailing vessel under way.

The stern light of a sailing vessel (or any other vessel), under way, would look like this.

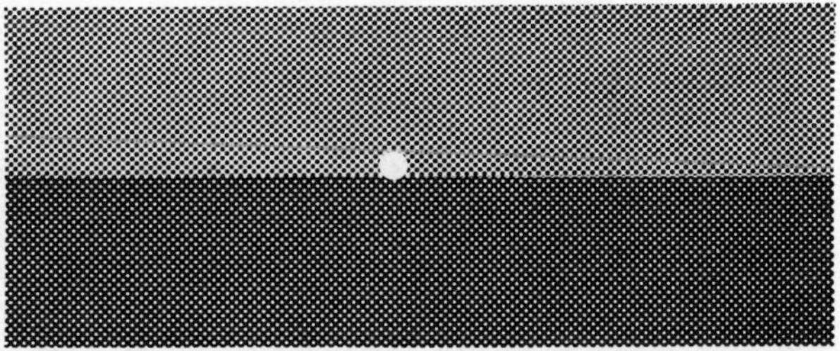

So, too, would a small boat's light, a distant steaming light, and many other vessels' lights.

You can seldom be sure what a single white light signifies until you have seen whether any other lights appear as you approach it.

In anchorage waters, however, you can be more positive, especially if the other vessel's portholes and upper works are lit up enough to show her shape.

A single all-round white light is displayed by a vessel less than 50 metres long, at ——— .

anchor

1. What type of vessel does each of the illustrations signify?
2. If you have sighted the lights in (B) on a steady bearing at a range of 2 miles and your course is dead into the wind, what action should you take?

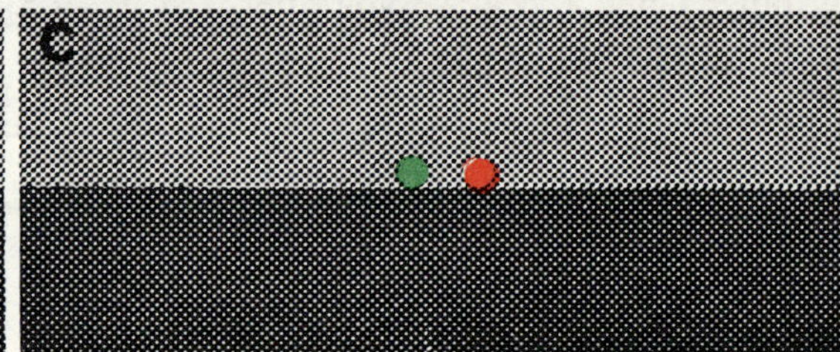

1. A sailing vessel under way.
2. Sound 2 short blasts (· ·) and alter course to port.

Vessels **under 50 metres** long **may** display two anchor lights, visible for at least 2 miles and **may** use their working lights.

Vessels **50 metres or over** in length **must** display two anchor lights, visible for at least 3 miles and **may** use their working lights.

Vessels over 100 metres in length **must** display two anchor lights **and** use their working or equivalent lights to illuminate their decks.

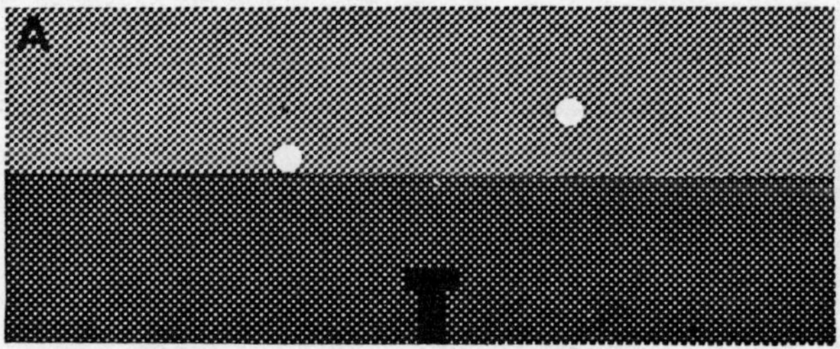

Anchor lights must be visible all round the horizon (i.e. through 360°). When two anchor lights are displayed, the forward light is higher (i.e. contrary to the masthead light positions when under way).

To either of the following questions, the answer may be that there is no way of telling.

In (A) in which direction is the anchored vessel's head lying, as you look at her?
In (B) are you approaching the anchored vessel's head or her stern?

(A) To the right (or starboard).
(B) There is no way of telling.

You sight these lights on a steady bearing at a range of about a mile inside a harbour.

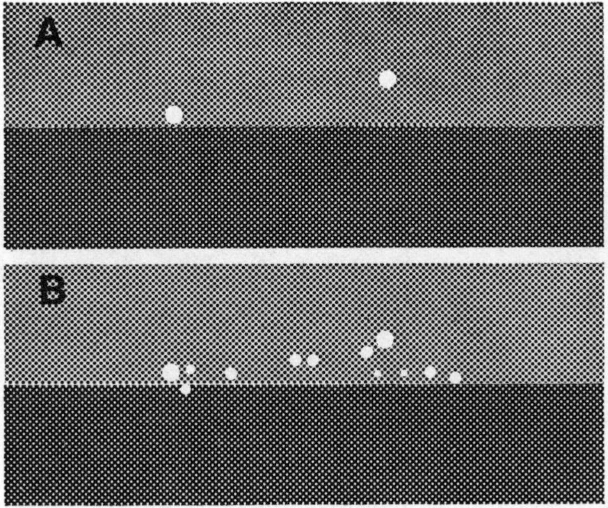

1. (a) What kind of vessel is signified in (A)?
   (b) After deciding what you have sighted, what should be the purpose of any action you take?

2. What kind of vessel **must** display the lights in (B)?

1. (a) A vessel at anchor; the length may be over, or under, 50 metres. (Remember that, unlike the positioning of masthead lights when under way, the after anchor light is lower than the forward anchor light.)
(b) To keep clear.
2. A vessel at anchor over 100 metres in length.

These lights shown in the illustrations below are displayed by a vessel **not under command** when **making way** through the water.

The red lights must be carried at least 2 metres apart in a vertical line, and they must be visible for at least two miles **all round** the horizon.

They are NOT distress signals.

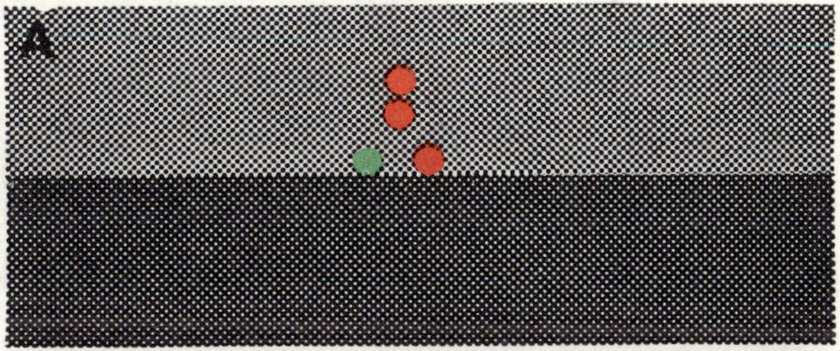

(A) Which way is this vessel heading?

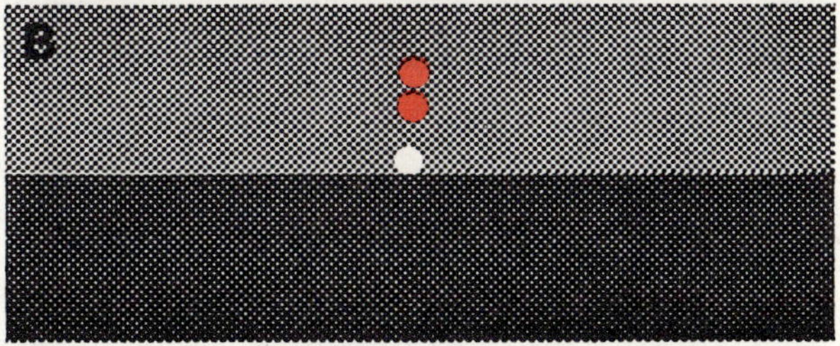

(B) Which way is this one heading?

(A) Directly towards you.
(B) Directly away from you.

Side lights and stern light must be displayed by a vessel not under command **only** when she is making way (moving) through the water.

So, if you see a vertical pair of red lights without any other lights, you know that they belong to a vessel not under command which is under way but ________.

stopped (i.e. not making way through the water)

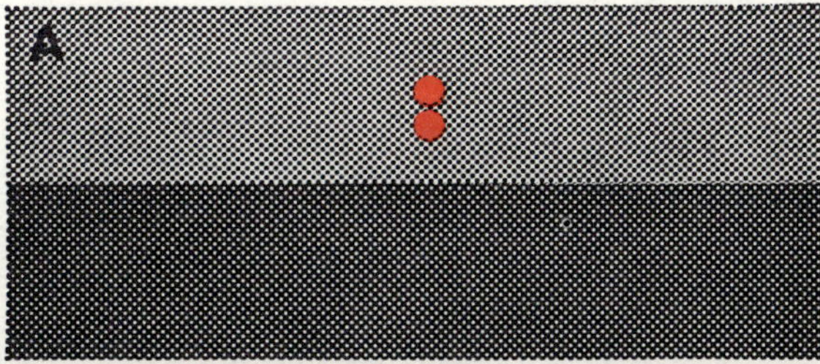

1. What do **all** these illustrations show?
2. Which vessels are **under** way?
3. Which ones are **making** way?

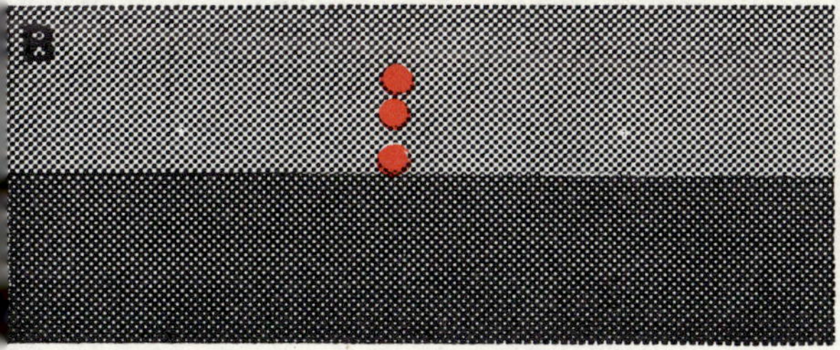

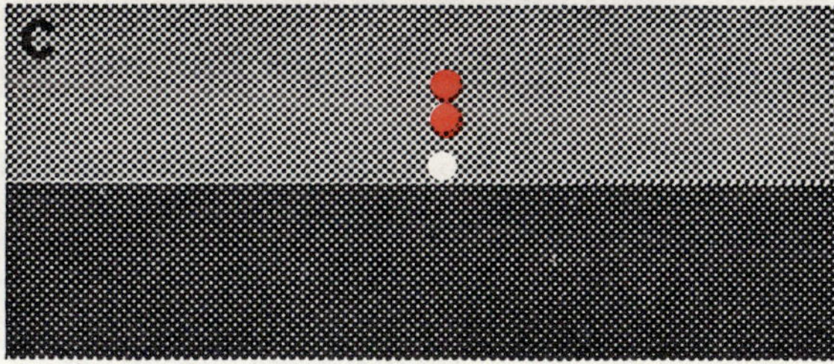

1. Vessels not under command.
2. All of them.
3. (B) and (C).

These lights signify a vessel aground.

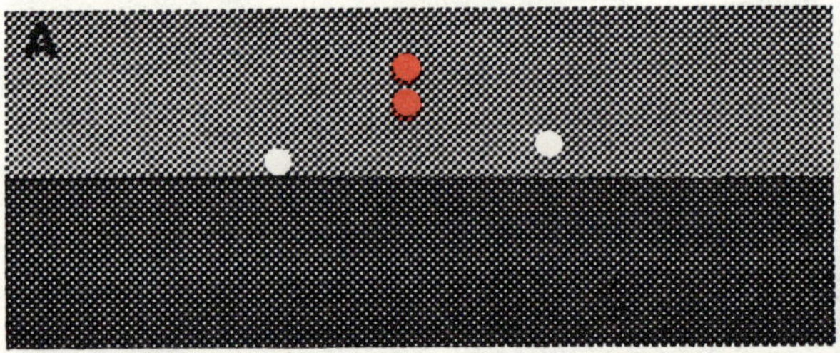

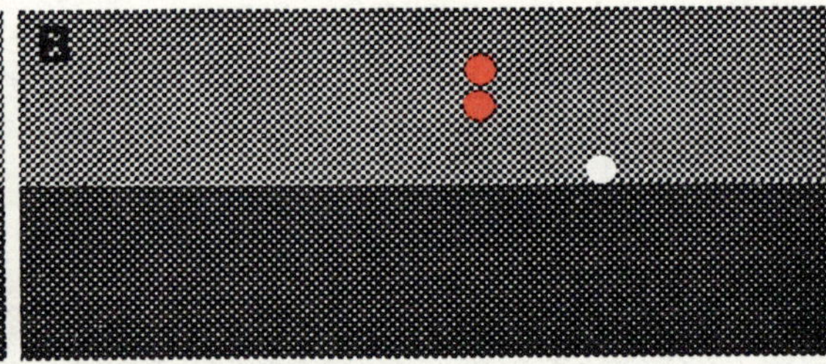

Which illustration shows a vessel definitely less than 50 metres long?

(B)

The lights shown in the illustration below are not distress signals. They may look like a vessel 'not under command, at anchor' but this is not so. Such a vessel would display only the ordinary anchor lights.

In fact, the lights have an extra meaning which is very important.

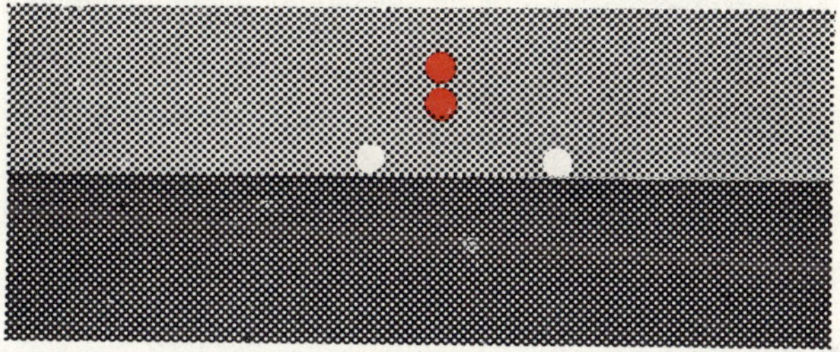

A vessel which has stuck fast on a reef or a sandbank, would need to warn other vessels of the fact.

The lights in the illustration indicate a vessel ______.

aground (Note: There are **two** red lights and anchor lights displayed at night as opposed to **three** black balls during the day.)

The lights for a vessel aground are **not** a distress signal, and neither are the lights shown here.

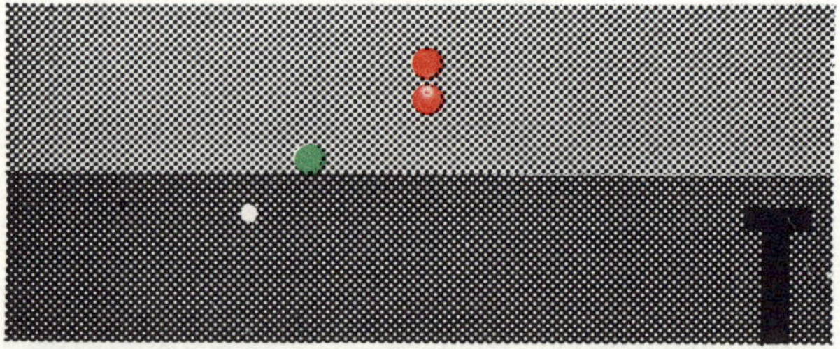

(a) What kind of vessel is shown in the illustration?
(b) What action should you take if you sighted these lights on your port bow at a range of three miles on a steady bearing?

[You will need to work out approximately how the other vessel is heading in relation to yours, before you can answer question (b) correctly.]

(a) A vessel not under command, making way.
(b) Sound 2 short blasts (· ·) and alter course to port.

In daylight, if the vessel in the illustration below was in the same circumstances, this signal would be replaced by a vertical line of three black balls.

(a) What do the lights in the illustration indicate?
(b) What do they indicate about her length?

(a) A vessel aground.
(b) Less than 50 metres.

The lights in these illustrations signify **a vessel restricted in her ability to manoeuvre, under way.**

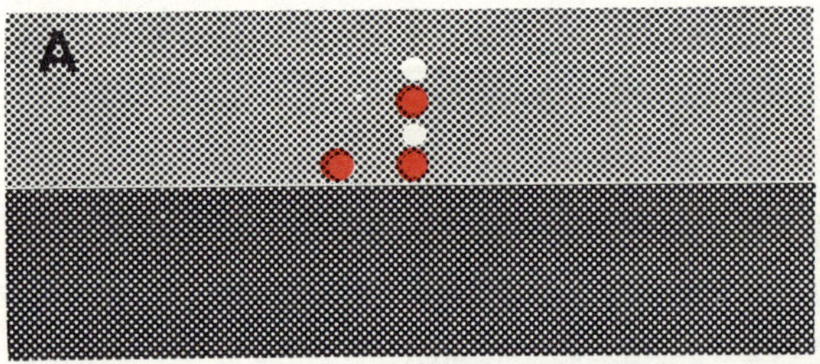

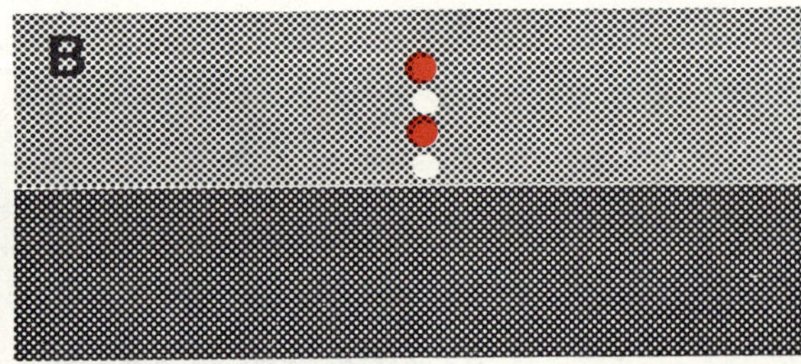

The term 'a vessel restricted in her ability to manoeuvre' was first referred to in Chapter 3 and includes vessels engaged in operations listed in Rule 3 (g), i.e. a vessel picking up a navigation mark, cable or pipeline, dredging, surveying or carrying out underwater operations, replenishing whilst under way, launching or recovering aircraft and towing operations that restrict alterations of course.

At night, in most cases, you would be unlikely to be able to identify the type of operation.

Which of the vessels in the above illustrations could you be overtaking?

(B)

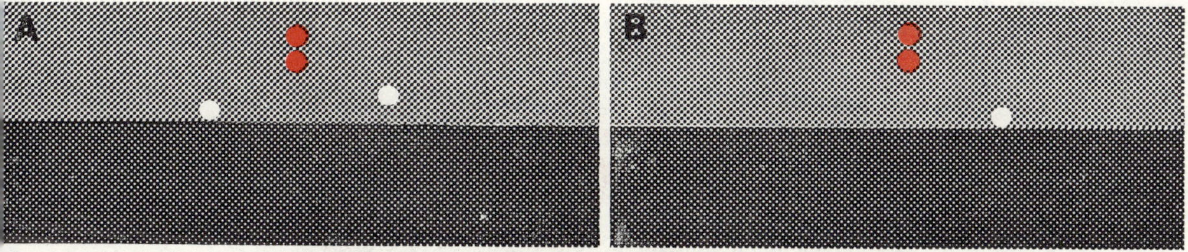

1. What is represented by the lights in both illustrations?
2. Vessel (B) has only a single white light. What does this signify?
3. Which way are the vessels headed?

1. A vessel aground.
2. She is less than 50 metres long.
3. To your right.

In daylight, the vessel shown below would display a signal which has 3 components i.e. black ball, diamond, black ball.

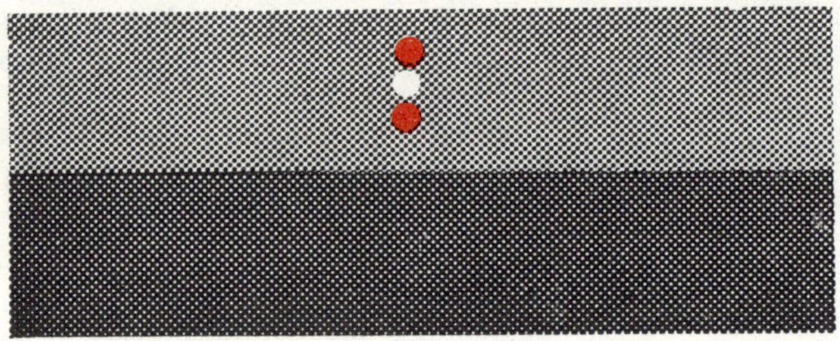

(a) What do these lights tell you about this vessel's activities?
(b) As you see, she is not displaying masthead light, side lights or stern light. What does this signify?

(a) She is restricted in her ability to manoeuvre.
(b) She is under way, but not making way.

These lights do not indicate a vessel aground. (There is a white light between the red lights.)

What do the lights indicate?

A vessel restricted in her ability to manoeuvre, at anchor, probably 50 metres or over in length.

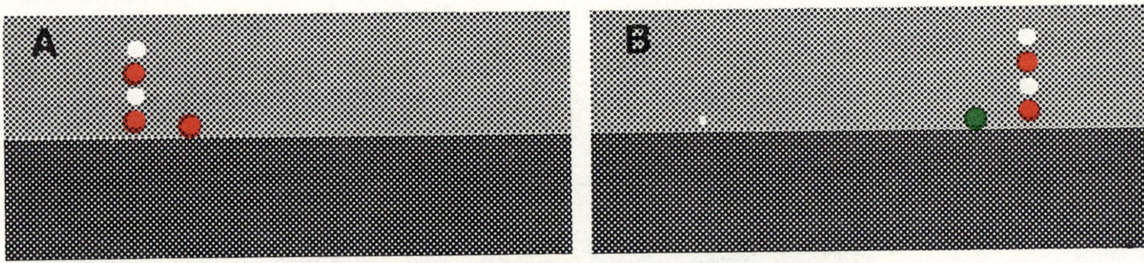

1. Which way is each of these vessels headed?
2. What should you do if you encounter either of these vessels?

1. (A) To your left.
   (B) To your right.
2. Keep clear.

(A) What do these lights indicate?

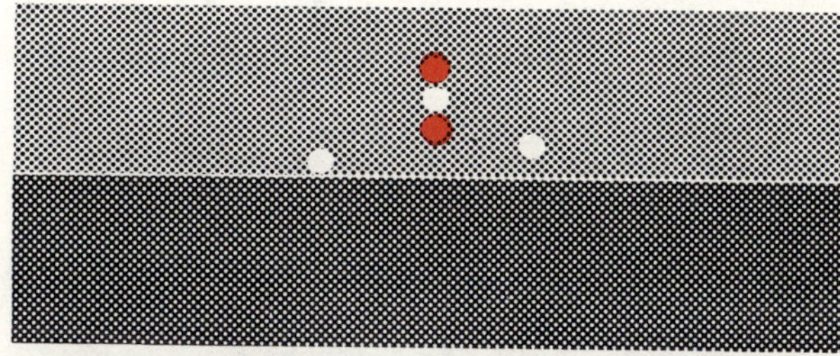

(B) What do these lights indicate?

(A) A vessel restricted in her ability to manoeuvre, at anchor.
(B) A vessel restricted in her ability to manoeuvre, making way.

A vessel **engaged in dredging or underwater operations when an obstruction exists** must, when **making way,** display the lights prescribed for any vessel restricted in her ability to manoeuvre and in addition, exhibit **two all-round red lights** in a vertical line **on the side on which the obstruction lies** and **two all-round green lights** to indicate **the side on which approaching vessels may pass.**

When these additional lights are displayed and the vessel is at anchor or under way but not making way, only the signal for a vessel 'restricted in her ability to manoeuvre' and the 'obstruction exists' signals will be displayed.

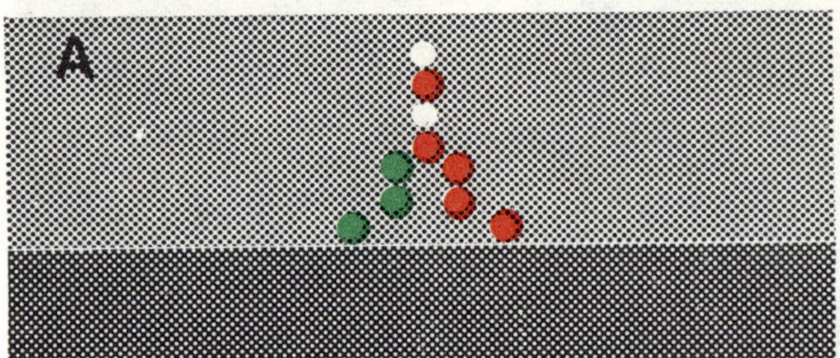

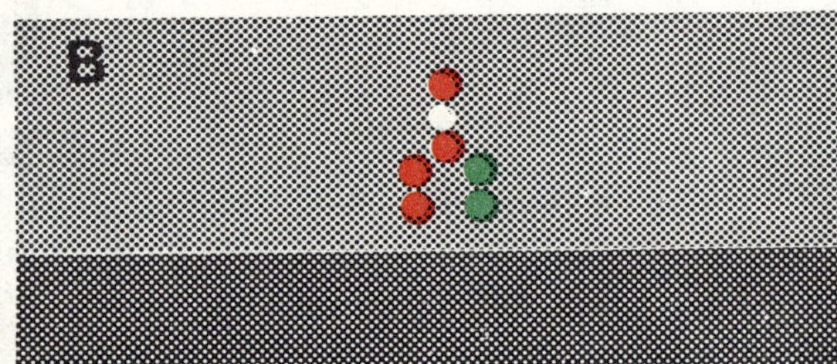

In respect of a vessel engaged in dredging or underwater operations,

(a) what, precisely, do the signals in (A) signify?
(b) what, precisely, do the signals in (B) signify?

(a) That the vessel is making way and an obstruction exists on her port side. Approaching vessels may pass to starboard.
(b) That the vessel is at anchor or under way but not making way. An obstruction exists on the side of the two red lights. Approaching vessels may pass on the side of the two green lights.

Another vessel which comes into the category 'restricted in her ability to manoeuvre' is a **vessel engaged in a towing operation** which **severely restricts her ability to deviate from her course.**

When this is the case, the vessel will display the lights appropriate to the towing situation **and** the lights for 'restricted in her ability to manoeuvre'.

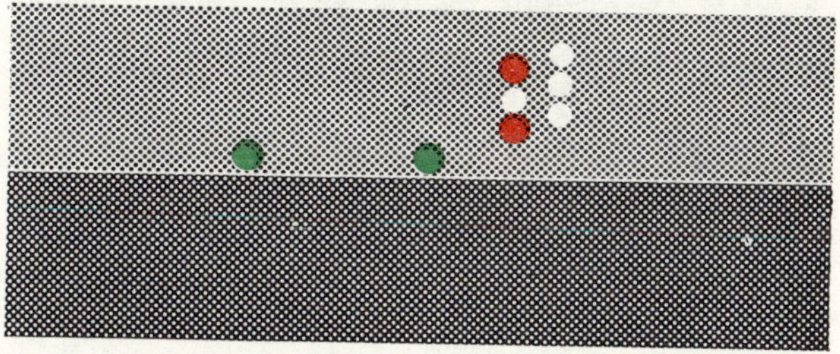

What do you understand from the signals shown in the illustration?

That the tow is over 200 metres in length. The towing vessel is less than 50 metres.
That the vessel cannot deviate from her course. (She is restricted in her ability to manoeuvre.)

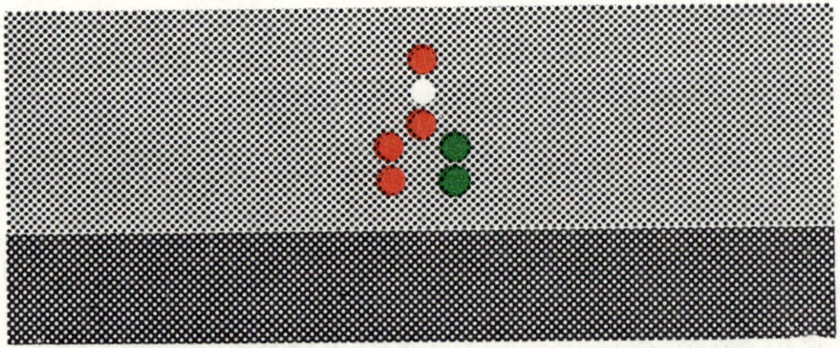

What action will you take when you approach a vessel in this situation?

Alter course to pass clear on the side of the two green lights.

A vessel **constrained by her draught may,** in addition to masthead lights, side lights and stern light, display 3 all-round red lights in a vertical line. (Rule 28.)

(Note: The **daytime** signal for a vessel constrained by her draught is a cylinder where it can best be seen.)

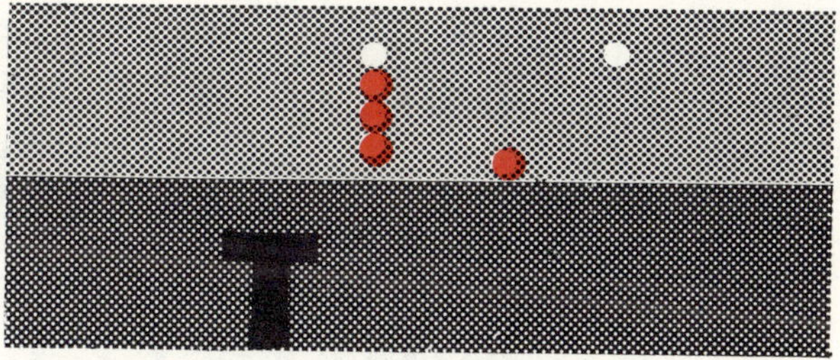

1. (a) What do the lights in the illustration signify?
   (b) In which direction is the vessel moving?
2. What action should you take?

1. (a) A vessel constrained by her draught.
   (b) Moving across your bow from right to left.
2. Alter course to starboard. (Sound one short blast.)

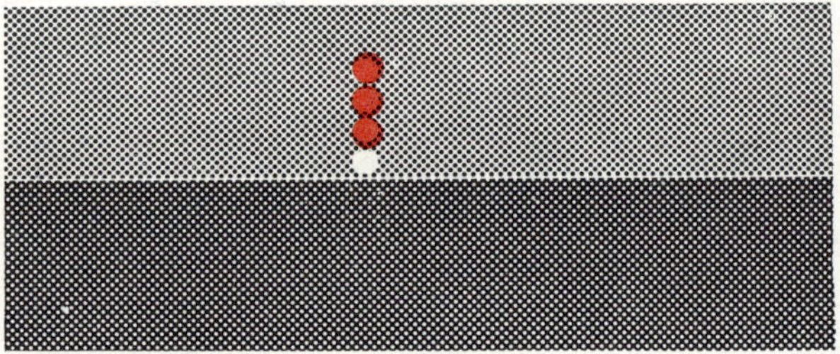

1. What do the lights in this illustration signify?
2. What action should you take?

1. You are overtaking a vessel constrained by her draught.
2. Avoid impeding her safe passage.

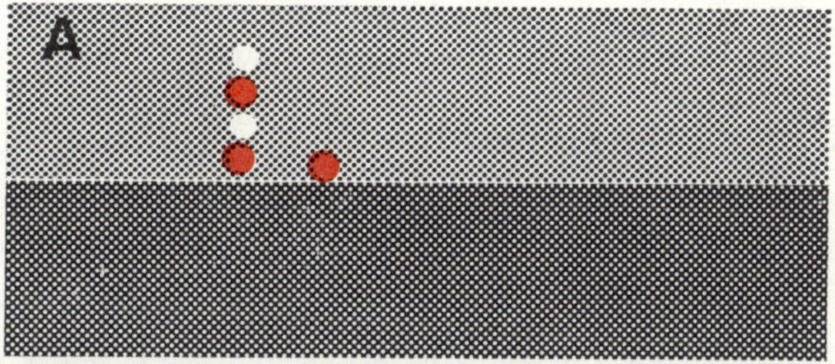

1. What do the signals in (A), (B) and (C) signify?
2. Which way are they moving?

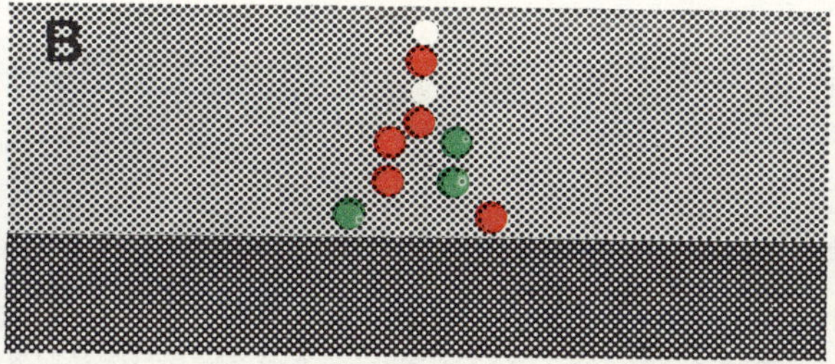

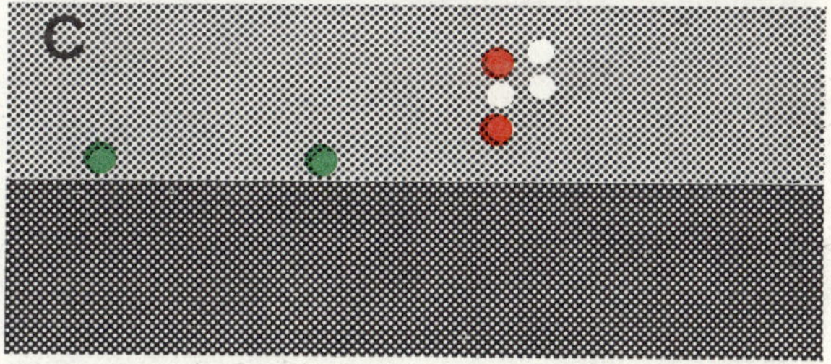

1. (A) A vessel under 50 metres in length, under way and making way, restricted in her ability to manoeuvre.
   (B) A vessel, making way, engaged in underwater operations. An obstruction exists on her starboard side. Other vessels may pass to port.
   (C) A vessel under 50 metres in length, engaged in towing and restricted in her ability to manoeuvre. The tow is less than 200 metres in length.

2. (A) From right to left.
   (B) Coming towards you.
   (C) From left to right.

The lights shown below indicate a vessel **engaged in minesweeping.** The green lights occupy the same positions as the black balls shown in daylight.
Which vessel is making way?

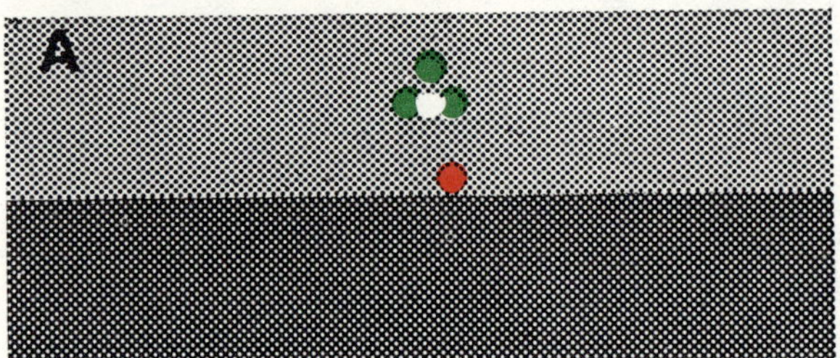

(A)

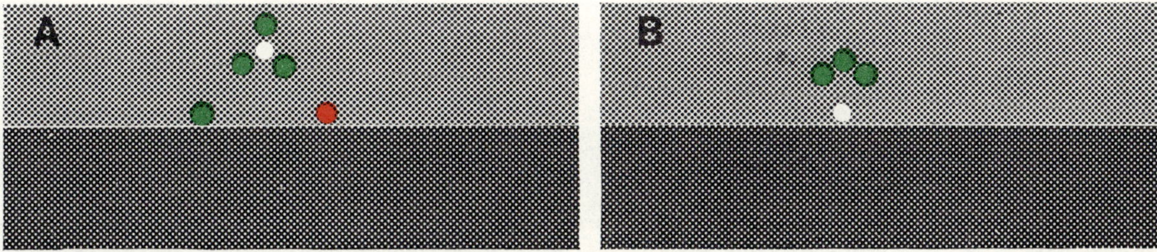

1. What are these vessels engaged in doing?
2. Which way is vessel (A) heading?
3. Which way is vessel (B) heading?

1. Minesweeping.
2. Towards you. Bows-on.
3. Away from you. Stern-on.

When you see a vessel minesweeping, you know that danger extends up to 1000 metres astern of her, and up to 500 metres on both sides.

Look carefully at the illustration and decide for yourself which way the other vessel is heading. The range is 2 miles and the bearing is steady.

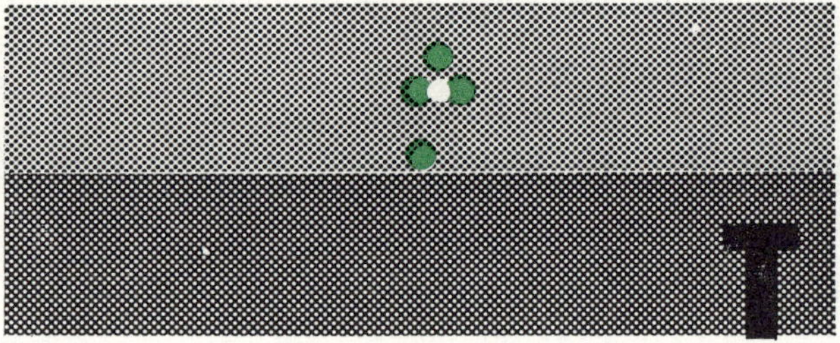

What should you do to ensure that you do not stand into danger?

Sound 2 short blasts (· ·) and alter course to port.
(You may also consider a reduction of speed.)

There is another class of vessel which carries a **green all-round light,** together with a **white all-round light:** vessels **engaged in trawling.** Vessels under 50 metres in length **may** and vessels of 50 metres or over **must** display a masthead light abaft of and higher than the green light.

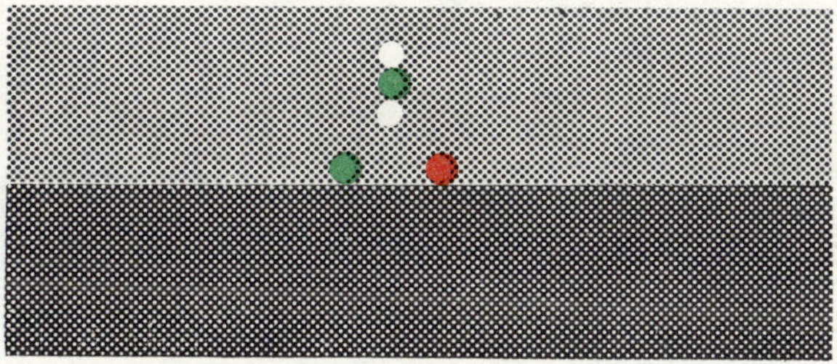

Under or over 50 metres. Bows-on.

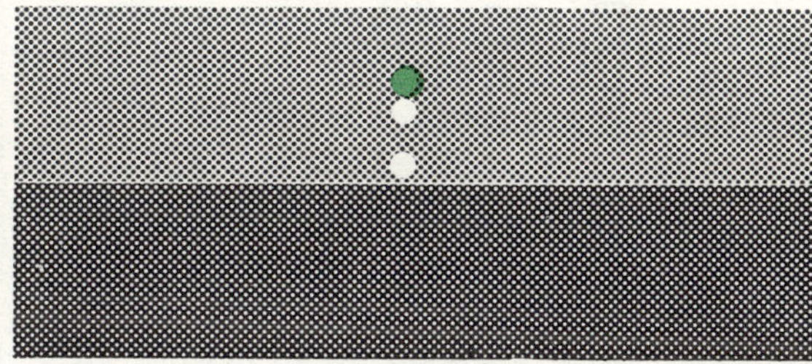

Under or over 50 metres. Stern-on.

Trawlers are grouped with other vessels under Rule 26, but it is only at night that they show any signal which distinguishes them from other fishing vessels.

What should you do if you encounter a vessel engaged in trawling?

Keep clear.

The range of the lights shown below is about 2 miles and the bearing is steady.

(a) What do the lights tell you about this vessel's activities?
(b) What action should you take?

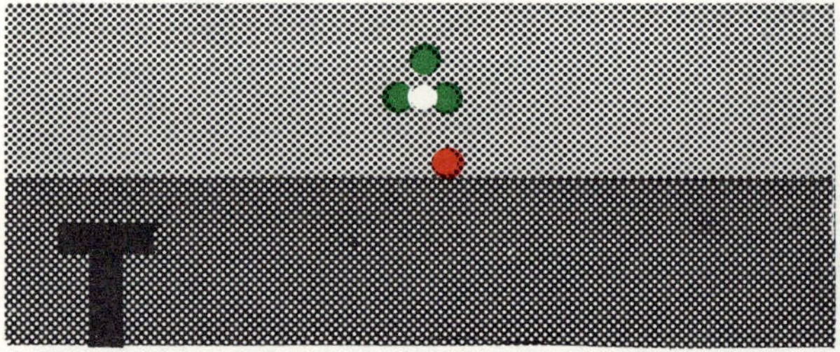

(a) She is engaged in minesweeping.
(b) Sound 1 short blast (·   ) and alter course to starboard.

Why does the stern-on view not show a masthead light.

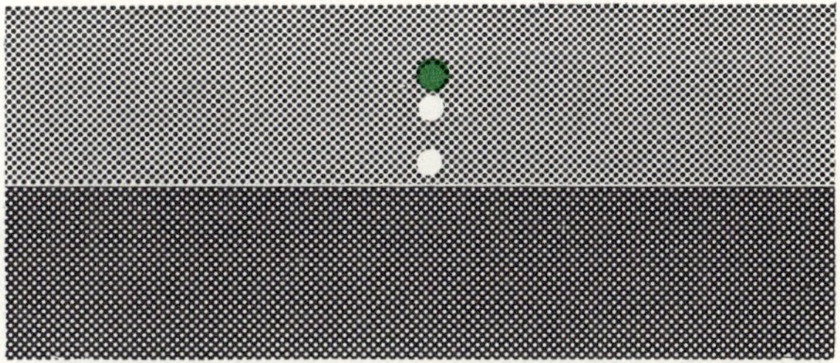

Stern-on with stern light.

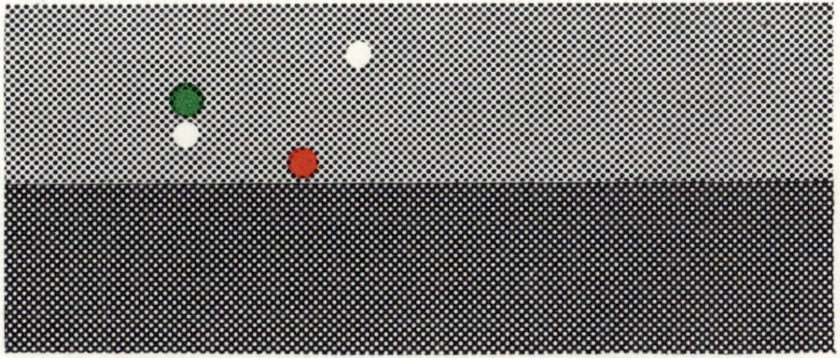

Port side with masthead light.

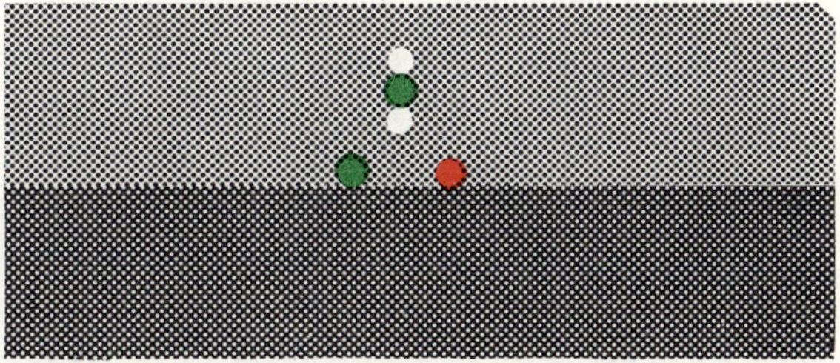

Head-on with masthead light.

Because the masthead light does not show more than 22·5° abaft the beam.

Vessels engaged in fishing without trawls show a red all-round light above a white all-round light. They do not show a masthead light.

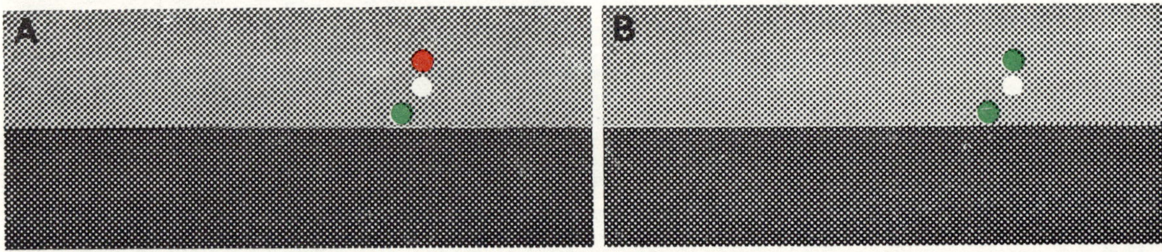

(a) What are vessels (A) and (B), respectively, engaged in doing?
(b) What is the length of the vessel in (B)?

(a) (A) Fishing.
(B) Trawling.

(b) Less than 50 metres.

Vessels engaged in fishing **(but not when trawling)** show an additional white all-round light if their outlying gear extends more than 150 metres, carried in the direction of the outlying gear. N.B. This white light is **not a masthead light;** it tells you nothing about the length of a fishing vessel.

Each of these vessels is about 2 miles away, on a steady bearing.

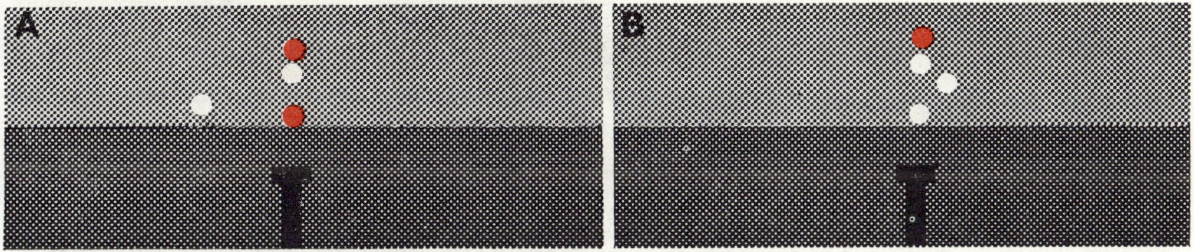

1. Indicate the vessel(s) with gear extending more than 150 metres.
2. Which ways should you alter course to avoid vessel (A) and vessel (B)?

1. Both. 2. (A) To starboard.
(B) To port.

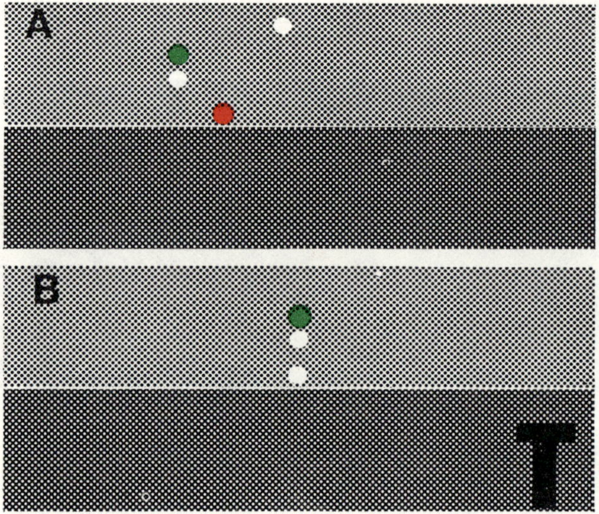

1. What are both these vessels engaged in doing?

2. What is the white light standing-off to the right of the others on vessel (A)?

3. If the bearing of vessel (B) is drawing aft, what are you doing in relation to her?

1. Trawling.
2. Her masthead light.
3. Overtaking her.

Just as in day-time, vessels engaged in fishing or trawling do not hoist signals to show when they are at anchor.

But, at night, you can at least tell when they are not making way.

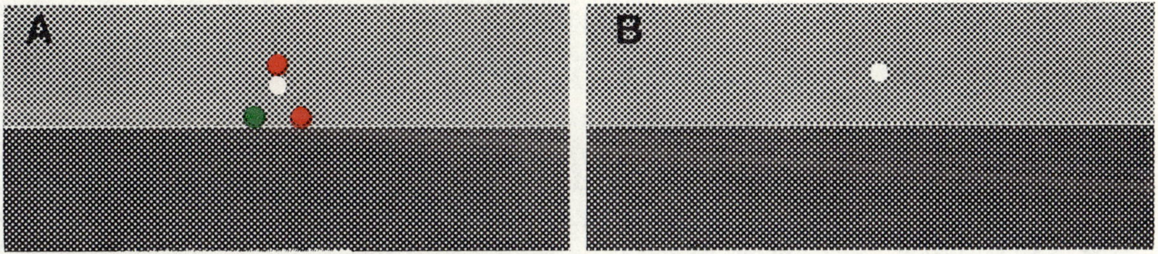

Which of these two vessels cannot be at anchor. What is she doing?

(A) The one with the side lights. She is engaged in fishing.

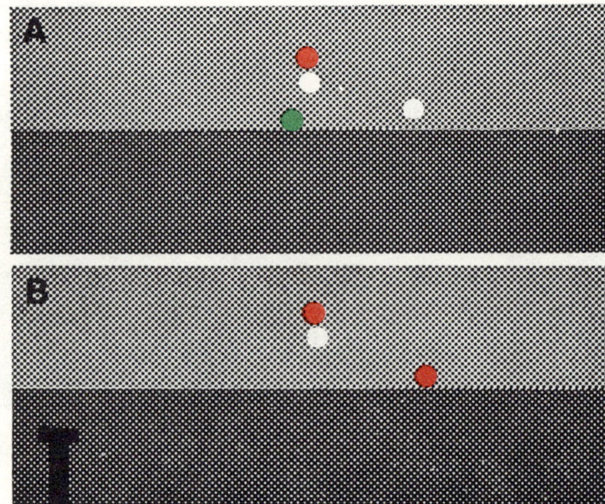

(A) What does the additional white light signify?

(B) The other vessel's bearing is steady. She is 2 miles distant. What action should you take?

(A) Outlying gear extending more than 150 metres in the direction of the white light.
(B) Sound 1 short blast (·   ) and alter course to starboard.

A vessel engaged in fishing in close proximity to other vessels engaged in fishing **may** exhibit the additional signals described in Annex II to the regulations.

Read Annex II.

The lights described must be at a lower level than those we have already considered (Rule 26). They must be visible all-round at a distance of 1 mile.

(a) What type of vessel is operating in (A) and (B)?
(b) What is she doing in (A)?
(c) What is she doing in (B)?

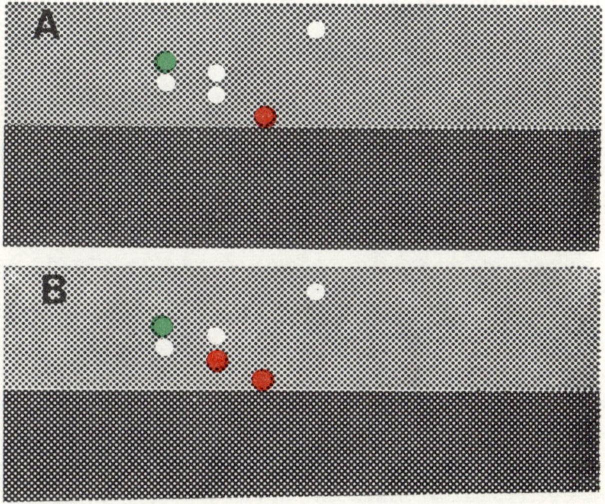

(a) A trawler. (b) Shooting her nets. (c) Hauling her nets

1. What has happened in (A)?
2. What do the lights in (B) indicate?
3. (a) What type of vessel is indicated in (C)?
   (b) What do the alternately flashing yellow lights indicate?

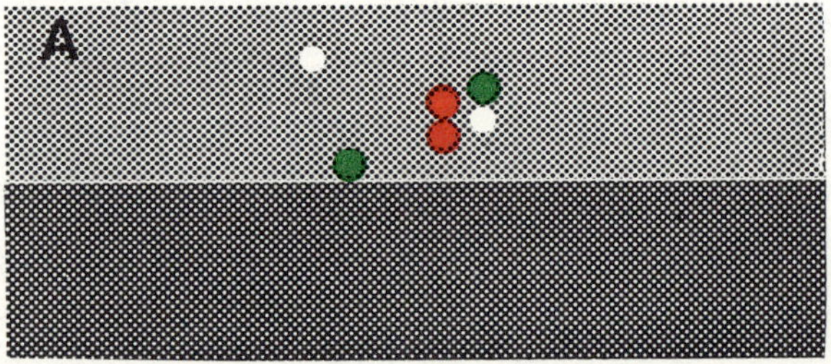

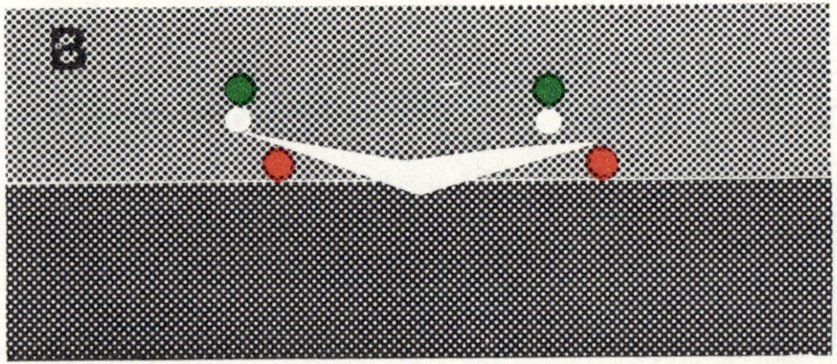

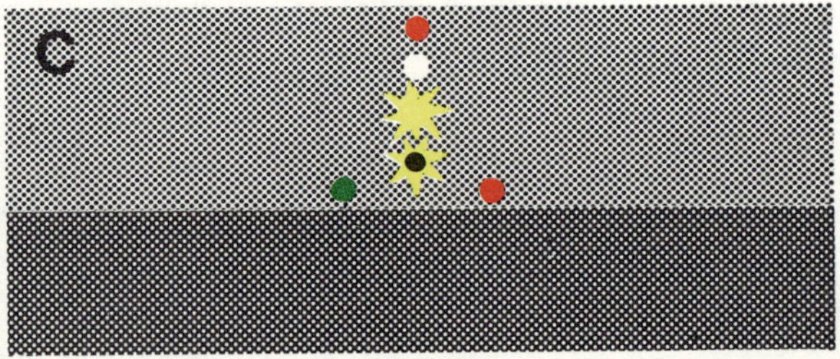

1. A trawler's nets have come fast upon an obstruction.
2. Trawlers trawling as a pair.
3. A fishing vessel is hampered by its purse seine gear.

Red and white lights are also carried on the mast by **pilot vessels** when on pilotage duty. They are all-round lights and the **white light is above the red one** (i.e. opposite to fishing vessels).

Is this pilot vessel under way?

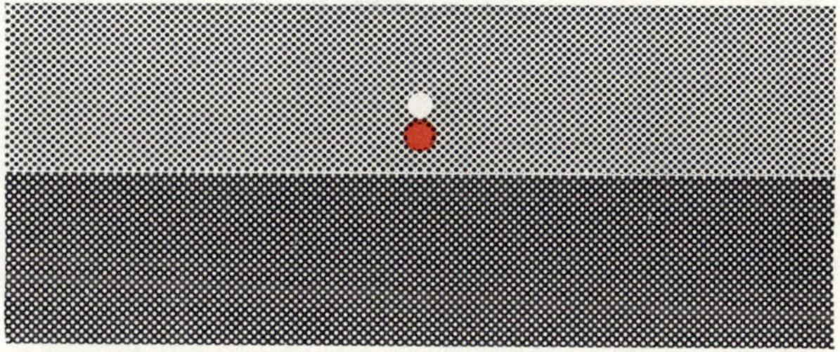

No. She is not displaying a stern light or side lights.

When under way a pilot vessel will display, in addition to the red and white lights, side lights and stern light but no masthead light.

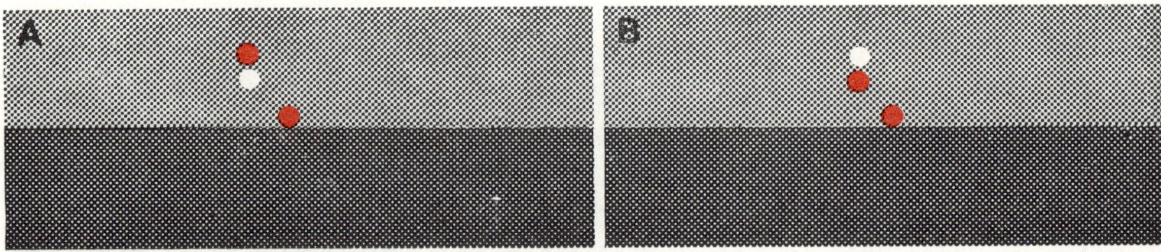

1. Which illustration shows a pilot vessel on pilotage duty?
2. What does the other illustration show (i.e. what is the other vessel engaged in doing)?

1. (B) is the pilot vessel.
2. (A) is a vessel engaged in fishing.

A pilot vessel **not on pilotage duty** is lit as any ordinary vessel of her type.

(a) Is (A) a pilot vessel?

(b) What is the vessel in (B)?

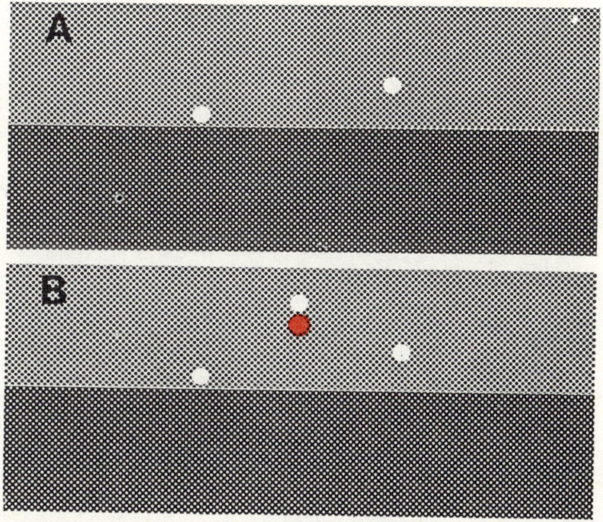

(a) It could be any vessel at anchor (including a pilot vessel not on pilotage duty).

(b) A pilot vessel on pilotage duty, at anchor.

Rule 31 says :

> 'When it is impracticable for a **seaplane** to exhibit lights and shapes of the characteristics prescribed in the Rules of this Part she shall exhibit lights and shapes as closely similar in characteristics and position as is possible.

Would you be able to identify a seaplane, at night, at a range of 1 mile?

It is unlikely because it displays the same lights as any other vessel of its size.

The air-cushion vessel is somewhat different.

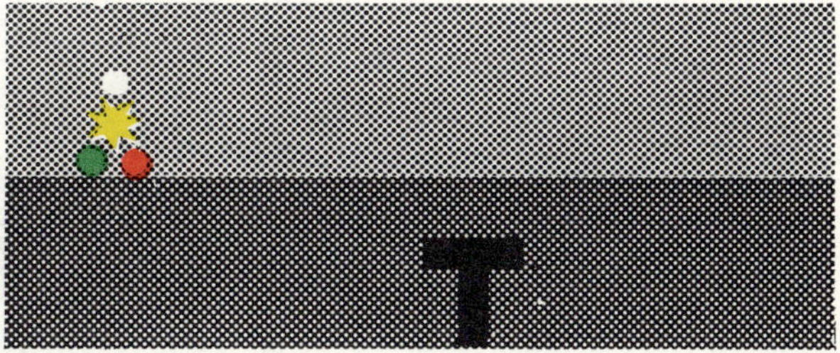

When operating in the non-displacement mode, it will carry the same lights as any other vessel of its size but in addition shall exhibit an all-round yellow light, flashing at a frequency of 120 flashes or more per minute.

It must be borne in mind that an air-cushion vessel may travel much faster than a conventional craft and when operating in the non-displacement mode in strong winds will be steering considerably off its course to maintain its track. Because of drift, the lights need not necessarily indicate the direction she is travelling over the ground.

What action would you take if you saw the lights illustrated at 45° on your port bow, on a steady bearing?

Stand-on with caution having regard for the possible high speed and drift of the air-cushion vessel.

What do the alternately flashing lights in this illustration represent?

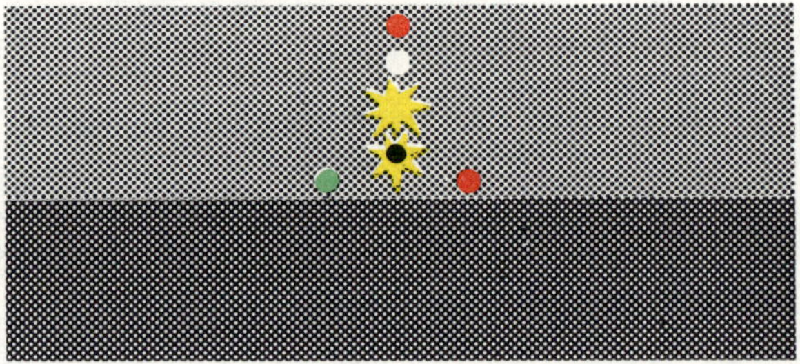

A fishing vessel hampered by its purse seine gear.

Test on Chapter 4

As in the last test, most of the questions in this test are based on interpreting illustrations. You must get 100% on all questions marked * before you go on to the next chapter.

Write down your answer to each question.

1. What are the arcs of visibility laid down for the following lights?

   (a) A masthead light.
   (b) A side light.
   (c) A stern light.

2. When **must** the lights in the Rules be displayed?

Test (continued)

3. *(A) (i) What kind of vessel is (A)?
   (ii) Is she under way, or at anchor?

   *(B) What do the lights indicate about the length of the vessel (B)?

   (C) What do they indicate about the length of vessel (C)?

4. *What should you do in situation (C), if you have sighted the vessel on a steady bearing at a range of 2 miles?

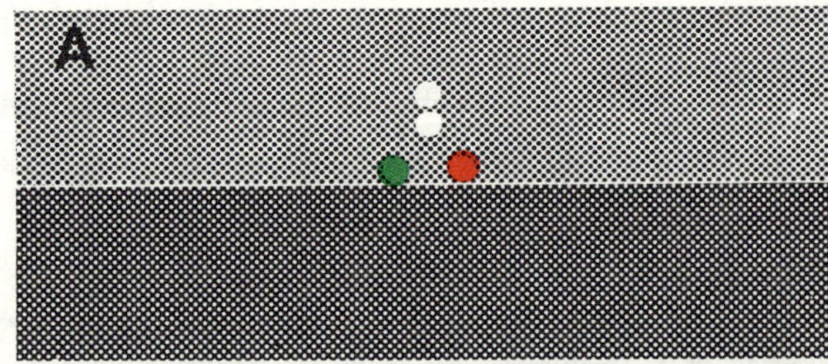

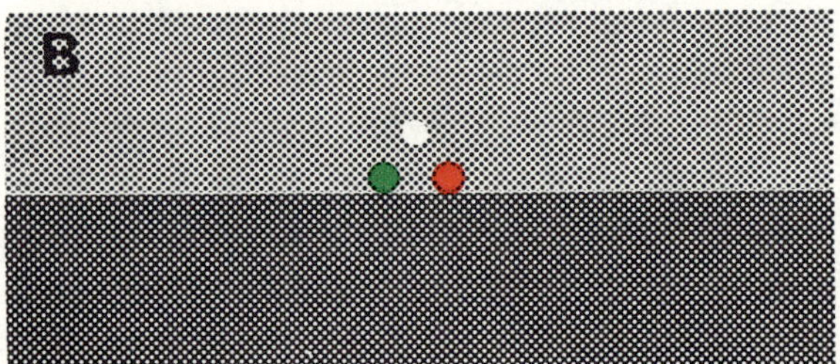

Test (continued)

*5. What is indicated in illustration (A)?

*6. (i) What is indicated in illustration (B)?
(ii) What length is indicated in (B)?

*7. (i) What is indicated in illustration (C)?
(ii) What **two** lengths are indicated in (C)?

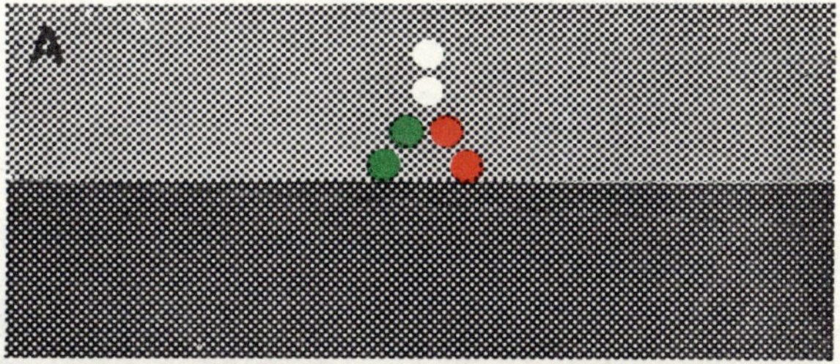

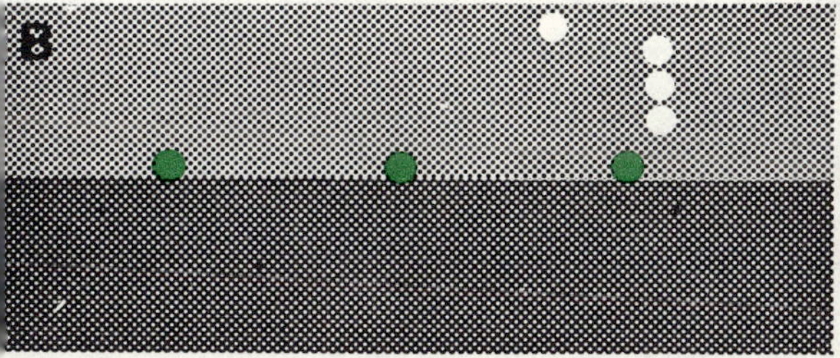

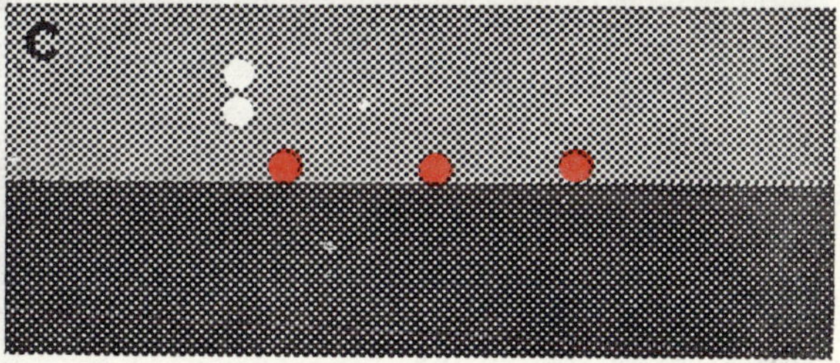

Test (continued)

*8. (i) What situation is depicted in both (A) and (B)?
(ii) In what direction are the vessels heading?
(iii) What action should you take in situation (A)?
(iv) What must you do in situation (B)?

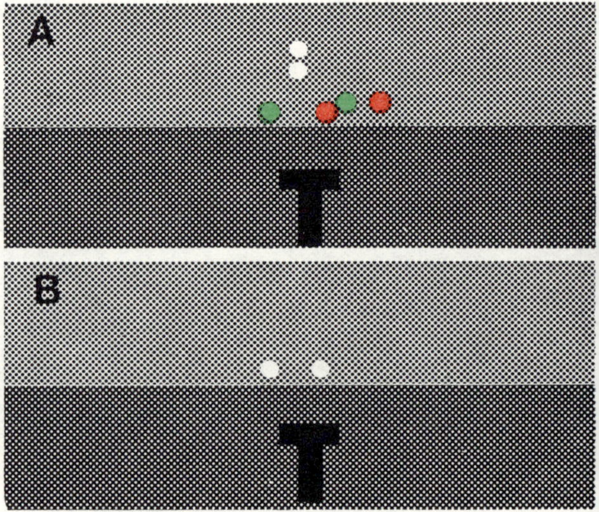

Test (continued)

*9. (i) What do the signals in (A), (B) and (C), signify?

(ii) What must you do when you approach each of the situations illustrated?

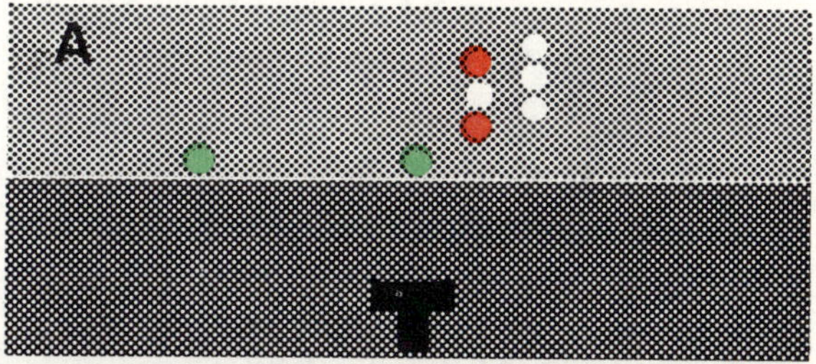

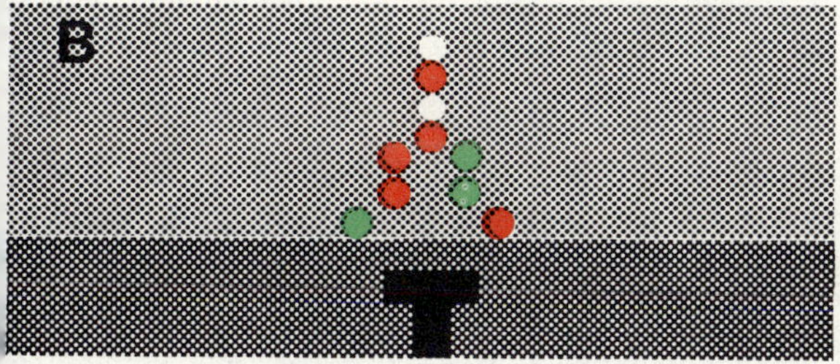

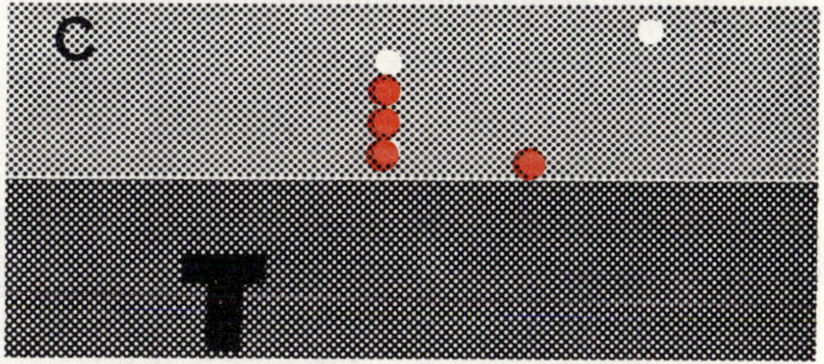

Test (continued)

10. *(i) What type(s) of vessels is/are indicated in illustrations (A) and (B)?
    (ii) Which way is the vessel in (B) heading as you look at it?

11. *(i) What would probably be indicated by the lights in (C), if you sighted them in a harbour?
    (ii) Which way is the vessel in (C) heading as you look at it?

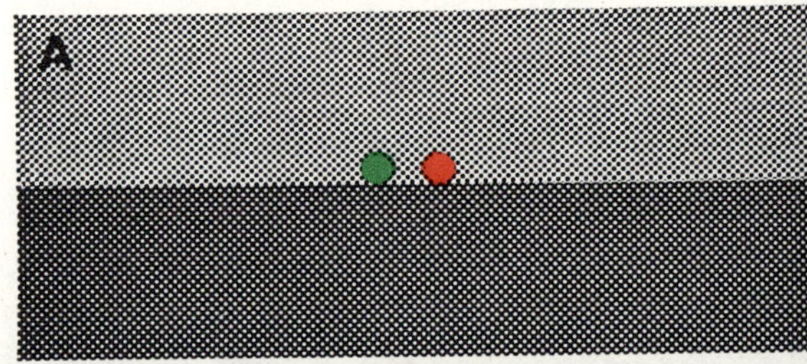

Test (continued)

*12. What does each of the illustrations (A), (B) and (C), represent?
(In each case state also whether the vessel is at anchor, making way, or under way but not making way.)

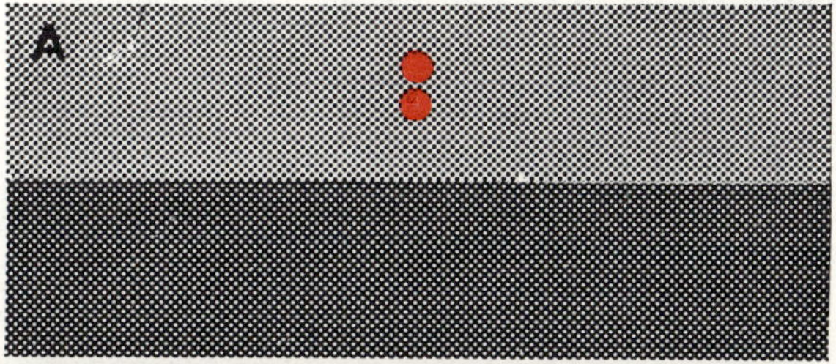

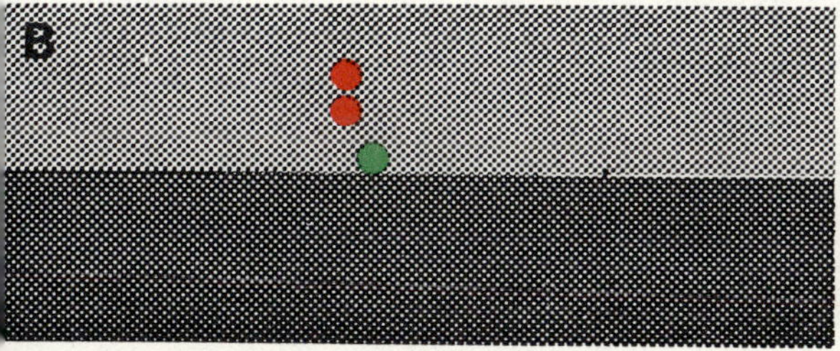

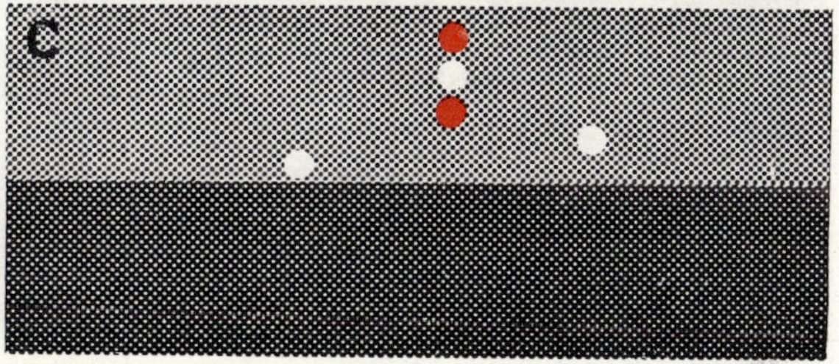

Test (continued)

*13. What does each of the illustrations (A), (B) and (C), represent?
(In each case, state whether the vessel is making way, under way but not making way, or not under way.)

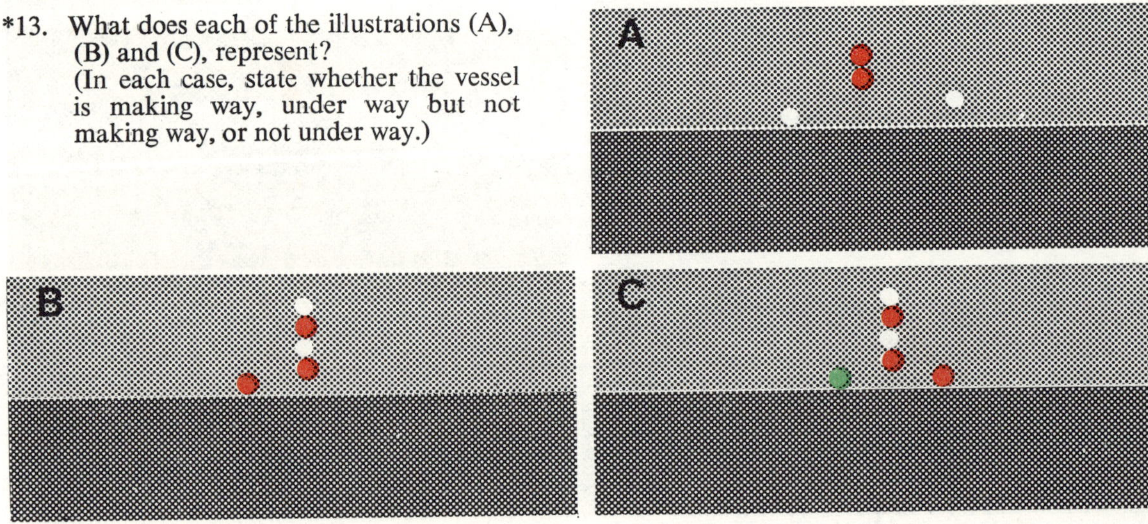

Test (continued)

14. (i) Which of the vessels in (A) and (B) would you be overtaking if the range was decreasing?
(ii) What must you do if you are overtaking any vessel?

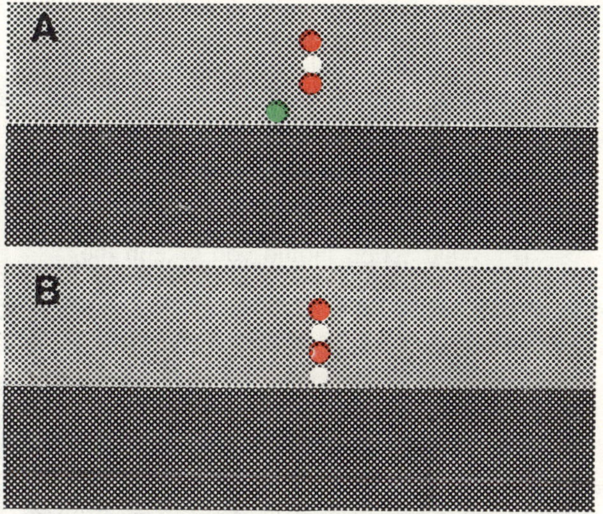

Test (continued)

*15. What does each of the illustrations (A), (B) and (C), represent? (In each case, state also whether the vessel is making way, under way but not making way, or not under way.)

*16. (i) How far astern and how far to the side of the vessel depicted in (C) does danger exist?
(ii) What action should you take in the situation illustrated in (C)?

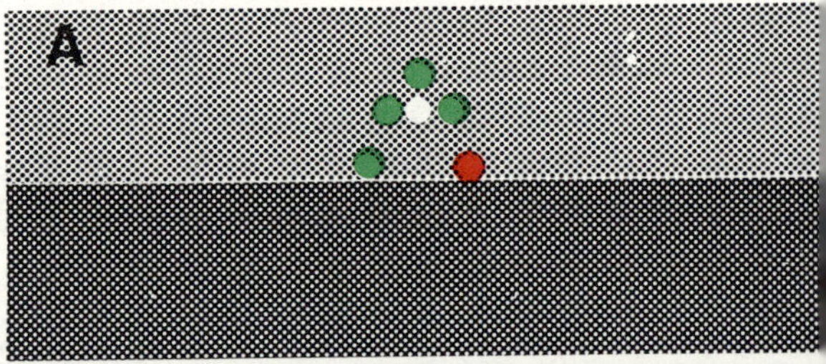

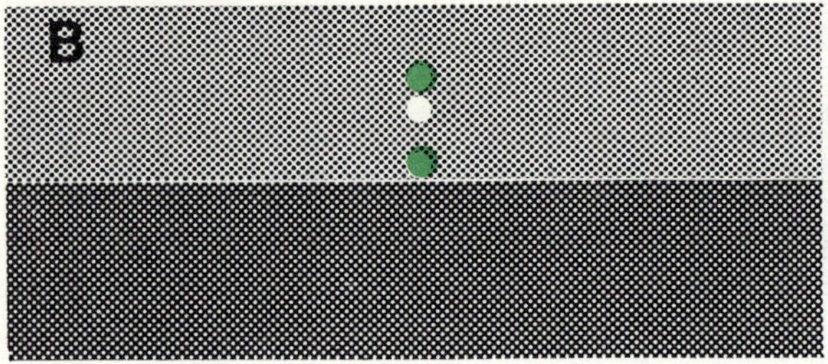

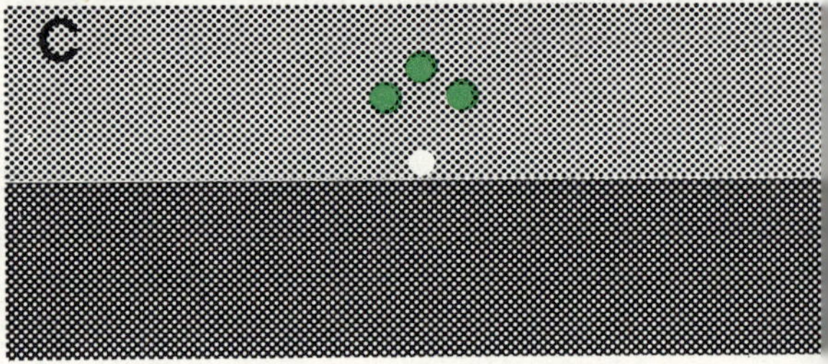

Test (continued)

17. What does each of the illustrations represent?
(Identify each one and state whether she is making way, etc.)

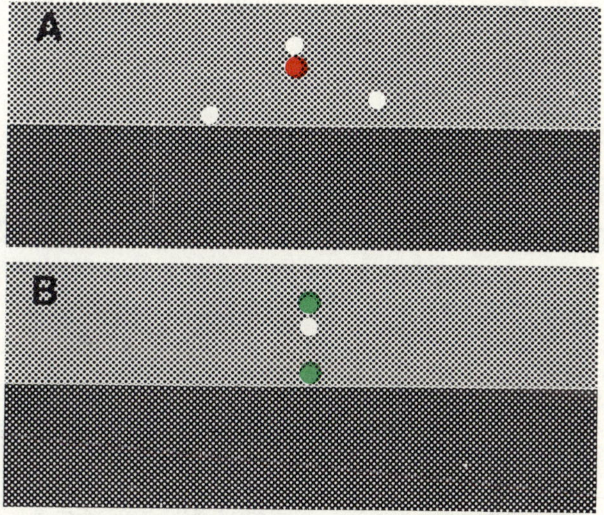

Test (continued)

*18. What does each of the illustrations (A), (B) and (C), represent?
(State whether the vessels are making way or not.)

19. What does the white light to the right in (A) indicate?

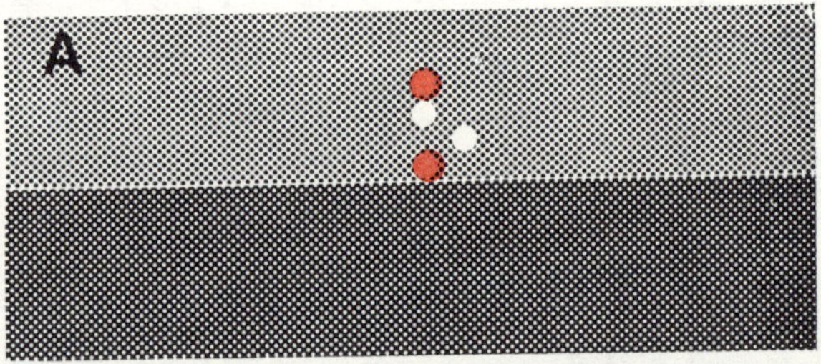

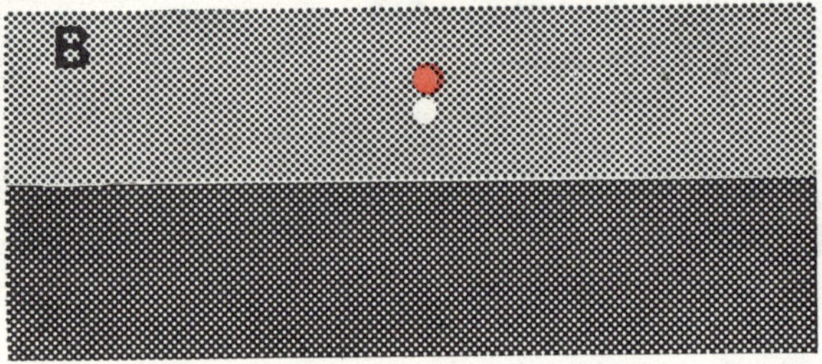

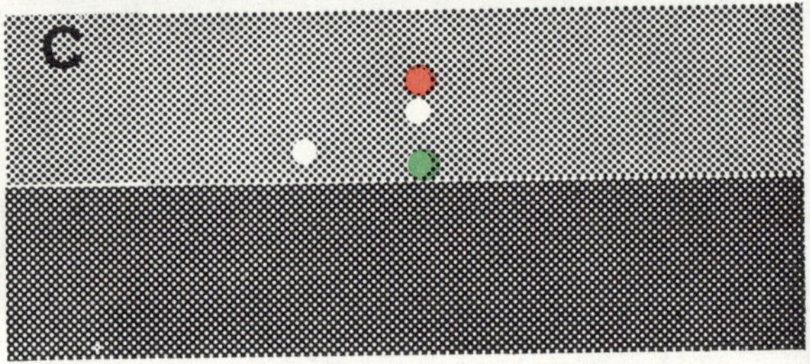

Test (continued)

20. *(i) The yellow light in (A) flashes at a frequency of 120 flashes per minute. What does it indicate?
    (ii) What factors must you take into account when you see the lights in (A)?

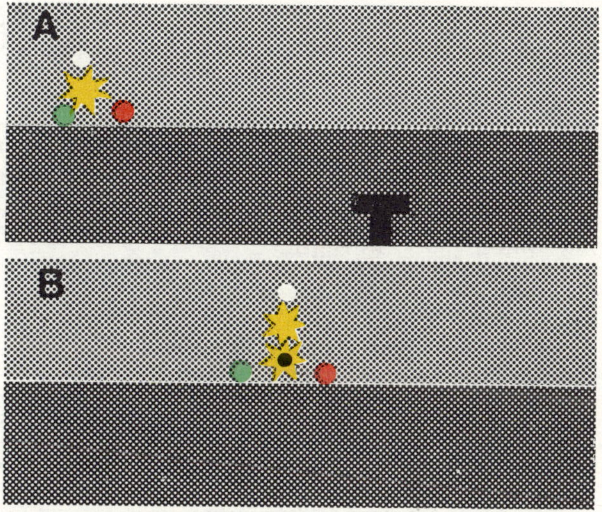

21. *What do the alternately flashing lights in (B) indicate?

Answers to Test

After every answer, a page reference is given in the column at the right. If you have any wrong answers, make a note of their references so that you can go over those sections again.

	Reference
1. (a) Through the **bows,** from 22·5° **abaft the beam** on **either** side. (b) From **right ahead,** to 22·5° **abaft the beam** on **one** side. (c) Through the **stern,** from 22·5° **abaft the beam** on **either** side.	pages 124–128
2. From sunset to sunrise.	122
3. *(A) (i) A **power-driven** vessel. (ii) **Under way.** *(B) Her length is **under 50 metres.** (C) Her length is **under 20 metres.**	123 134–137
*4. Sound 1 short blast (·) and alter course to starboard.	53–55
*5. A power-driven vessel of less than 50 metres in length **pushing** one or more other vessels.	138–147

Answers to Test (continued)

		Reference
6.	*(i) A power-driven vessel towing two other vessels. (ii) The length of the tow is **over 200 metres.**	pages 138–149
7.	*(i) A power-driven vessel towing two other vessels. (ii) The length of the **tow** is **under 200 metres** and the length of the **towing vessel** is **under 50 metres.**	
8.	*(i) A vessel **towing** another **alongside.** (ii) (A) Towards you. Head-on. (B) Away from you. Stern-on. *(iii) Sound one short blast and **alter course to starboard.** *(iv) **Keep out of the way until past and clear.**	143 53–55
9.	*(i) (A) The vessels are **restricted in their ability to manoeuvre** by being severely restricted in their ability to deviate from their course. (B) The vessel is **engaged in dredging or underwater operations.** An **obstruction exists on the side of the red lights. Approaching vessels may pass on the side of the green lights.** (C) A vessel **constrained by her draught.** *(ii) (A) Keep clear. (B) Sound one short blast and alter course to starboard. (C) Avoid impeding her safe passage.	171 170 173

Answers to Test (continued)

			Reference
10.	*(i)	Sailing vessels, under way.	pages 151–153
	(ii)	From right to left.	
11.	*(i)	A vessel at anchor.	155–156
	(ii)	From left to right.	
12.	*(A)	A vessel **not under command,** under way but **not making way.**	157–158
	*(B)	A vessel **not under command, making way.**	
	(C)	A vessel **restricted in her ability to manoeuvre, at anchor.**	167
13.	*(A)	A vessel **aground,** not under way.	161
	(B)	A vessel **restricted in her ability to manoeuvre, making way.**	164
	(C)	A vessel **restricted in her ability to manoeuvre, making way.**	164
14.	*(i)	Vessel (B).	53–55
	*(ii)	Keep out of the way until past and clear.	
15.	(A)	A vessel engaged in **minesweeping, making way.**	176–178
	(B)	A vessel engaged in **trawling, making way.**	179–181
	(C)	A vessel engaged in **minesweeping, making way.**	176–178
16.	*(i)	**1000 metres astern. 500 metres to both sides.**	176–178
	(ii)	**Immediately** alter course to port or starboard to **keep clear** of the **danger areas.**	
17.	*(A)	A **pilot vessel** on **pilotage duty,** at anchor.	189–191
	*(B)	A vessel engaged in **trawling, making way.**	179–181

Answers to Test (continued)

		Reference
18.	*(i) (A) A vessel engaged in **fishing, making way.** (B) A vessel engaged in **fishing, not making way.** (C) A vessel engaged in **fishing, making way.**	pages 182–187
19.	*That the vessel has **outlying gear** extending more than **150 metres.**	
20.	*(i) An air cushion vessel operating in the non-displacement mode. (ii) The vessel's speed and drift.	193
21.	*A fishing vessel hampered by her purse seine gear.	188

Before going on to the next chapter, look up the reference of any questions, marked with an asterisk, that you answered wrongly. If you have more than **four** different references to look up, you should work through the chapter again.

CHAPTER 5. CONDUCT IN NARROW CHANNELS, TRAFFIC SEPARATION SCHEMES AND IN RESTRICTED VISIBILITY

This chapter will deal with Rules 2: 5: 9: 10: 19: 34 (c), (e): 35.

Turn to these Rules now and read them before continuing this chapter.

Most situations with which we are concerned will occur on the open sea. However, you will remember that the Rules also apply to navigable waters connected with the sea.

These 'navigable waters' may well be narrow channels, and so, obviously, some modifications to the normal Rules will be necessary.

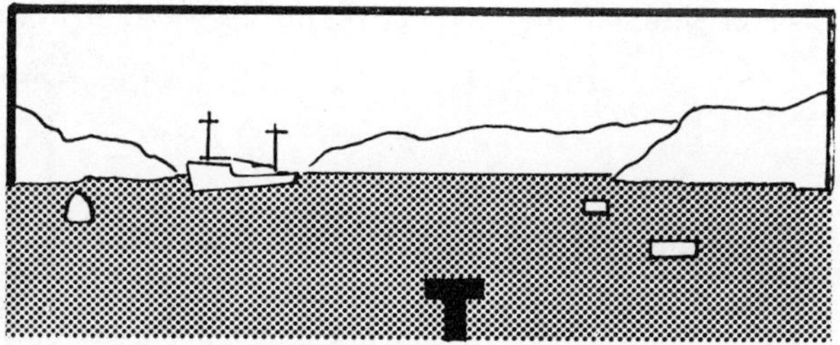

The buoys mark the entrance to a narrow channel. The other ship is just leaving the channel.

To which side of the channel should you go?

The starboard side.

Rule 9 (a) states:

> 'A vessel proceeding along the course of a narrow channel or fairway shall keep as near to the outer limit of the channel or fairway which lies on her starboard side as is safe and practicable.'

You are entering this fiord, which is steep-to on both sides.

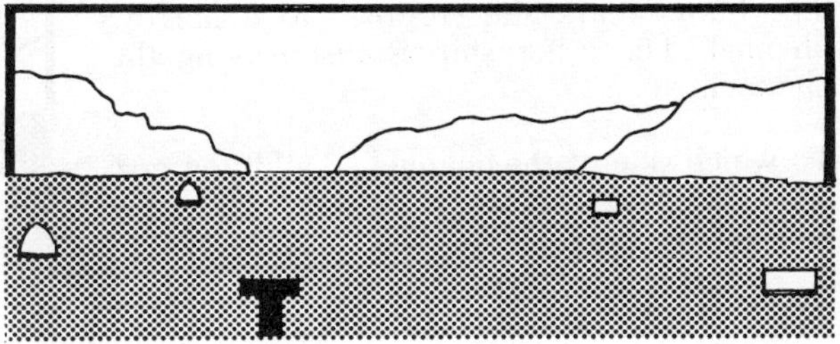

To which side of the fiord should you keep?

The starboard side.

There is a further point you should note about navigation in a channel.

Rules 9 (f) and 34 (e) state that you must sound a prolonged blast when nearing a blind bend in a channel.

We will represent a prolonged blast with the symbol (–). A prolonged blast is of four to six seconds in duration.

You are approaching this bend in the channel.

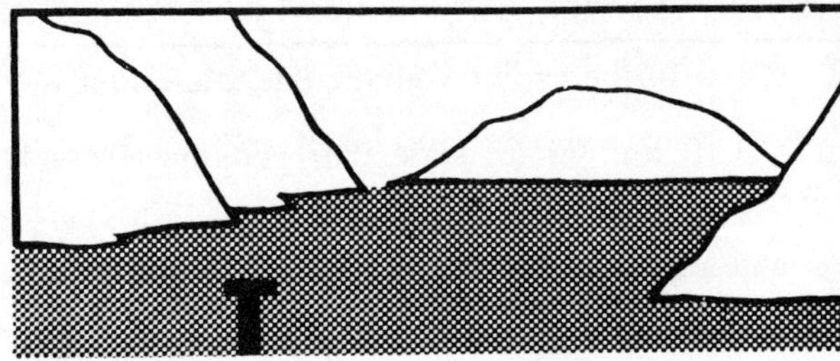

What signal would you make?

One prolonged blast (–).

You hear one prolonged blast from round the bend on your starboard bow.

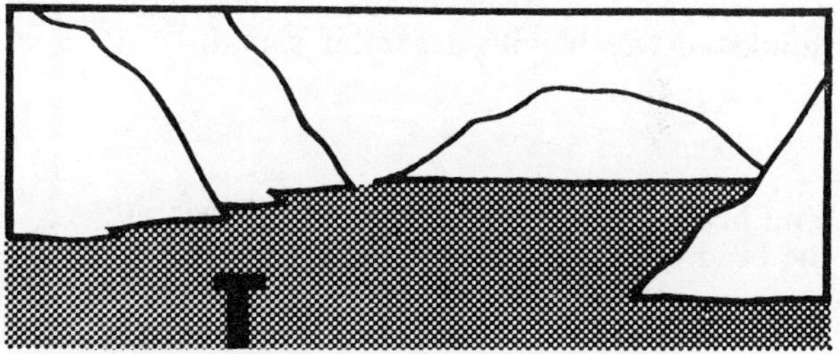

Would you swing out to port to get the earliest possible view of the approaching ship?

No—you must keep to the starboard side of the channel.

Rule 34 (e) also states that when you hear a prolonged blast from behind a bend, you should answer it with a similar signal.

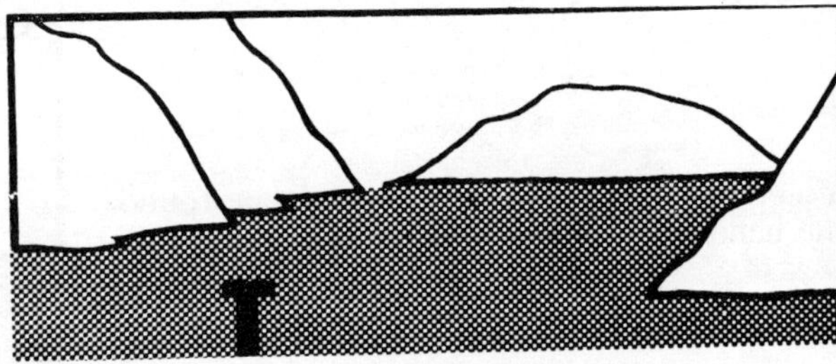

You hear a prolonged blast (–) from behind the bend on your starboard bow.

What signal do you make? Of what duration is it?

One prolonged blast (–).
Four to six seconds' duration.

To which side of the channel should you keep?

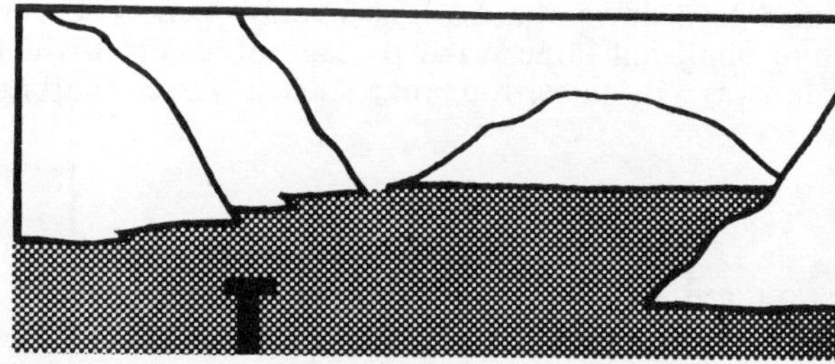

The starboard side.

Rule 9 says that no vessel should anchor in a narrow channel if it can be avoided.

It also lays down that sailing vessels, vessels less than 20 metres in length and vessels engaged in fishing shall not impede the passage of a vessel which can only navigate safely in a narrow channel or fairway. It states, too, that such a vessel shall not be impeded by a vessel crossing the channel.

If you are the Officer of the watch of a power-driven vessel proceeding in the narrow channel marked by the buoys in the illustration and the actions of the vessel approaching on your starboard bow cause you to **doubt her intentions,** what whistle signal will you give?

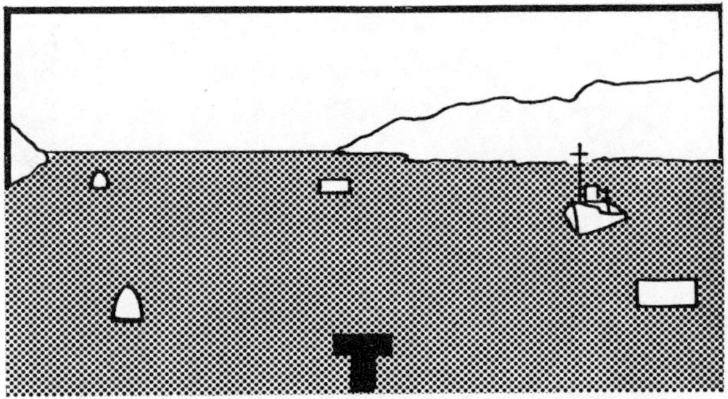

The 'wake-up' signal, at least 5 short blasts (. . . . .).

If the vessel continued to approach on the same heading at the same speed you would have to take whatever action was appropriate to avoid a collision. The precise action would depend upon the speeds of both vessels but assuming that the approaching vessel either altered course to avoid entering the channel or stopped, to which side of the channel would you keep?

The starboard side.

Overtaking in a narrow channel may not be possible unless the vessel to be overtaken alters course to allow the overtaking vessel to pass. Under these circumstances the overtaking vessel must indicate her intention by whistle signals.

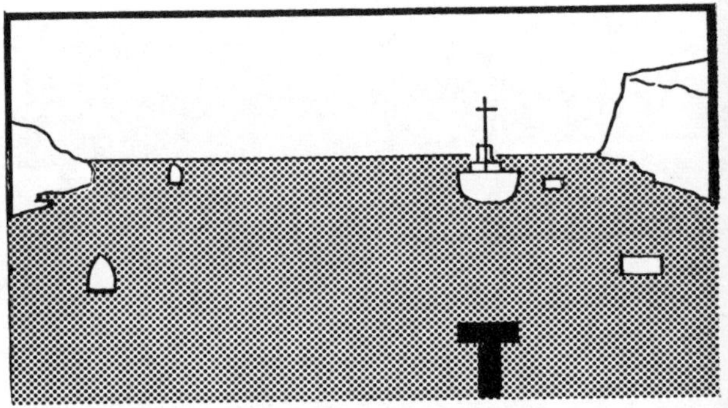

If she wishes to overtake on the **starboard** side she must sound **two prolonged blasts followed by one short blast** (– – ·).

If she wishes to overtake on the **port** side she must sound **two prolonged blasts followed by two short blasts** (– – · ·).

The vessel being overtaken will then take whatever action is necessary to give a clear passage to the **overtaking vessel** and sound **one prolonged blast, one short blast, one prolonged blast and one short blast** (– · – ·) to signify agreement with the overtaking vessel's intention. This signal does not absolve the overtaking vessel from her responsibility to keep clear.

You wish to overtake in the circumstances illustrated. On which side will you overtake?

Since both vessels are keeping to the right-hand side of the channel, and the way ahead is clear, you will leave the other vessel to starboard.

Assuming that there is not, in your view, enough water between the vessel ahead and the left-hand side of the channel for you to pass safely without some action by her. What sound signal will you give?

Two prolonged blasts followed by two short blasts (– – · ·). ("I intend to overtake you on your port side.")

---

1. What would you expect the vessel ahead to do?
2. When would you start to pass?
3. What signal would you expect the vessel ahead to give if she was in doubt about the situation?

1. Sound one prolonged blast, one short blast, one prolonged blast and one short blast (–·–·) and then alter course slightly to starboard.
2. When the vessel to be overtaken has signalled her agreement and the channel is clear for you.
3. At least five short blasts (·····).

The vessel you are in charge of here is a small power-driven vessel heading to **cross** a narrow channel, and a larger vessel, obviously limited to using the channel, is approaching on your port bow.

What, in general terms, should you do?

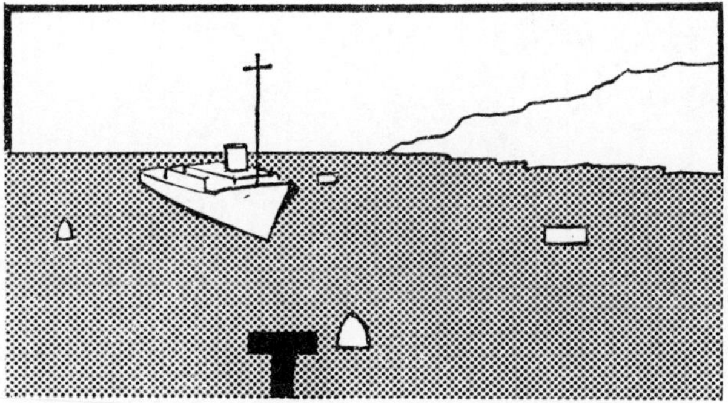

Keep out of her way.

The Rules in respect of **overtaking in narrow channels** in no way relieve the overtaking vessel of her obligations under Rule 13.

What is the duty of the overtaking vessel under Rule 13?

To keep out of the way until she is past and clear.

In the circumstances illustrated, what signals would you give if you decided you wished to pass on the starboard side of the vessel ahead?

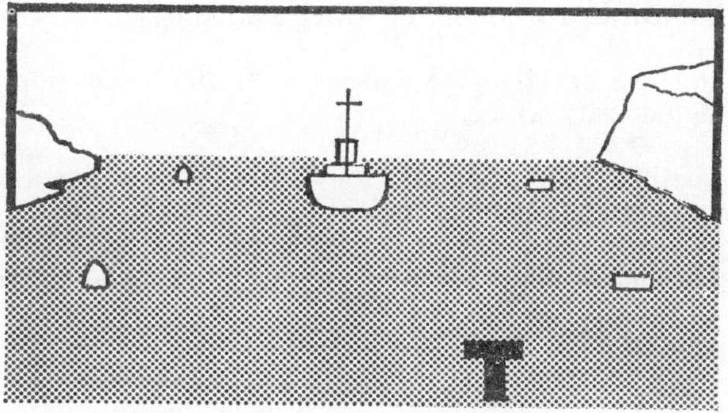

Two prolonged blasts and one short blast (– – ·).

The Rules for the avoidance of collision in narrow channels are based upon necessity due to the limited area or depth of water available.

Now we come to the Rules for **Traffic Separation Schemes** which are adopted for sea areas of **high-density traffic.**

The illustration opposite shows the Western part of the Dover Straits with Traffic Separation zones and separation lines indicating the traffic lanes.

Through traffic shall **not**, normally, **use inshore zones** if an adjacent traffic lane can be used safely.

The vessel in the illustration is a power-driven vessel en route from London to Tangiers.
Is she following a proper course for such a vessel?

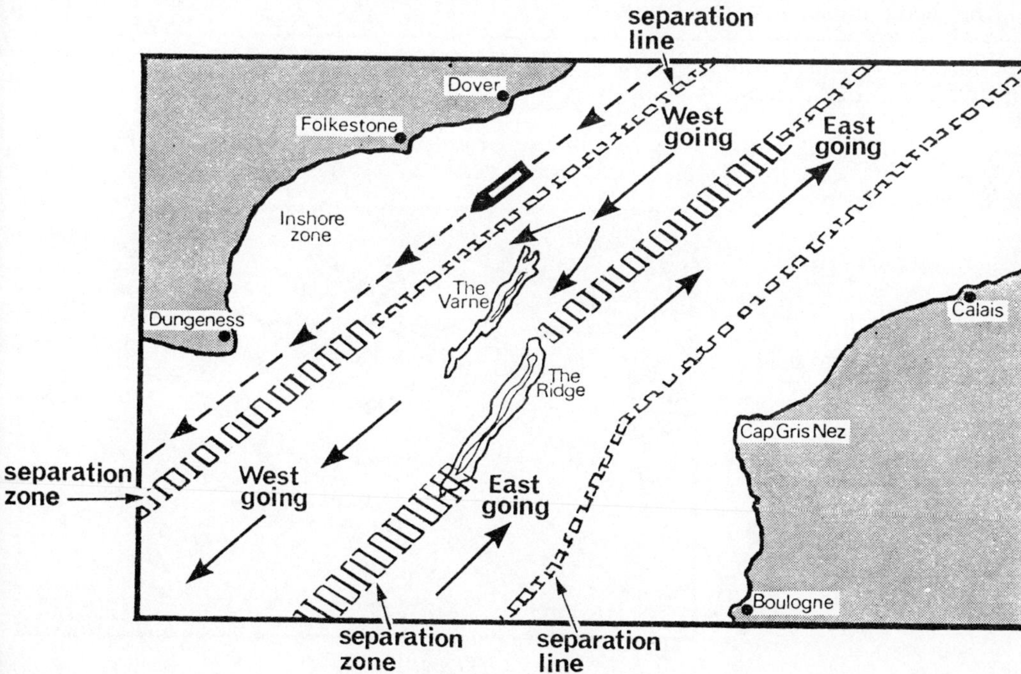
separation line
Dover
Folkestone
West going
East going
Inshore zone
The Varne
Dungeness
Calais
The Ridge
Cap Gris Nez
separation zone
West going
East going
Boulogne
separation zone
separation line

No. She should be in the adjacent traffic lane.

Through traffic on this course would unnecessarily add to the already high density of inshore traffic plying between local harbours.

Further, the Rules say that vessels **not** using a traffic separation scheme should avoid it by as wide a margin as possible. In this case, Vessel A may cause doubt about her intentions among vessels properly using the traffic lane.

Vessel B is proceeding from Calais to Boulogne. Is she following a proper course?

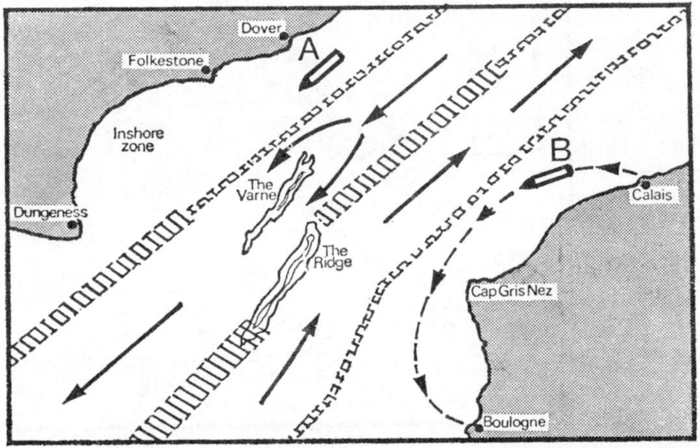

Yes, she is not 'through traffic'.

Vessels **engaged in fishing** must not impede the safe passage of **any** vessel following a traffic lane. **Sailing vessels and vessels under 20 metres in length** shall not impede the safe passage of **power-driven vessels** following a traffic lane and **no vessel** should **anchor** in a traffic separation lane or near its termination if it can be avoided.

However, fishing vessels **may fish** in **traffic separation zones** provided that they do not impede vessels in traffic lanes.

Except when crossing, no other vessel should normally enter a traffic separation zone except in emergencies to avoid immediate danger.

If, when navigating through a traffic separation lane you sighted the vessel illustrated, apparently about to cross close across your bows, what signal would you give?

If you consider that by altering course your safe passage is endangered, then sound the 'wake-up' signal, at least five short blasts. If, however, you can safely alter course to keep out of the way, it is your duty to do so.

If when proceeding through a traffic lane, you see a vessel stopped in the centre of a traffic separation zone, what two possible reasons will you look for?

That the vessel is either fishing or in an emergency situation.

Normally, a vessel shall **join or leave a traffic lane at its termination** but there are times when this is, obviously, impracticable and it is necessary to join from the side.

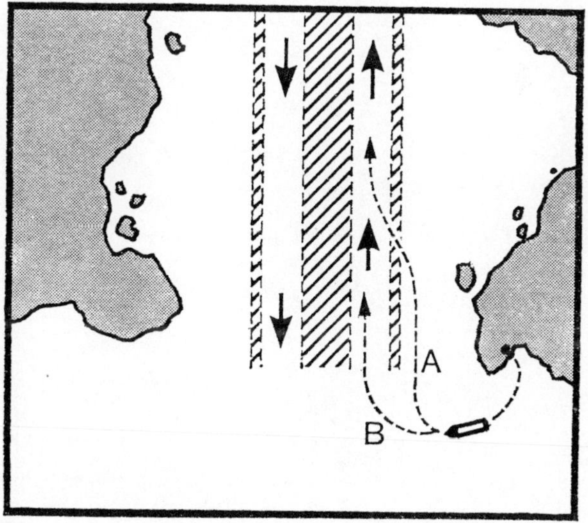

Following the principle that a vessel moving through a traffic lane must move in the general direction of the flow in that lane, a vessel joining the lane should enter at as small an angle as possible.

If you were in charge of the vessel in the illustration, which of the two courses A or B would you choose as more properly conforming to the Rules?

Course B, because the Rules say that a vessel shall, normally, join or leave a traffic separation scheme at its termination.

Which would be the correct course to follow in this case?

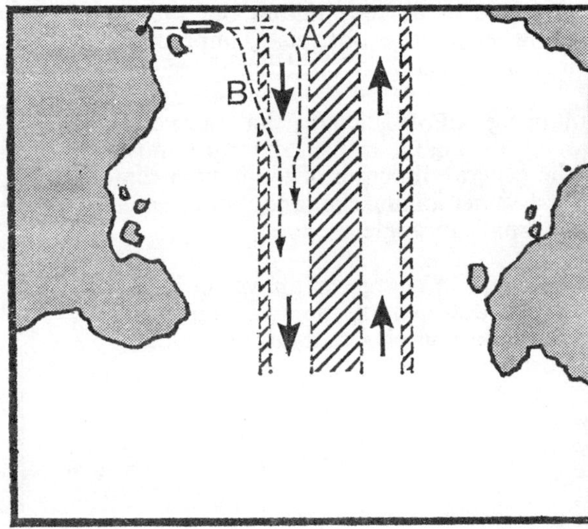

Course B (because it joins the traffic lane at a small angle).

When actually **crossing traffic separation schemes** it **is** correct to enter the traffic lanes **at right-angles to the flow of traffic**. Thus, the intention of the vessel cannot be mistaken.

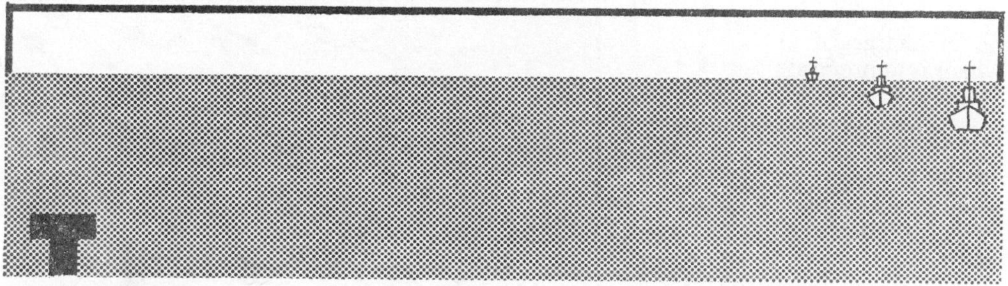

You are steaming in inshore waters. Your planned course is to cross a traffic separation scheme. The traffic separation line is on your starboard side and there are oncoming vessels in the first traffic lane to be crossed.

Having regard for the general Rules for avoidance of collision, what would you do and what signal would you give?

Your precise action would depend upon the range and speeds of the oncoming vessels. At the appropriate moment, make an alteration of course to starboard so as to cross the direction of the traffic lane at 90° or as near as possible. Sound one short blast.

Study the illustration.

You are in charge of a vessel which is to proceed from Dungeness to Calais.

Which of the four routes shown would most nearly accord with the intentions of the Rules?

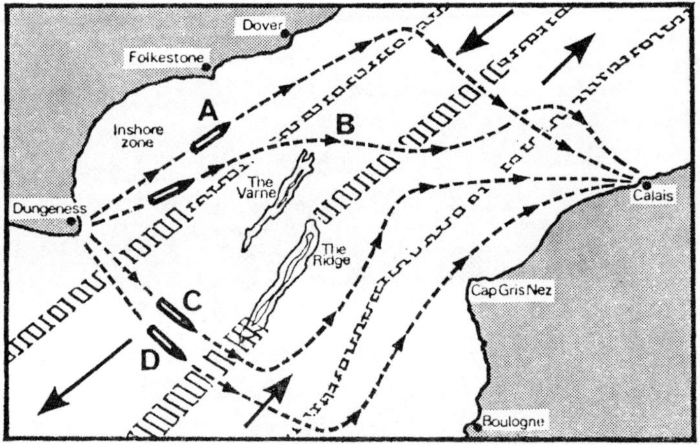

Route A or route D.

In using route A or D, you are crossing the lanes at right-angles in accordance with the Rules. As you are not 'through' traffic, you are not obliged to use the traffic lanes and you may use the inshore zones.

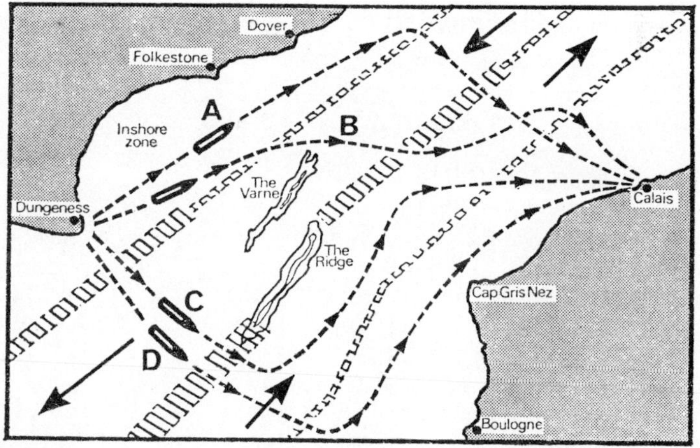

Route B would take your vessel against the flow of traffic in the south-west bound lane and leaving the north-east bound lane at right-angles to the flow of traffic would not be in accordance with the Rules.

On route C, crossing the south-west bound traffic lane at right-angles to the traffic flow, and entering and leaving the north-east bound lane at small angles are correct actions. However, on entering, crossing and leaving the north-east bound lane, your intentions may not be entirely clear to other vessels. So A or D would be the best course of action.

Apart from crossing, under what circumstances would you enter a traffic separation zone?

In a case of emergency to avoid immediate danger.

Now we come to an extremely important section of the Rules.

Rule 19 covers The Conduct of Vessels in Restricted Visibility.

The Rule applies to vessels not in sight of one another in or near an area of restricted visibility.

Rule 19 (b) states :

> 'Every vessel shall proceed at a safe speed adapted to the prevailing circumstances and conditions of restricted visibility. A power-driven vessei shall have her engines ready for immediate manoeuvre.'

You are proceeding at 20 knots in clear visibility. You sight a fog bank ahead.

Should you reduce speed before you enter the fog and, if so, why?

Yes.
The Rule says that you must proceed at a safe speed adapted to the prevailing circumstances and conditions of restricted visibility. Since it will take time for your speed to reduce, you must slow down in time to be travelling at a safe speed when you enter the fog.

The shorter the range at which you sight a ship, and the faster you go, the less time you have for action in accordance with the Rules. So if the visibility is restricted (i.e. less than maximum) you must go at a ____ speed.

safe

Accidents due to excessive speed in fog are numerous. Any ship that is involved in a collision, and whose speed was excessive, must always be blameworthy to some degree, whatever the other ship did.

It is vital that, in restricted visibility, you go at a ___ _____.

You may be wondering what is the definition of 'safe speed'.

The Rules state that your speed in restricted visibility must depend on the 'existing circumstances and conditions'. This, of course, includes the visibility, the stopping power of your own ship, density of traffic, sea-room available and other factors listed in Rule 6.

If the visibility is about two miles, and you are doing 12 knots, would you say that this speed would be safe for:
(a) a destroyer?
(b) a heavily laden tanker?

It might be safe for the destroyer, with her considerable astern power, but probably not for the tanker. (If you said that you did not know enough of the conditions to be **certain,** you are quite right.)

A good rule of thumb is that your speed, in restricted visibility, should be such that you could stop **within** half the visibility distance.

However remember that the other ship might not be conducted as prudently as yours and may not be able to stop within this distance.

What speed would you consider safe in a visibility of half a mile?

It would depend upon the circumstances but, in general, it should be a speed that would enable you to stop **within** $\frac{1}{4}$ mile.

This is a most important point, so let us go over it once more.

In any vessel, you must proceed at a ____ _____ consistent with the prevailing circumstances and conditions of restricted visibility.

And finally, to end this section, a quotation from Mr. Justice Willmer who was giving judgment on a collision case in the Admiralty Court in 1955. (Arnold Bratt–Coquette, 1955: Lloyds List Law Report, 1955, Vol. I, page 24.)

'I appreciate . . . that in judging what is and what is not a moderate speed in fog regard must always be had to the nature of the vessel, to her engine power, and, in particular, to her power of pulling up under reversed engines. What is a proper speed for vessel A may be highly improper for vessel B, having regard to their different characteristics. But . . . it is not enough to say that because a vessel has remarkable pulling up power she is therefore justified in proceeding at high speed in fog . . .'

Next, we will consider Rule 35. This deals with sound signals in restricted visibility (usually called 'fog signals').

So far in the programme it has been possible to present the material in such a way that each page has been a fairly small step forward. With fog signals this is not quite so easy: they simply have to be learned by heart.

There are five different fog signals for power-driven vessels under way.
These are set out in the next four pages.

Look at page 246 and learn these fog signals by heart.

The signals listed below must be sounded in **restricted visibility** by vessels under way.

Signal	Vessel	**Learning aid**
– (at intervals of not more than 2 minutes)	Power-driven vessel under way, making way through the water.	('Here I come sounding one')
– – (at intervals of not more than 2 minutes with 2 seconds between blasts)	Power-driven vessel under way, but not making way.	(I'm waiting **too** long')
– · · (at intervals of not more than 2 minutes)	Vessels which are:	('Long blast'—vessel under way, plus two short blasts equal to:
	(i) Not under command	two balls
	(ii) Restricted in their ability to manoeuvre	two balls, parted
	(iii) Constrained by their draughts	two balls plus one
	(iv) Towing or Pushing	two ships
	(v) Fishing	two fish
	(vi) Sailing	two sails)
– · · · (at intervals of not more than 2 minutes)	Last vessel of tow.	(Last vessel has the longest signal.)
· · · · (when necessary, in addition to signals required by a vessel of her size)	A power-driven pilot vessel on duty.	(Pilot flag is like 'H'.)

Note that vessels pushing or being pushed as a composite unit, shall be regarded as one power-driven vessel.

State what **kind of vessel** sounds each of the following signals.

Signal		Vessel	
– · · ·	(at intervals of not more than 2 minutes)	____________ (Longest signal)	
– –	(at intervals of not more than 2 minutes with 2 seconds between blasts)	____________ (I'm waiting too long)	
· · · ·	(when necessary, in addition to signals required by a vessel of her size)	________ (Flag 'H')	
–	(at intervals of not more than 2 minutes)	____________ (Here I come)	
– · ·	(at intervals of not more than 2 minutes)	(i) ____________	(two balls)
		(ii) ____________	(two balls, parted)
		(iii) ____________	(two balls plus one ball)
		(iv) ____________	(two ships)
		(v) ____________	(two fish)
		(vi) ____________	(two sails)

Check your answers with the previous page—if you have any wrong, re-learn them.

State what **kind of vessel** sounds each of the following signals.

· · · · (when necessary) ____________________

– · · (at intervals of not more than 2 minutes) ____________________

– (at intervals of not more than 2 minutes) ____________________

– · · · (at intervals of not more than 2 minutes) ____________________

– – (at intervals of not more than 2 minutes with 2 seconds between blasts) ____________________

Check your answers with page 246—if you have any wrong, re-learn them.

Now learn the list the other way round.
For each vessel state right **fog signal** and **time interval.**

Power-driven vessel under way, making way through the water.	______ ('Here I come')	(at intervals of not more than ______)
Power-driven vessel under way, but not making way.	______ ('I'm waiting')	(at intervals of not more than ______ with ___ seconds between blasts)
Vessels which are: (i) Not under command. (ii) Restricted in their ability to manoeuvre. (iii) Constrained by their draughts. (iv) Towing or Pushing. (v) Fishing. (vi) Sailing.	______ ('Vessel under way plus')	(at intervals of not more than ______)
Last vessel of the tow.	______ ('Longest signal')	(at intervals of not more than ______)
A power-driven pilot vessel on duty. (In addition to signals required by a vessel of her size.)	______ ('Pilot flag')	(when ______)

For each vessel state the right **fog signal** and **time interval.**

Last vessel of tow.	__________	__________
Power-driven vessel under way but stopped in the water.	__________	__________
A power-driven pilot vessel on duty.	__________	__________
Vessels which are: (i) Not under command. (ii) Restricted in their ability to manoeuvre. (iii) Constrained by their draughts. (iv) Towing or Pushing. (v) Fishing. (vi) Sailing.	__________	__________
Power-driven vessel under way, making way through the water.	__________	__________

Check your answers with page 246—if you have any wrong, work through pages 245 to 250 again

Two extra points about signals to be sounded in restricted visibility (fog signals):

1. When practicable, as soon as the last vessel of the tow hears the towing ship sound her signal, she should sound her own, so the signal – · · · should be heard immediately ______ the signal – · ·

2. A power-driven pilot vessel on duty obeys the Rules for a normal power-driven vessel, so if the identification signal · · · · is used, it is used in ________ to the signals for a power-driven vessel under way.

1. after
2. addition

Remember then that, when practicable, the fog signal of the last vessel of the tow is sounded immediately after the fog signal of the ______ ______.

Also, that when the pilot vessel identification fog signal is used, it is used in addition to the fog signals for a ______-______ ______.

towing vessel
power-driven vessel

Rule 5 states, among other things, that a proper look-out must be maintained at all times.

Rule 2 makes it clear that nothing shall exonerate you from the consequences of neglecting any precautions which may be required by the ordinary practices of seamen or special circumstances.

In low visibility a proper look-out can be taken to mean a more careful look-out than normal and kept by every means—eyes, ears and radar.

For instance, you may put a man in the eyes of the ship or, if the fog is low-lying, up the mast.

Therefore, before entering restricted visibility, place ______ look-outs and set a watch on the ______ .

extra (you may have said 'special' or a similar word)
radar

In poor visibility there is usually little time for action when you sight a ship; so use your radar to give you early warning of its presence and ensure that it is actually sighted at the earliest possible moment.

In fog, or other weather restricting visibility, you must keep the best possible look-out so, before the visibility closes down, always place ______ look-outs, and set a watch on the ______ .

extra radar

What other two actions must you take in entering restricted visibility?

Reduce to safe speed. (Remember, Rule 19(b) states that a power-driven vessel shall have her engines ready for immediate manoeuvre.)
Sound a fog signal.

And you must also place ______ ______-______ and set a watch on the ______ .

extra look-outs
radar

Rule 19 (e) states:

> 'Except where it has been determined that a risk of collision does not exist, every vessel which hears apparently forward of her beam the fog signal of another vessel, or which cannot avoid a close-quarters situation with another vessel forward of her beam, shall reduce her speed to the minimum at which she can be kept on her course. She shall, if necessary take all way off and in any event navigate with extreme caution until danger of collision is over.'

The visibility is ½ mile. You have already reduced speed to 4 knots and hear one prolonged blast apparently on your starboard bow.

What do you do immediately.

Take all way off the ship and sound two prolonged blasts.

The Rule clearly implies that you should not make assumptions about the other vessel's position and heading just on the evidence of her fog signal.

If you hear two prolonged blasts apparently on your **port** bow, should you :

1. Stand on?
2. Stop engines and take all way off the ship?

2. Stop engines and take all way off the ship.

The hearing of one prolonged blast gives you no indication of a vessel's course and speed. You cannot rely on estimating the direction of the sound accurately in fog. You must navigate with caution **until all danger of collision is past.**

The visibility is 1 mile, your speed is 8 knots. You hear a fog signal ahead, very faintly, which you cannot identify.

1. What action do you take?
2. For how long?

1. Reduce speed to a minimum and navigate with caution.
2. Until danger of collision is past.

As soon as you can see the other ship then, of course, the Rules for vessels in sight of one another will apply.

The visibility is about ½ mile in rain. You hear one prolonged blast ahead and you stop your engines. You keep a sharp look-out, and see a ship approaching head-on from right ahead.

What should you do?

Alter course to starboard and sound one short blast. (You may also have added 'put your engines ahead' if you had decided that you had lost steerage way.)

What five things must you do on entering fog?

Sound fog signal.
Reduce to safe speed.
Place extra look-outs.
Set a watch on the radar.
Have engines ready for immediate manoeuvre.

There are, of course, other measures that you may consider on entering restricted visibility, such as calling the Captain and ensuring that you have full power available, but the five points above are the essential minimum.

There is a second major group of fog signals which you should learn. These are the fog signals for vessels at anchor or aground. There are five of these signals and they are set out on the next few pages.

Turn to page 263 and learn these fog signals by heart.

Vessels at anchor, or aground, sound special fog signals, shown below.

		Learning aids
A vessel of under 100 metres, at anchor.	Rapid ringing of a bell for 5 seconds (at intervals of not more than 1 minute).	('A rapidly ringing bell is a warning.')
A vessel of 100 metres and over.	Rapid ringing of the bell forward for 5 seconds (at intervals of not more than 1 minute). Rapid sounding of a gong aft for 5 seconds (at intervals of not more than 1 minute).	('At anchor and long, a bell and a gong.')
A vessel of under 100 metres, aground.	3 strokes on bell. 5 seconds' ringing on bell. 3 strokes on bell.	('Three balls or three bells mean aground.')
A vessel of 100 metres and over, aground.	3 strokes on bell. 5 seconds' ringing on bell. 3 strokes on bell. 5 seconds' sounding of gong aft. (May also sound an appropriate whistle signal.)	('Three balls or three bells mean aground.')
A vessel at anchor giving warning of her position.	Signal for vessel at anchor followed by · – · on the whistle.	('Are you coming near me?')
A power-driven pilot vessel on duty, at anchor.	Signal for vessel at anchor and · · · · on the whistle.	('Pilot flag is like H.')

Learn the meaning of each of these signals before you go on to the next page.

For each vessel, give the complete details of each **fog signal.**

A vessel of under 100 metres, at anchor.	______ ('A warning.)
A vessel at anchor giving warning of her position.	______ ('Are you coming?')
A vessel of under 100 metres, aground.	______ ('Three balls.')
A vessel of 100 metres or over, aground.	______ ('Three balls.')
A power-driven pilot vessel on duty, at anchor.	______ ('Pilot Flag.')
A vessel of 100 metres or over, at anchor.	______ ('At anchor and long.')

Check your answers with the previous page—if you have any wrong re-learn them.

For each vessel, give the complete details of each **fog signal.**

A vessel at anchor giving warning of her position. __________

A power-driven pilot vessel on duty, at anchor. __________

A vessel of under 100 metres, aground. __________

A vessel of 100 metres or over, aground. __________

A vessel of under 100 metres, at anchor. __________

A vessel of 100 metres or over, at anchor. __________

Check your answers with page 263—if you have any wrong, re-learn them.

Now learn the list the other way round.
State **what kind of vessel** will sound each of the following signals.

Rapid ringing of a bell for 5 seconds (at intervals of not more than 1 minute). ______

('A warning.')

Rapid ringing of a bell forward for 5 seconds (at intervals of not more than 1 minute). Rapid ringing of a gong aft for 5 seconds (at intervals of not more than 1 minute). ______

('A bell and a gong.')

3 strokes on bell.
5 seconds ringing on bell.
3 strokes on bell. ______

('Three balls.')

3 strokes on bell.
5 seconds ringing on bell.
3 strokes on bell.
5 seconds sounding of gong aft.
(May also sound an appropriate whistle signal.) ______

('Three balls.')

Signal for vessel at anchor, and · · · · on the whistle. ______

('Flag H.')

Check your answers with page 263—if you have any wrong, re-learn them.

State what kind of vessel will sound each of the following signals.

Rapid ringing of a bell for 5 seconds (at intevals of not more than 1 minute). ____________________

3 strokes on bell.
5 seconds' ringing on bell.
3 strokes on bell. ____________________

Signal for a vessel at anchor, and · · · · on the whistle. ____________________

Rapid ringing of a bell forward for 5 seconds (at intervals of not more than one minute). Rapid ringing of a gong aft for 5 seconds (at intervals of not more than 1 minute). ____________________

3 strokes on bell.
5 seconds' ringing on bell.
3 strokes on bell.
5 seconds' sounding of gong aft. (May also sound an appropriate whistle signal.) ____________________

Check your answers with page 263—if you have any wrong, work through pages 263 to 266 again.

Now, some revision.

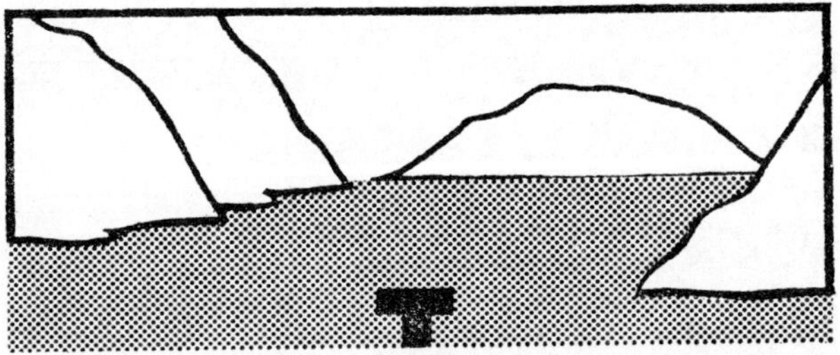

1. To which side of the channel should you keep?
2. If, when you are in the situation above, you hear one prolonged blast, what does it indicate?
3. What must you immediately do?

1. Starboard.
2. There is a ship approaching round the blind bend.
3. Sound 1 prolonged blast (–) in answer.

You are in a narrow channel and wish to overtake on the port side of the vessel ahead.

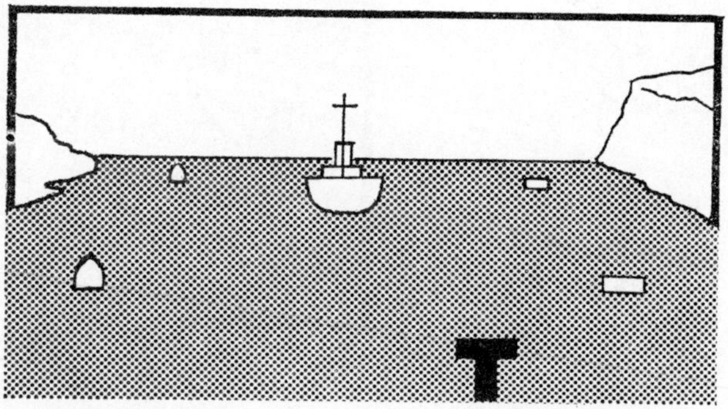

1. What sound signal will you give?
2. When will you pass?

1. Two prolonged blasts followed by two short blasts (– – · ·).
2. When you hear the sound signal signifying agreement by the vessel ahead. One prolonged blast, one short blast, one prolonged blast, one short blast (– · – ·) and you consider she has made sufficient room for you to pass.

Which of these two courses would you select to join the traffic separation lane?

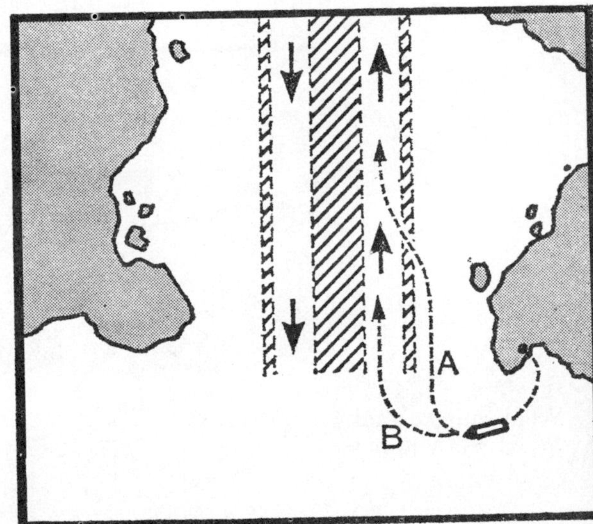

Course B.

What actions must you take before entering restricted visibility?

Sound fog signal.
Reduce to safe speed.
Place extra look-outs.
Set a watch on the radar.
Have engines ready for immediate manoeuvre.

The visibility is about $\frac{1}{4}$ mile and you are proceeding dead slow. The look-out reports that he hears a fog signal on the port bow.

What must you do?

Take all way off the ship and navigate with caution until danger of collision is past.

What sound signal is made in restricted visibility by each of the following?

1. A power-driven vessel under way, but not making way.
2. A vessel fishing.
3. A vessel of 100 metres or over in length, at anchor.
4. A sailing ship.

1. – – (at intervals of not more than 2 minutes).
2. – · · (at intervals of not more than 2 minutes).
3. Rapid ringing of a bell forward for 5 seconds (at intervals of not more than 1 minute).
   Rapid ringing of a gong aft for 5 seconds (at intervals of not more than 1 minute).
4. – · · (at intervals of not more than 2 minutes).

This completes the chapter. Now turn to the test on page 275.

Test on Chapter 5

You must get 100% on all questions marked * before going on to the next chapter.

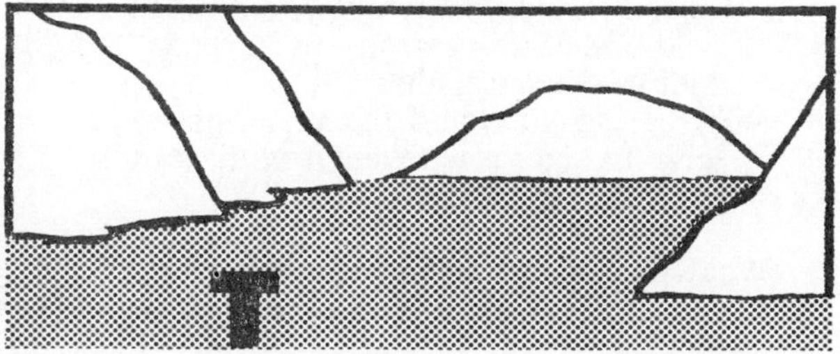

*1. To which side of this channel will you keep?

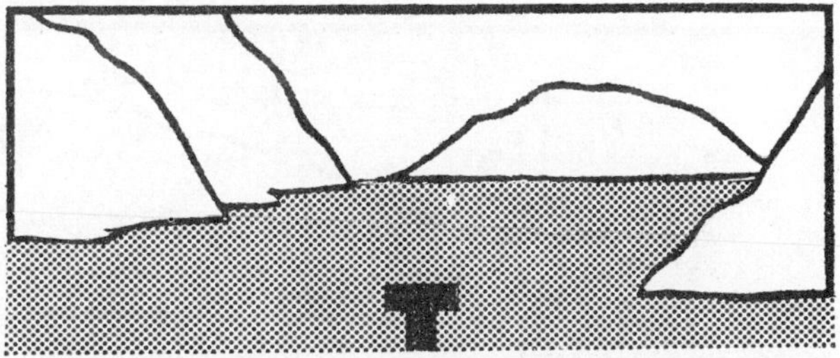

*2. Approaching this bend, what should you do?

*3. You have been in clear visibility but you note that it is closing in rapidly. What actions should you take?

Test (continued)

*4. (a) In the circumstances illustrated, what signal would you give if you decided you wished to pass on the starboard side of the vessel ahead?
(b) What signal would the vessel ahead give to signify agreement with your intention to pass?

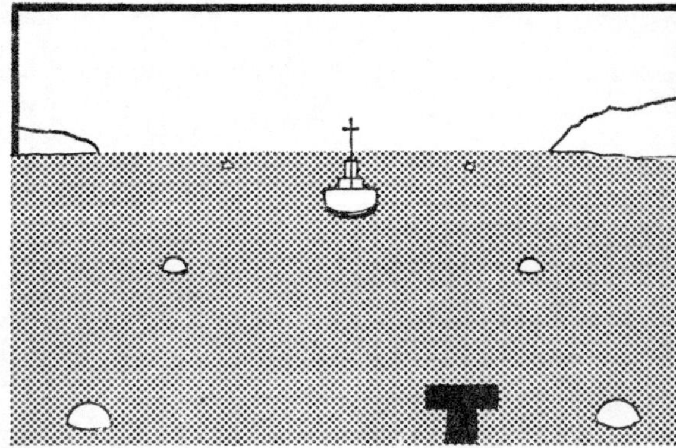

*5. What, in general terms, should you do if you are heading to cross this narrow channel?

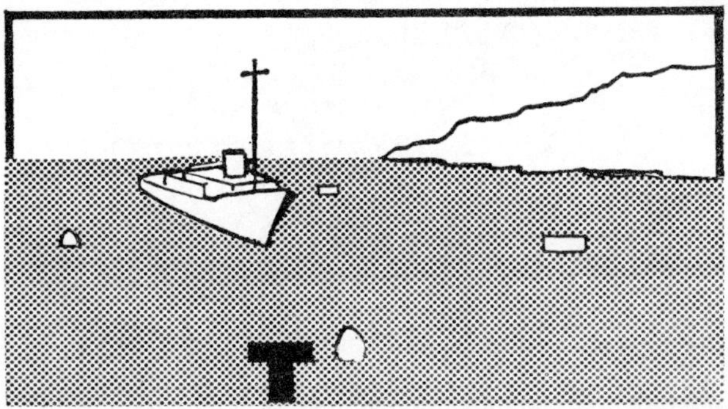

Test (continued)

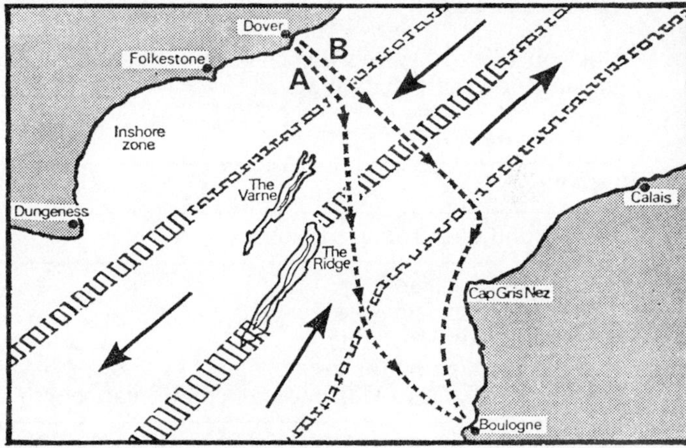

*6. Which of the two routes illustrated would be a more nearly correct route from Dover to Boulogne?

*7. What do the following signals mean when heard in fog?

(a) – · · (every 2 minutes on the whistle.
(b) – – (every 2 minutes on the whistle.
(c) · · · · (when necessary) on the whistle.

*8. What signals would you sound in fog if you were in each of the following?
(a) A vessel under 100 metres, at anchor.
(b) A vessel of 100 metres or over, aground.
(c) A power-driven pilot vessel on duty, at anchor.

*9. The visibility is 2 miles. No ships are in sight. You hear two prolonged blasts on your starboard bow. What must you do?

Answers to Test

You must get 100% on this chapter—if any answer is incorrect go back to the relevant section, as shown below, and study it again.

		Reference
*1.	Starboard.	pages 213–214
*2.	Sound one prolonged blast.	215–217
*3.	Sound fog signal. Reduce to safe speed. Place extra lookouts. Set a watch on the radar. Have engines ready for immediate manoeuvre.	252–261
*4.	(a) Two prolonged blasts followed by one short blast (– – ·) (b) One prolonged blast, one short blast, one prolonged blast, one short blast (– · – ·)	222–227
*5.	Keep out of the way of the vessel using the channel.	225
*6.	Route B.	228–237

Answers to Test (continued)

	Reference
*7. (a) It could be any one of the following: A vesssel not under command. A vessel restricted in her ability to manoeuvre. A vessel constrained by her draught. A vessel towing or pushing. A fishing vessel. A sailing vessel. (b) Power-driven vessel under way but not making way. (c) A pilot vessel on duty.	pages 245–250
*8. (a) Rapid ringing of a bell for 5 seconds at intervals of not more than 1 minute. (b) 3 strokes on a bell, 5 seconds' ringing on a bell, 3 strokes on a bell, 5 seconds' sounding of a gong aft. (May also sound appropriate whistle signal.) (c) Signal for vessel at anchor and four short blasts on the whistle (· · · ·).	261–266
9. Reduce to a safe speed and navigate with caution until danger of collision is over.	238–243

CHAPTER 6. RULES FOR SAILING VESSELS

In this chapter you are asked to change your point of view and to imagine yourself as the helmsman in charge of a sailing vessel. For most of the chapter you will be considering your course of action upon encountering another sailing vessel in various circumstances.

Read Rule 12 carefully, as it is the basis of this chapter. Also, read **once** through Rules 2, 13, 15, 16, 17 and 18. You have read through these before but you should revise them from the point of view of sailing vessels.

Having read through the relevant Rules you will have realised that there are special provisions for sailing vessels which approach each other on crossing courses or head-on. Otherwise they have the same obligations as power-driven vessels, as far as the Rules are concerned.

Thus, if you are in charge of a sailing vessel that must give way, you must take positive early action to keep clear of the other sailing vessel (Rules 12 & 16).

If you are obliged to stand-on, you must do so (although tacking and shift of wind may affect your course and speed), unless you must take action to avoid immediate danger (Rules 2 & 8).

If you are overtaking any vessel (from more than 22·5° abaft her beam), you must keep out of her way until you are finally past and clear (Rule 13).

Rule 18 (a) gives you the right of way over a power-driven vessel, in most circumstances. However, Rule 18 (b) says that a sailing vessel must keep out of the way of vessels not under command, restricted in their ability to manoeuvre and engaged in fishing and Rule 18 (d) says that if you encounter a power-driven vessel constrained by her draught you ______ ______ impede her safe passage.

must not

In a sailing vessel, you have the right of way over a power-driven vessel (unless you are overtaking her, she is fishing, not under command or restricted in her ability to manoeuvre) but you must not impede her safe passage in a narrow channel or a traffic separation lane.

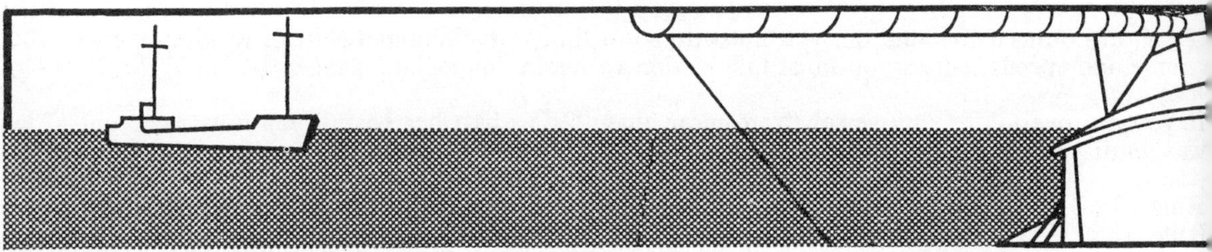

Suppose you encounter a large power-driven vessel on a steady bearing **in the open sea.**

What must you do?

Stand on with caution.

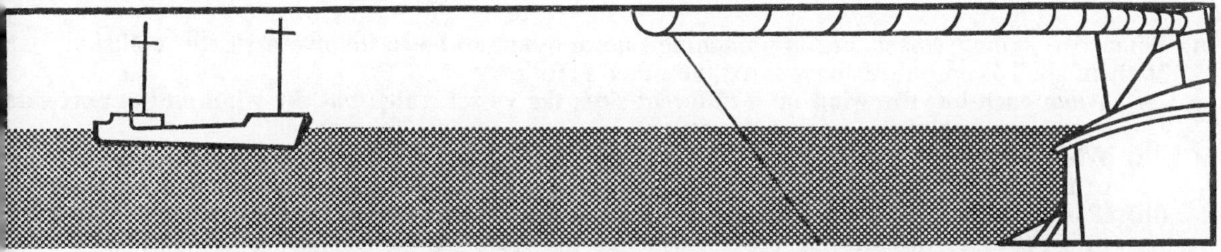

You encounter a power-driven vessel similar to the one on the last page, on a steady bearing, in a narrow channel. The channel is 10 metres deep, the draught of your vessel is 2 metres and there is a wide stretch of water 3 metres deep, on each side of the channel.

Who should give way in this situation?

You.

The greater part of this chapter is based on Rule 12 which states:

‘(a) When two sailing vessels are approaching one another, so as to involve a risk of collision, one of them shall keep out of the way of the other as follows:

(i) **When each has the wind on a different side, the vessel which has the wind on the port side shall keep out of the way of the other.**

(ii) **When both have the wind on the same side, the vessel which is to windward shall keep out of the way of the vessel which is to leeward.**

(iii) **If a vessel with the wind on the port side sees a vessel to windward and cannot determine with certainty whether the other vessel has the wind on the port or on the starboard side, she shall keep out of the way of the other.**

(b) For the purposes of this Rule the windward side shall be deemed to be the side opposite to that on which the mainsail is carried or in the case of a square-rigged vessel, the side opposite to that on which the largest fore-and-aft sail is carried.’

The following pages will teach you the use of the Rule, but not the Rule itself.

You should learn (i), (ii) and (iii) by heart, **now.**

Rule 12 (a)(i) states:

'When each has the wind on a different side, the vessel which has the wind on the port side shall keep out of the way of the other.'

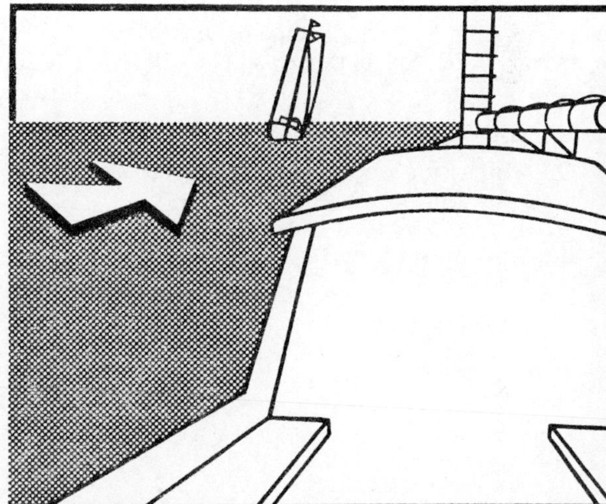

The direction of the wind is shown by the arrow.

The other vessel is coming towards you, so the wind is on her starboard side. The bearing is steady.

Should you stand on, or keep out of the way?

Keep out of the way.

The other vessel is approaching you on a steady bearing.

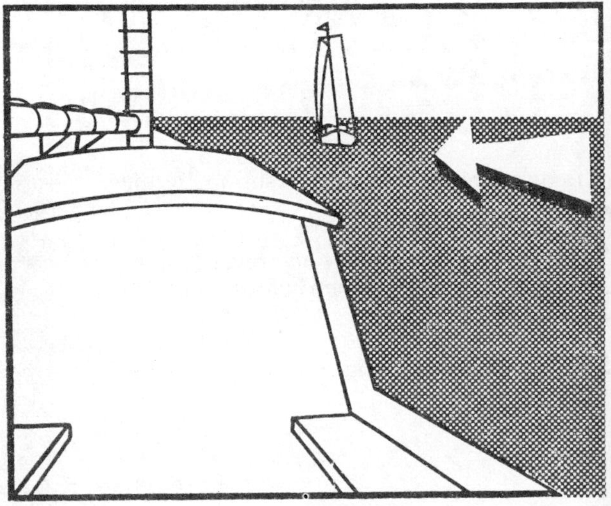

Remember that the wind (shown here by the arrow) is on the opposite side to the mainsail.

(a) On which side do you have the wind?
(b) On which side does the other vessel have the wind?
(c) What should you do (i.e. keep out of the way or stand-on)?

(a) Your **starboard** side.
(b) Her **port** side.
(c) Stand-on.

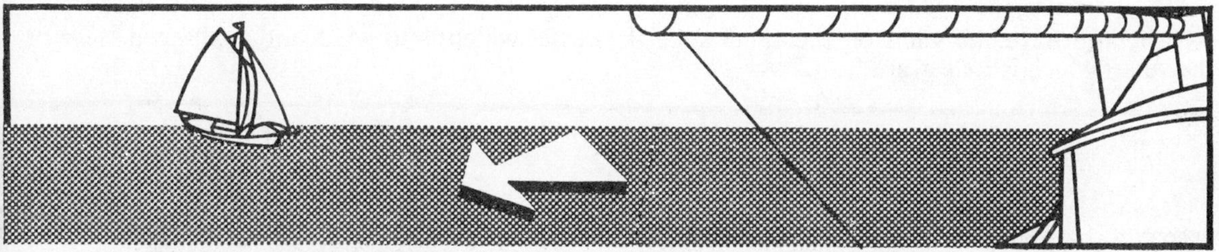

(a) On which side of your vessel do you have the wind?
(b) On which side of the other vessel does her helmsman have the wind?
(c) What should you do if the bearing is steady?

(a) The **starboard** side.
(b) The **port** side.
(c) Stand-on.

Rule 12 (a)(ii) states:

'When both have the wind on the same side, the vessel which is to windward shall keep clear of the vessel which is to leeward.'

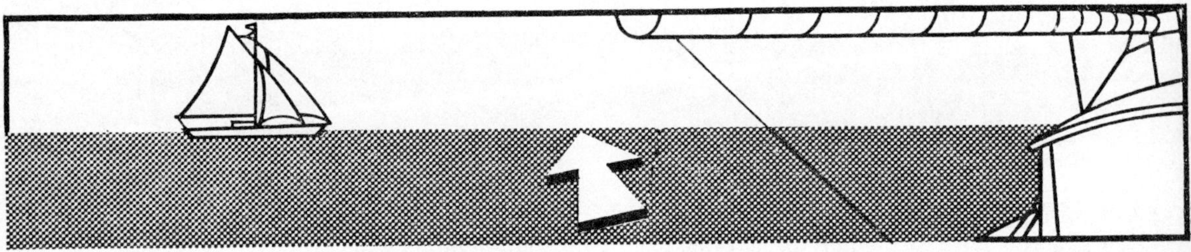

(a) On which side does your vessel have the wind?
(b) On which side does the other vessel have the wind?
(c) Is yours the windward vessel or the leeward vessel?
(d) What should you do if the bearing is steady?

(a) The **starboard** side.
(b) The **starboard** side.
(c) Windward.
(d) Keep out of the way.

Rule 12 (a)(iii) states:

'If a vessel with the wind on the port side sees a vessel to windward and cannot determine with certainty whether the other vessel has the wind on the port or on the starboard side, she shall keep out of the way of the other.'

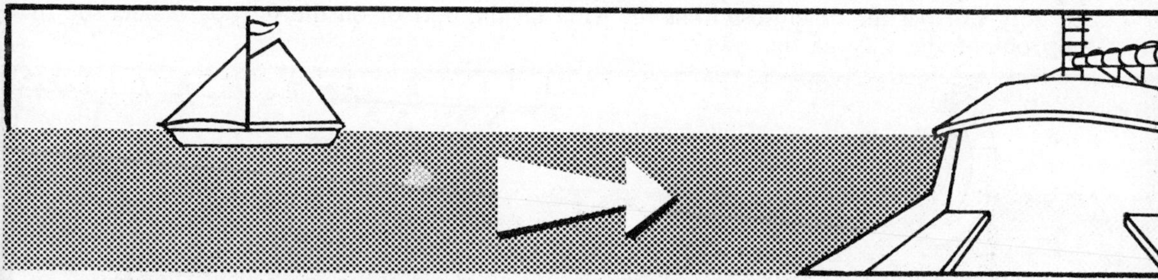

(a) On which side do you have the wind?
(b) On which side does the other vessel have the wind?
(c) Is yours the windward or the leeward vessel?
(d) What should you do?

(a) On the **port** side.
(b) You are not sure.
(c) Leeward.
(d) Keep out of the way.

Here are the three parts of Rule 12 (a), which will not be quoted again in this chapter.

'(i) When each has the wind on a different side, the vessel which has the wind on the port side shall keep out of the way of the other.

(ii) When both have the wind on the same side, the vessel which is to windward shall keep out of the way of the vessel which is to leeward.

(iii) If a vessel with the wind on the port side sees a vessel to windward and cannot determine with certainty whether the other vessel has the wind on the port or on the starboard side, she shall keep out of the way of the other.'

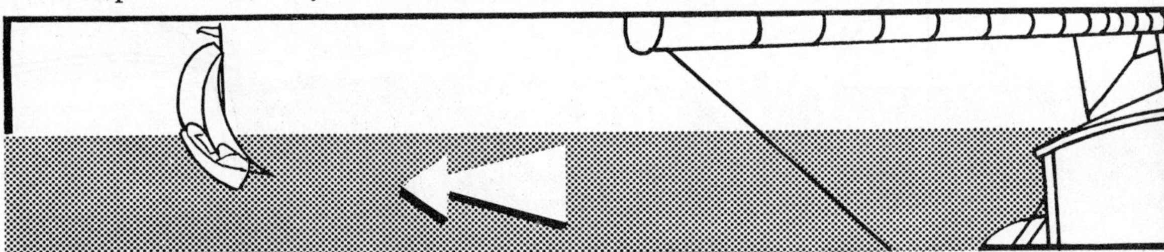

(a) On which side do you have the wind?
(b) On which side does the other vessel have the wind?
(c) Is your vessel to leeward or windward?
(d) If the bearing is steady, what should you do and why?

(a) Starboard.
(b) Port.
(c) Windward.
(d) Stand-on. (Because the two vessels have the wind on different sides.)

On this page, and the next two, the other vessel is shown as it appears by night, as well as by day. The bearing of the other vessel is steady.

(a) On which side do you have the wind?
(b) On which side does the other vessel have the wind?
(c) Are you the windward vessel or the leeward vessel?
(d) What should you do and why?

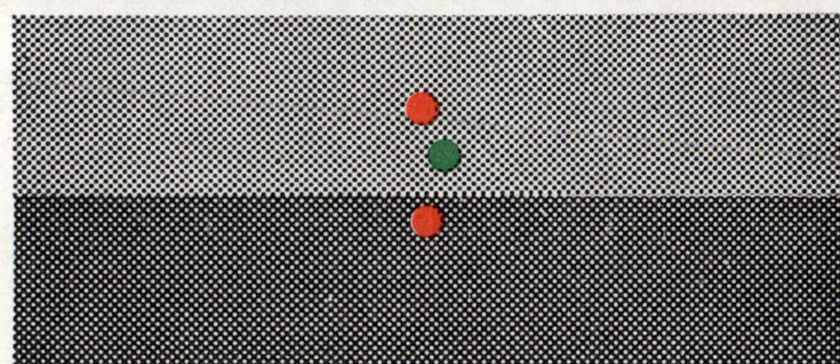

(a) Starboard.
(b) Port.
(c) Leeward.
(d) Stand-on, because you have the wind on the starboard side and the other vessel has the wind on the port side.

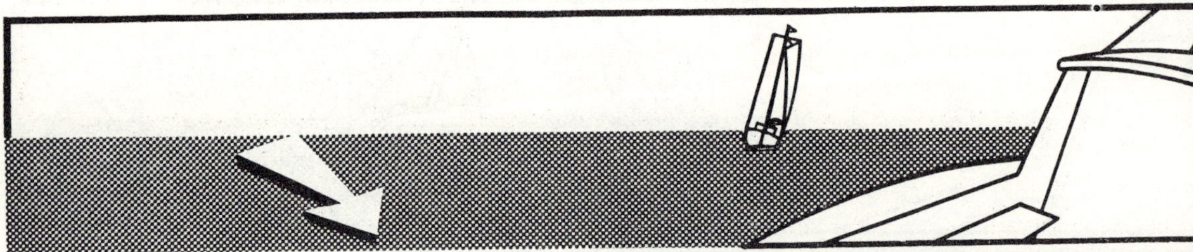

(a) On which side do you have the wind?
(b) On which side does the other vessel have the wind?
(c) Are you the windward vessel or the leeward vessel?
(d) What should you do, if the other vessel is on a steady bearing, and why?

(a) Port.
(b) Starboard.
(c) Leeward.
(d) Keep out of the way, because you have the wind on the port side and the other vessel has the wind on the starboard.

The bearing of the other vessel is steady.

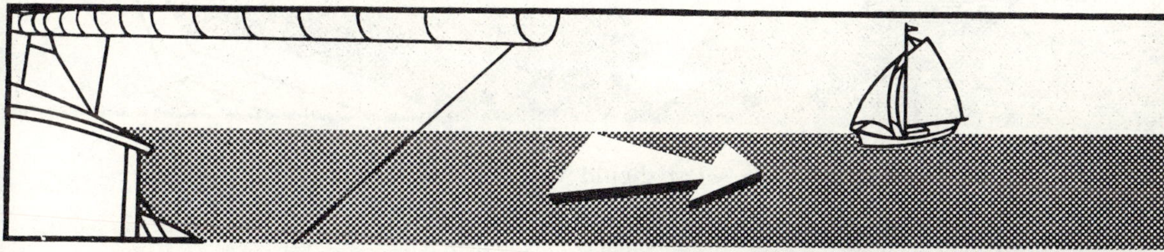

What should you do in this situation?

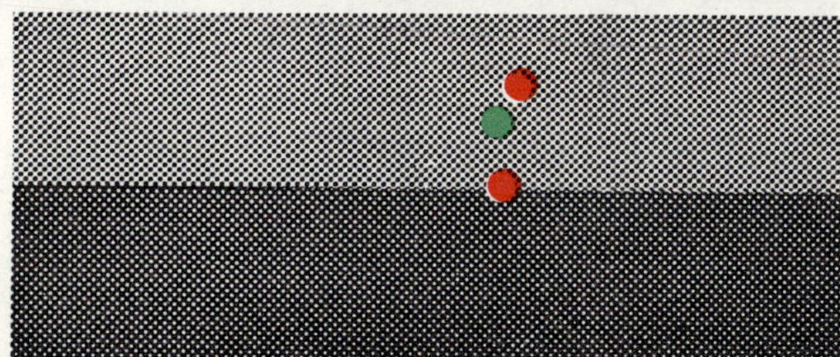

Give-way. (Because you have the wind on the port side and the other vessel has the wind on the starboard side.)

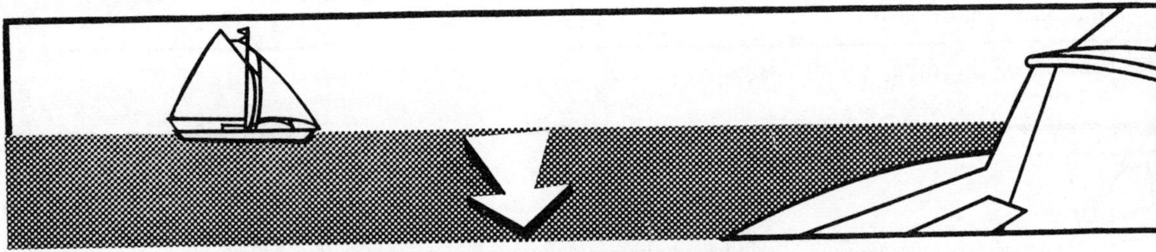

If the other vessel's bearing is steady, what should you do in this situation?

Stand-on. (Both vessels have the wind on the same side, and your vessel is to leeward.)

Study the illustration carefully.

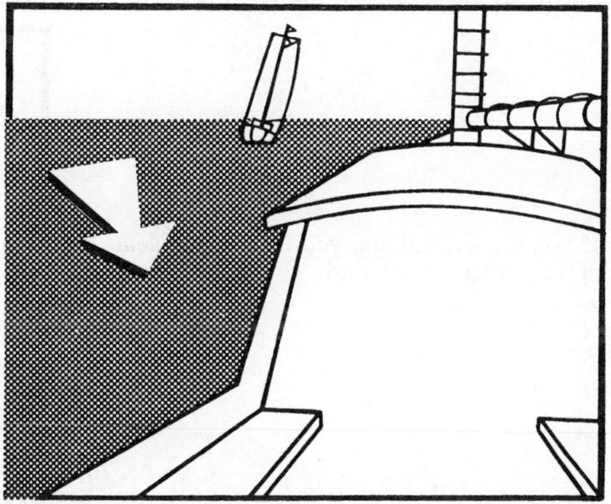

You can see the other vessel's stern, the bearing is steady and the range is decreasing.

Both vessels have the wind on the same side, and your vessel is to leeward.

But you should **keep clear** of the other vessel, because you are ____________ her.

In the sort of situation shown here, if the range is decreasing, you always have the same obligation. This is so, regardless of the wind direction or type of vessel involved.

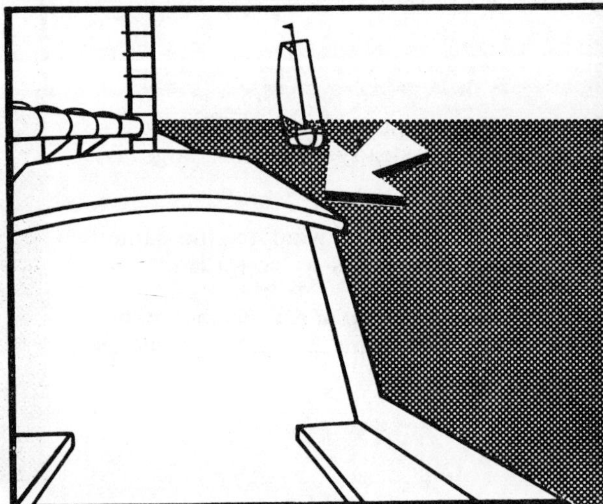

If you are overtaking, you must **keep clear** of the other vessel until you are ______ ______ ______ .

past and clear

Sailing vessels are often obliged to approach each other fairly closely, especially on sheltered waters. There are no sound signals laid down for sailing vessels in sight of one another, and their crews frequently communicate by hailing each other.

Suppose you had the wind on your starboard side, and there was risk of collision with a vessel which had the wind on her port side. You would have the right of way and should stand-on.

If, at any time, you thought that nothing the giving-way vessel could do alone would prevent a collision, you should act as ____________ to ____________________.

necessary avert (or avoid) collision

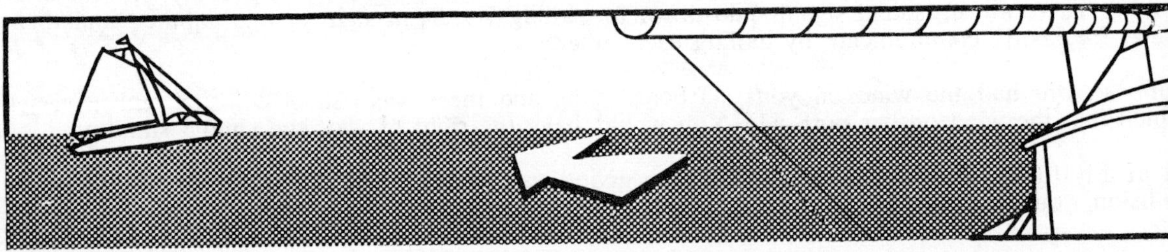

The vessel on your port bow is on a steady bearing.

In this situation, you should ______ ______ .

keep clear (You are probably overtaking the other vessel.)

In the situation shown below, if there is a risk of collision, you have the right of way.

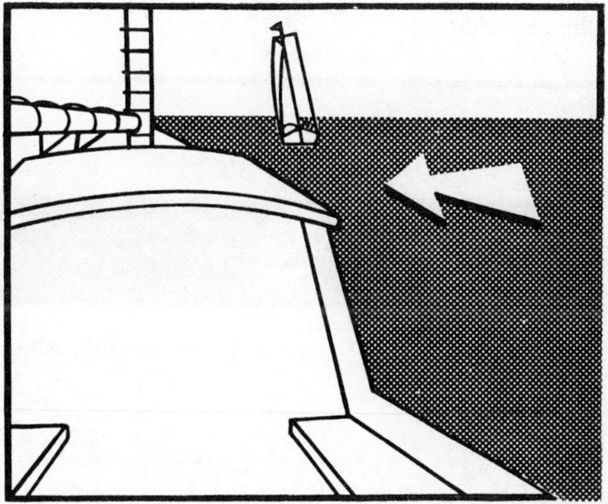

If, however, the other vessel appears to be giving-way too little or too late, it may become likely that her action alone will not avert a collision.

What should you do then?

Act as necessary to avert a collision.

Test on Chapter 6

There are five questions in this test. You must get at least three of them right before you go on to the next chapter.

1. If the other vessel is on a steady bearing, what must you do?

Test (continued)

2. The bearing of the other vessel is steady. What should you do?

Test (continued)

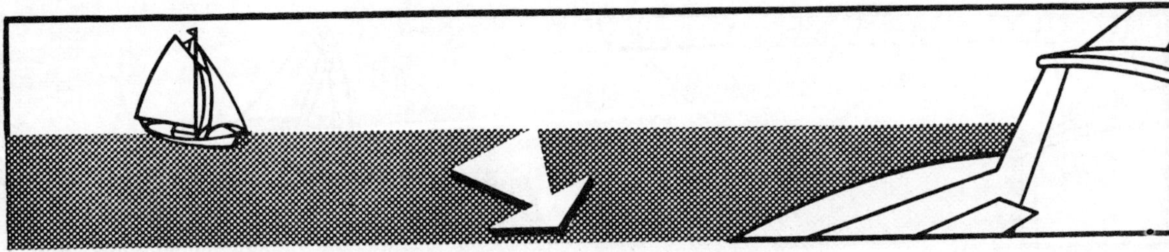

3. What should you do, if the other vessel's bearing is steady?

Test (continued)

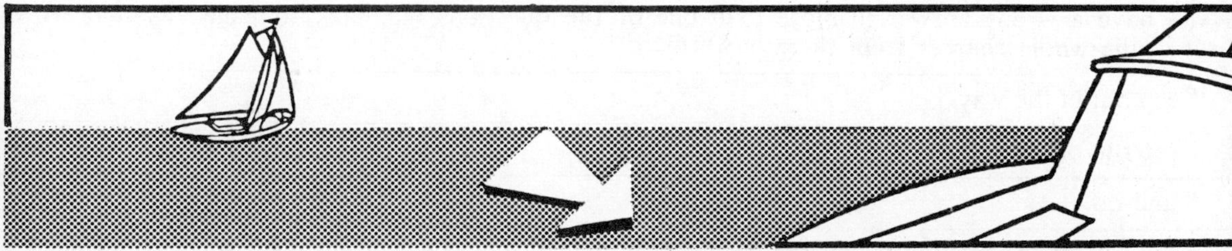

4. What must you do in this situation, if the bearing is steady and the range is decreasing?

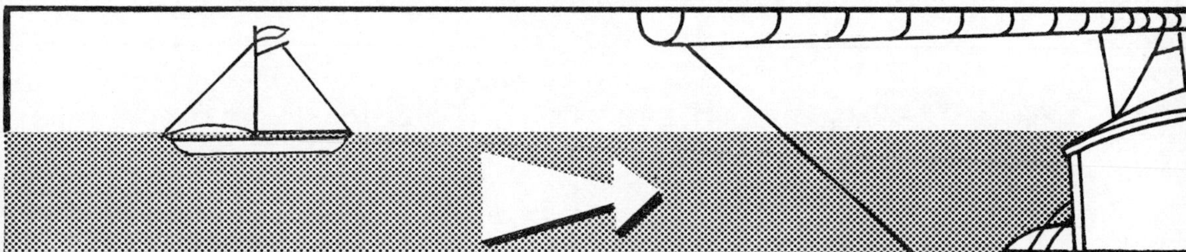

5. What must you do in this situation?

Answers to Test

If you have a wrong answer to more than one of the questions, go back to page 284 and work through the whole chapter **from there onwards.**

1. Keep out of the way.
2. Keep out of the way.
3. Stand-on.
4. Keep out of the way until you are finally past and clear, since you are probably overtaking the vessel.
5. Keep out of the way, since you will probably not know on which side the other vessel has the wind.

CHAPTER 7 RADAR AND THE RULES

Read Rules 6 (b), 7 (b), 7 (c) and 19 (d) which all refer to the use of radar.

This chapter will relate the points made in these Rules to practical situations.

On most pages in this chapter you will see the picture of a radar screen, like this:

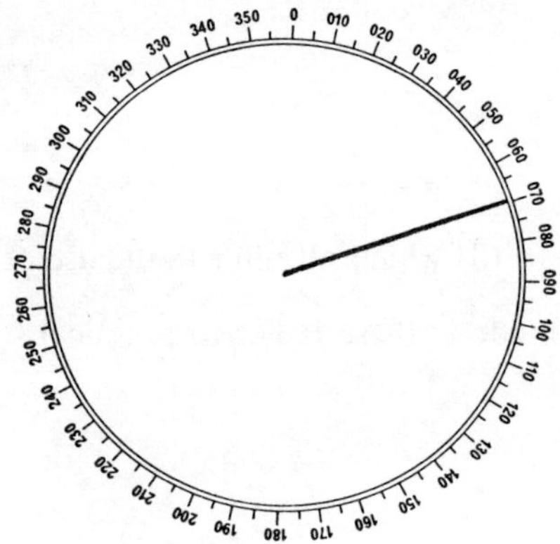

Your own ship is always in the centre. The radar picture is compass stabilised: that is to say that ________ is always at the top of the picture.

North (or 000°)

The direction of the ship's head is indicated by the ship's head marker. The ship's head marker will move as your ship alters course.

Here is your radar picture.

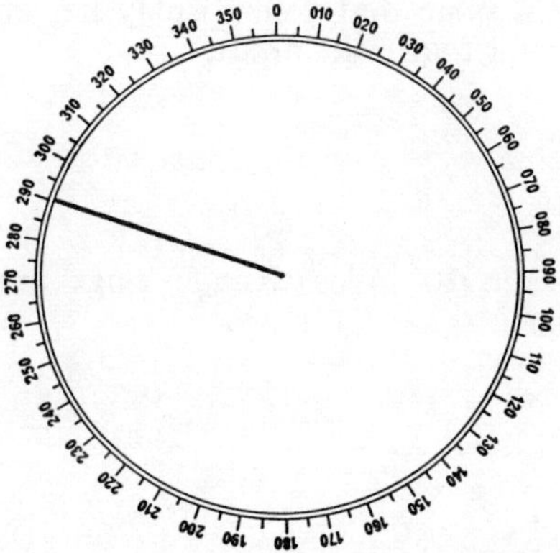

Your ship's course is ____°.

290°

One final point should be noted about the conventions of the radar pictures in this sequence.

We shall assume that your display has electronic range rings which can be switched on and will be either two or four miles apart.

Range scale 10 miles. Range rings are 2 miles apart.

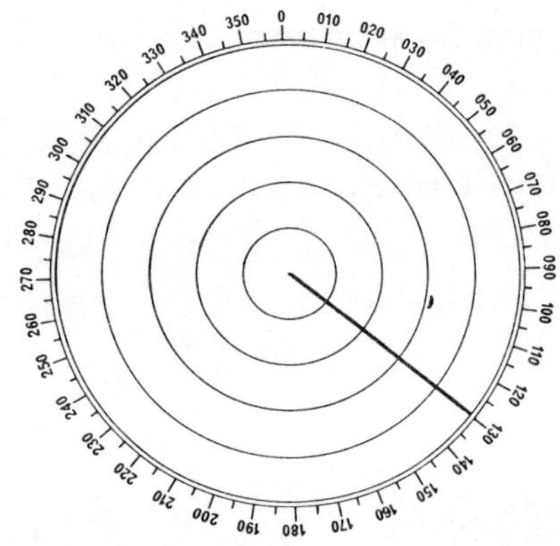

The range of the echo on the display shown on this page is ____ miles.

So, to recapitulate:

(i) North is always at the top.
(ii) Your own ship is always in the centre.
(iii) The ship's head marker indicates your heading.
(iv) Electronic range rings may be switched on.

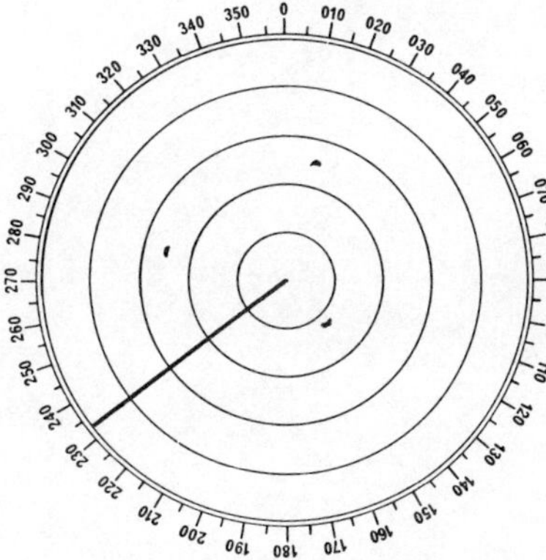

One important thing we shall be teaching is a method of plotting a radar echo. However, we shall only be teaching you one method—there are many others. The important thing to remember is that you must always ______ an echo.

Here is your radar picture.

The range rings are 2 miles apart.

You can see on this display that there is a contact on your starboard bow.

Previous positions of this echo have been plotted with crosses which form a line or 'back track'.

This line can be projected forward so that you can see where she will be relative to you in the future.

The projected relative track of this contact passes down your starboard side, and its closest range will be 2½ miles. Its **C**losest **P**oint of **A**pproach (CPA) is, therefore, said to be ____ ______ to starboard.

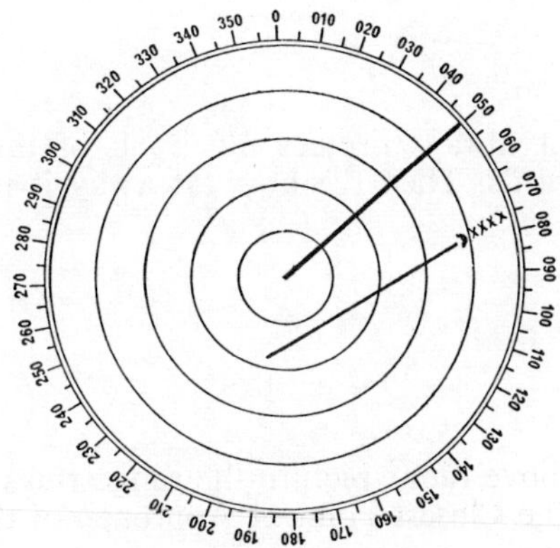

$2\frac{1}{2}$ miles

You must always project the track of the other ship onwards. Then see how far away it is going to pass.

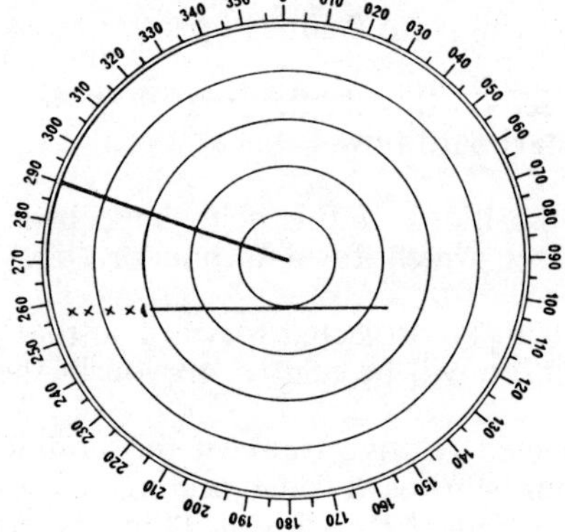

On the above radar picture the range rings are two miles apart. What is the **C**losest **P**oint of **A**pproach of the other ship?

2 miles.

The range scale in use is 20 miles.

Whenever you are watching an echo to see if risk of a close-quarters situation exists, you must plot its position at regular intervals until you have built up a track.

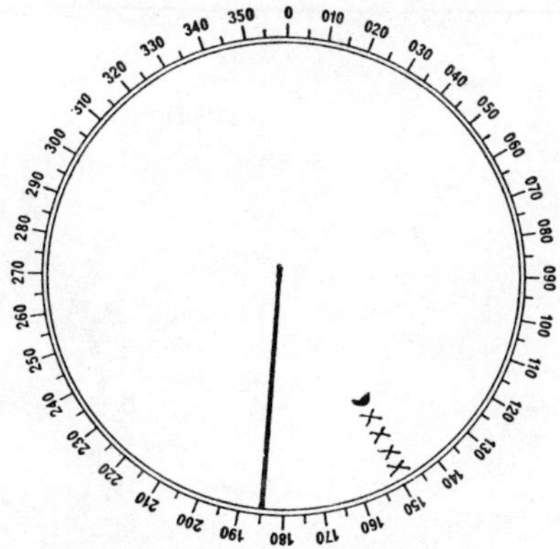

1. What is the next thing you do to see how far away the ship will pass?
2. What is the C.P.A. in this case?

1. Project the track onwards.
2. The C.P.A. is zero (or something very near it).

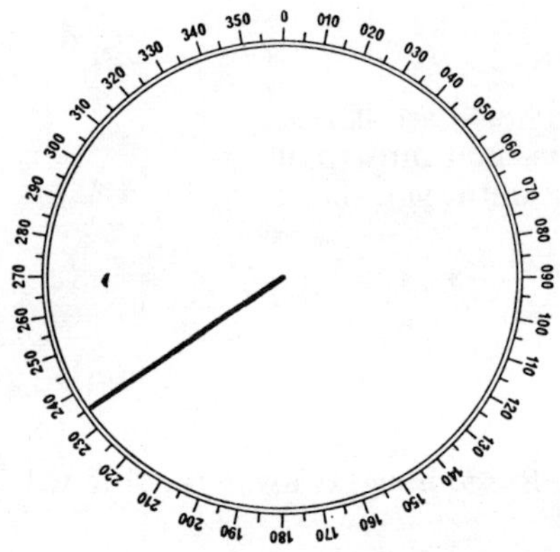

1. How do you build up a track to see if a risk of a close-quarters situation exists?
2. What do you do after the track is built up?

1. Plot the echo at regular intervals.
2. Project it onwards.

The range scale is 20 miles.

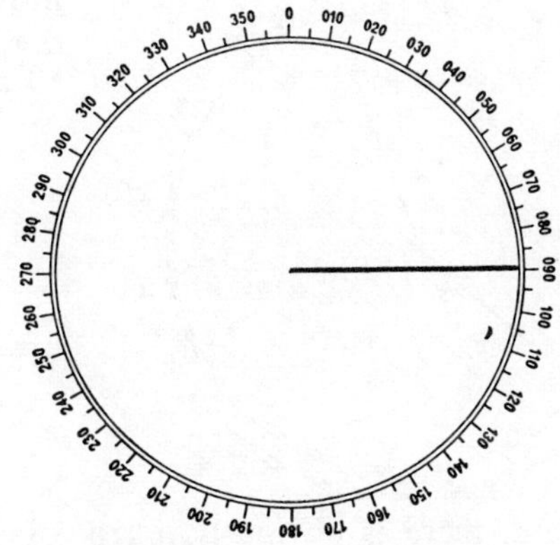

What action do you always take first, when you are watching an echo to see if a risk of a close-quarters situation exists?

Plot the echo at regular intervals, to build up a track.

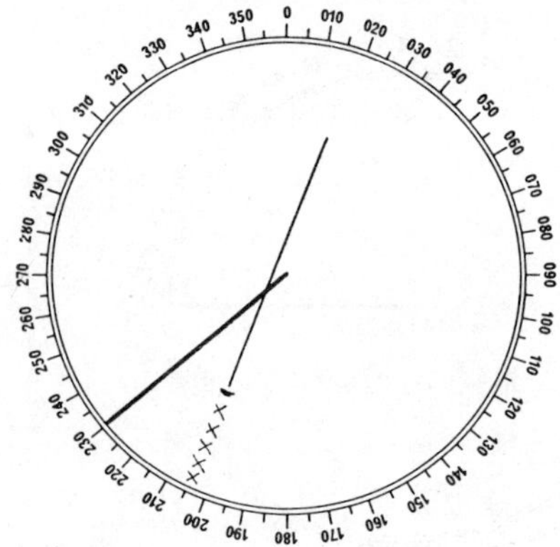

In both illustrations range scale in use, 10 miles.

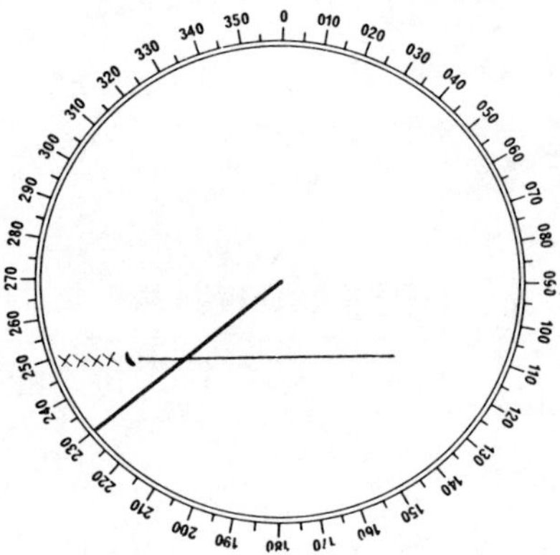

In this case, there is obviously a risk of a close-quarters situation. If the other ship is visible, then the Rules for vessels in sight of one another will apply. However, if the other vessel is **not** visible, you should consider altering course and/or speed. This alteration should be **substantial,** so that you will pass well clear of the other ship. An alteration to starboard is generally preferable to an alteration to port.

In this case there is probably no risk of collision.

You should continue to watch and plot the echo, until it is well past and clear. (The other ship may alter course or speed.)

Range scale in use, 10 miles.

Risk of a close-quarters situation exists here. The other vessel is not visible.

The action that you take must ensure that if you alter course or speed, then its effect will be seen as soon as possible on your radar, and on that of the other ship (if it has radar).

1. In general terms, what action should you consider?

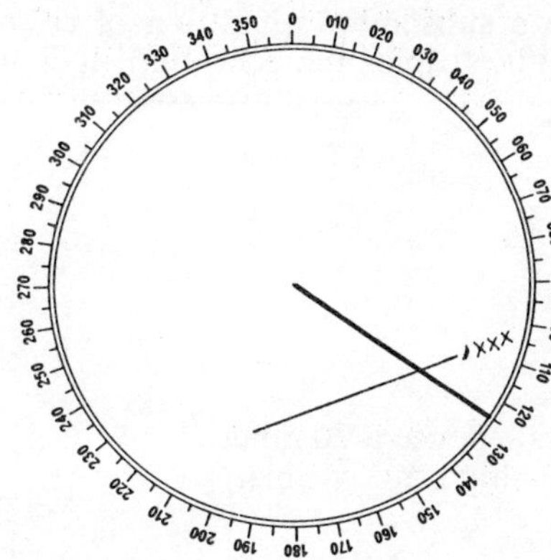

Range scale in use, 10 miles.

In this case there is no risk of a close-quarters situation.

2. What action should you take to ensure that you would notice immediately if there were to be a risk of a close-quarters situation?

1. Make a **substantial** alteration of course and/or speed.
2. Continue to plot the echo until it is finally past and clear.

Range scale in use is 20 miles.
The other ship is not visible.

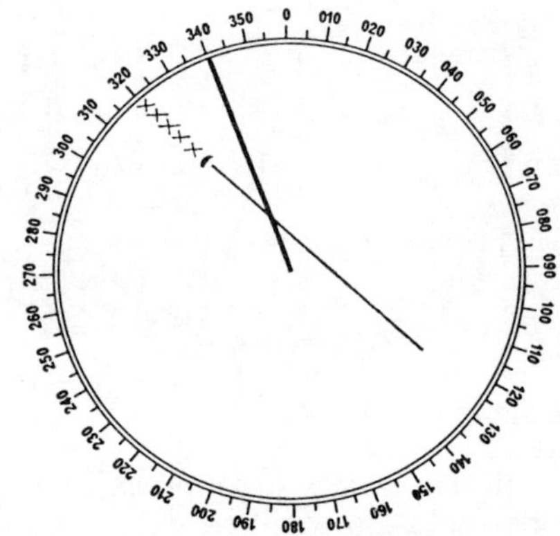

1. In general terms, what action would you consider here?
2. In order to see whether the other ship draws clear as planned, what would you do after you have taken action?

1. You should have considered a **substantial** alteration of course to pass well clear of the other ship, bearing in mind that the Rules say that an alteration to starboard is generally preferable to an alteration to port.

   If you gave a specific answer (e.g. alter a 'certain number' of degrees to starboard) then, to count your answer as right, your alteration should have been at least 45°.

2. You should continue to plot the echo until it is well past and clear.

This situation represents the moment just before you take action to avoid the other ship.

Range scale in use, 10 miles.

Having taken the action, what should you do?

You should continue to plot the other echo, to build up a new track and measure the new C.P.A., so that you can confirm that the ship is drawing clear as planned, until it is well past and clear.

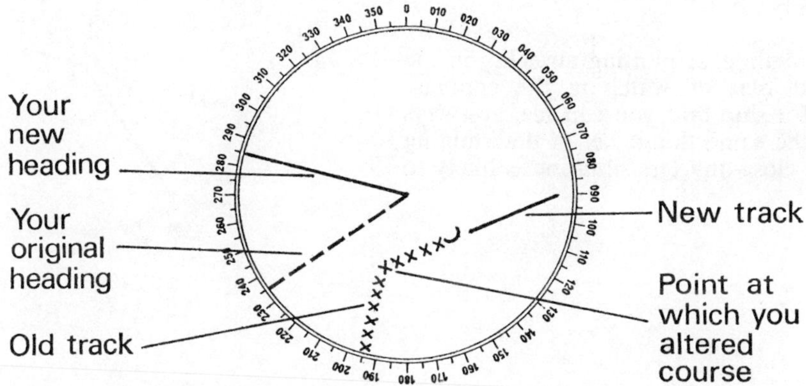

You will probably have realised by now that, when the projected track of a ship passes through your own ship (i.e. the centre of the display) this means that the bearing of the ship is steady.

Thus the method of plotting an echo on the radar, and that of watching the compass bearing of a ship that you can see, are ways of doing the same thing: i.e. of determining whether a close-quarters situation is likely to exist.

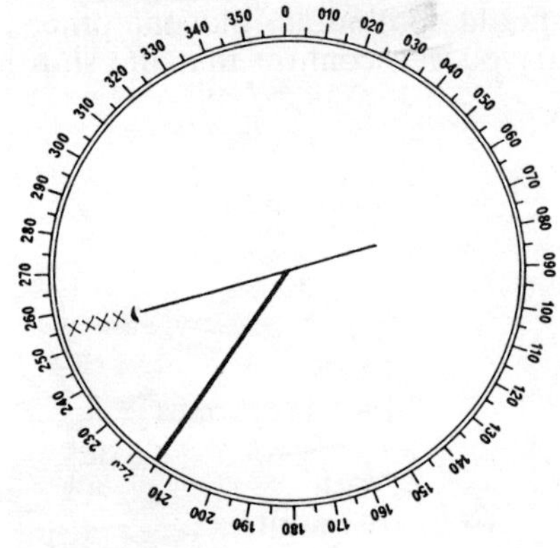

Now let us consider the next point concerning the use of radar. Some objects, including small vessels (particularly wooden ones) and small icebergs, do not reflect radar pulses very effectively, so they may be detected only at close range or not at all.

This is one reason why, even when using radar, you **must** obey Rule 19: i.e., you must proceed at a safe speed for the prevailing circumstances and conditions of restricted visibility.

Put yourself in this position: your radar screen is clear of ship contacts out to 15 miles and you sight a bank of fog ahead. You decide to reduce to 'safe speed'.

In which of the following areas do you think that you would be justified in proceeding at a higher safe speed than if you did not have radar.

In the English channel.	Go to 324.
In mid-Pacific.	Go to 325.
Neither.	Go to 326.

You think that in low visibility in the English Channel, with a clear radar screen, you would be justified in proceeding at a higher speed than if you did not have radar.

'Safe speed' must, of course, be a matter for individual judgement in each case, considering every circumstance.

One circumstance, however, that you must consider in this case, is the likelihood of small sailing or fishing boats being in the Channel and, our opinion is that you would be wrong in proceeding at a higher speed. Go back to page 323, re-read it and choose another answer.

You think that in low visibility in mid-Pacific, with a clear radar screen, you would be justified in proceeding at a higher speed than if you did not have radar.

'Safe speed' must, of course, be a matter for individual judgement in each case. If, in this case, you considered it unlikely that you would meet ice or small vessels, then undoubtedly your clear radar screen would be a factor that might legitimately lead to a decision that a higher speed was safe. If you looked at it this way, then you are right.

However, do not forget that if you were on the spot and felt **any** doubt, then the slower the better.

Go to 327.

You do not think that, in low visibility and with a clear radar screen, you would be justified in proceeding at a higher speed than if you did not have radar, whether you were in the English Channel or mid-Pacific.

Your answer is quite right—to go at a lower speed is never wrong.

If you were actually on the spot, you might decide that the risk of meeting small craft that might be detected late (or not at all) was very remote, and you might consider that a higher speed was safe; but if there was any doubt, the slower the better. Go to page 327.

If you are navigating in restricted visibility, but particularly in fog or heavy rain, and you hear a fog signal, it is not possible to be **certain** which radar echo is that of the ship that made the signal.

Rule 19 (e) states:

'Except where it has been determined that a risk of collision does not exist, every vessel which hears apparently forward of her beam the fog signal of another vessel, or which cannot avoid a close-quarters situation with another vessel forward of her beam, shall reduce her speed to the minimum at which she can be kept on her course. She shall, if necessary, take all her way off and in any event navigate with extreme caution until danger of collision is over.'

Here is your radar picture (range rings are 2 miles apart, visibility is about 1 mile). You have plotted the echoes as shown.

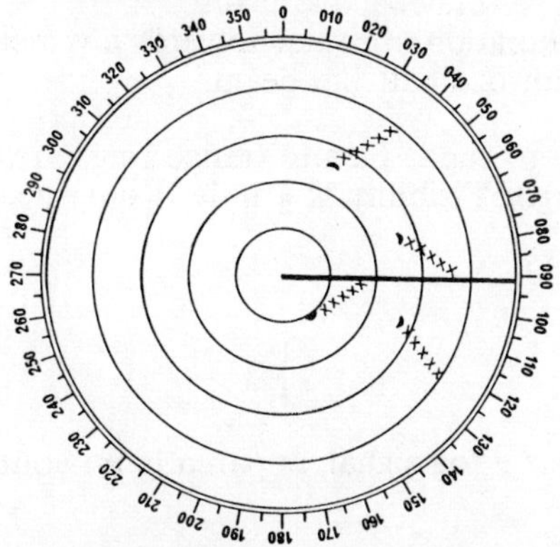

You hear a fog signal apparently forward of your starboard beam. What should you do?

Reduce speed to a minimum and navigate with caution until danger of collision is over.

Rule 19 (d) states:

'A vessel which detects by radar alone the presence of another vessel shall determine if a close-quarters situation is developing and/or risk of collision exists. If so, she shall take avoiding action in ample time, provided that when such action consists of an alteration of course, so far as possible the following shall be avoided:

(i) an alteration of course to port for a vessel forward of the beam, other than for a vessel being overtaken;

(ii) an alteration of course towards a vessel abeam or abaft the beam.'

Here is your radar picture (range rings are 2 miles apart). Visibility is ½ mile. Your speed is 5 knots.

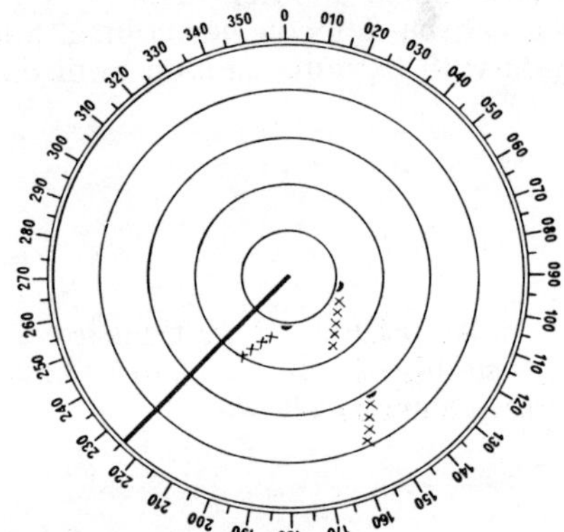

If you hear a fog signal, apparently on your port bow, what should you do?

Reduce speed to a minimum and navigate with caution until danger of collision is over.

If in answer to the last question you said that you should alter course to starboard, whether you mentioned taking off all way or not, you were wrong.

Even if there is only one vessel on your radar screen, you could not assume that the fog signal came from her. Why? (Remember what we said about the difficulty of detecting some vessels.)

The signal may have come from a vessel not detected by your radar.

Whenever there are drops of moisture in the air (as in fog, rain or snow) then radar detection ranges may be reduced. These conditions also produce restricted visibility.

It is possible for radar echoes to be completely obliterated in some weather conditions.

Here is your radar picture. The range scale in use is 10 miles. The visibility is good, but you see a bank of rain ahead, in which you estimate visibility will be reduced.

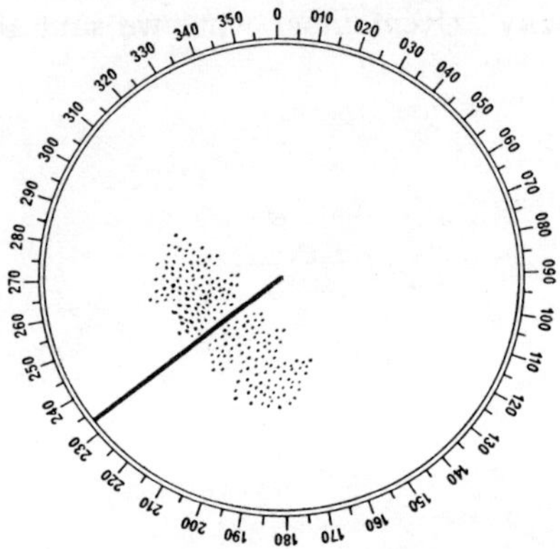

Before you enter the rain, you must reduce to a safe speed. In deciding on the speed, would you assume that there are no vessels in the area of rain?

No. (Because rain affects radar detection ranges and there may be a ship hidden in the area of rain.)

Radar is only one aid to preventing a collision; you must make use of **all** aids.

You will remember that Rule 2 states, in part, nothing in the Rules shall exonerate you from any consequences of neglect to keep a proper look-out.

A proper look-out means as good a look-out as your resources allow. In restricted visibility this means use radar properly, listen and look.

When using radar, you should ensure that a ______ look-out and an aural look-out are kept.

visual

If, as the Officer of the Watch in restricted visibility, you were to spend most of your time watching the radar, this would **not** constitute a proper look-out.

You must arrange that a continuous radar look-out, a continuous ________ look-out and a continuous ________ look-out are always kept.

visual aural

When using your radar as an aid to avoid collision, you must know what its limitations are.

We are not going to discuss all those limitations here, except to remind you that the very moment when you need your radar most (i.e. in restricted visibility) is just the time when you must assess its information with the most care.

When there are drops of moisture in the atmosphere detection ranges may be ________ and in severe conditions the weather echoes may even ________other echoes completely.

reduced obliterate
(Or any words having similar meanings.)

Here is your radar picture.

Range scale in use is 20 miles.

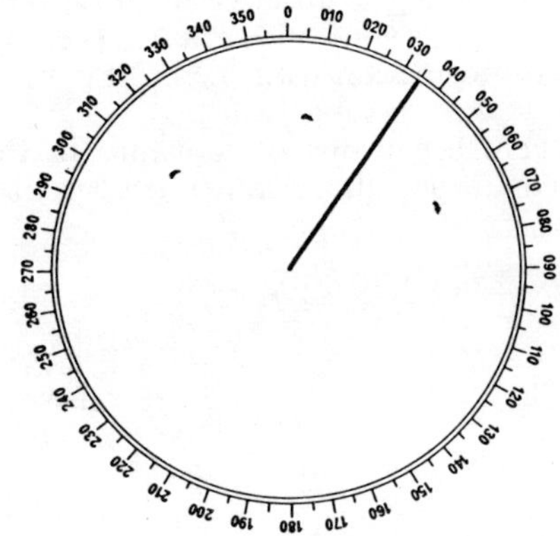

As the Officer of the Watch you are quite satisfied with the working of your radar, and a good watch is being kept upon it.

Is it necessary to keep a visual look-out as well:

1. In good visibility?
2. In restricted visibility?

1. Yes.
2. Yes.

Most radar sets have controls to lessen the effect of weather, and you must be familiar with their effects on the radar picture.

However, even with these controls, the same weather that causes restricted visibility may ____ detection ranges or even ______ echoes completely.

reduce obliterate

You are the Officer of the Watch and you see that the radar has detected the echo to the north-east.

Range scale in use is 20 miles.

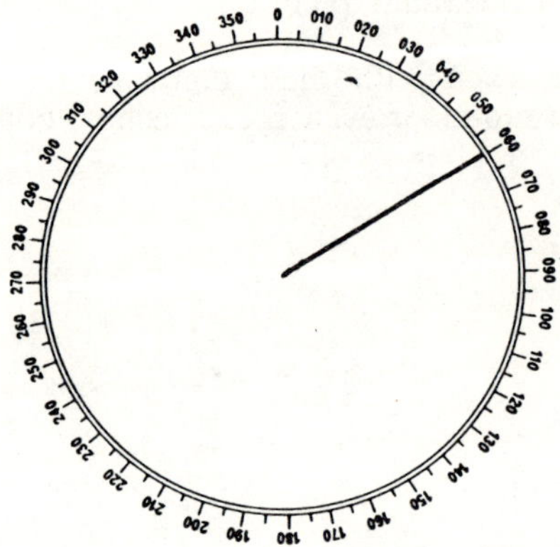

You must avoid a close-quarters situation. Before you decide whether avoiding action is necessary, what should you do?

Plot the echo, project its track onwards and determine the C.P.A.

A little while later, your picture looks like this. Range scale in use, 20 miles.

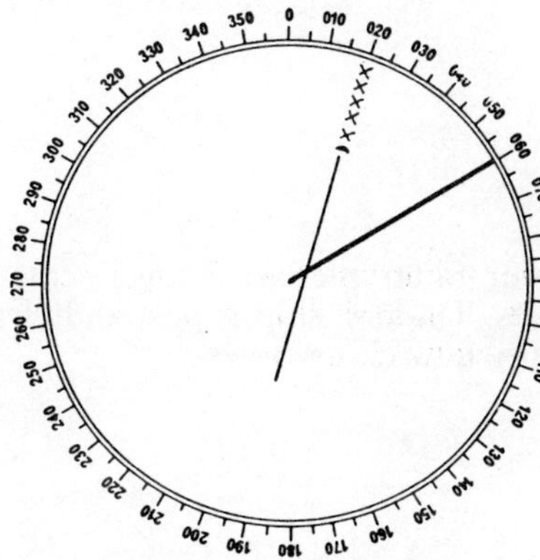

Then the look-out reports that a masthead light and starboard bow light are visible on the bearing of the echo.

What should you do?

Maintain your course and speed (stand on) with caution.
(You would also take a visual bearing. You may have mentioned this.)

Here is your radar picture. Range scale in use, 10 miles. The first ship is past and clear. The visibility now closes down.

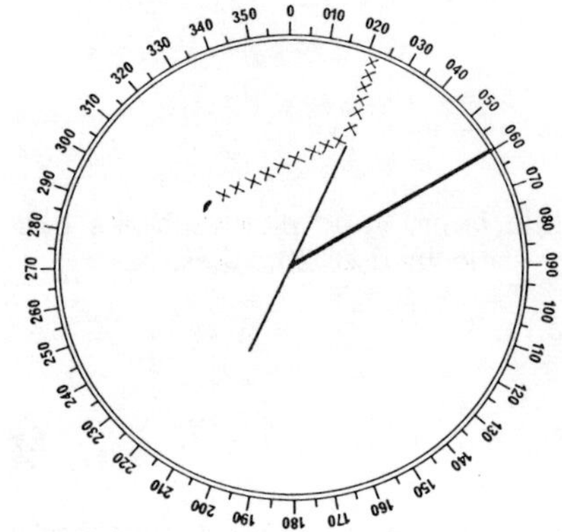

What must you do?

Reduce to safe speed. Sound fog signal. (One prolonged blast, at intervals of not more than 2 minutes.) Place extra look-outs. Have engines ready for immediate manoeuvre.

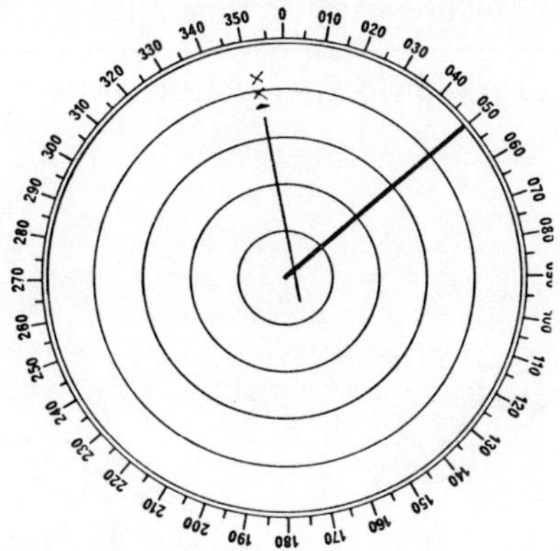

You now detect and track the echo to the north. (Range rings 2 miles apart.)

The visibility is now about one mile.

What sort of action should you consider, and when must it be taken?

Action to avoid a close-quarters situation i.e. substantial alteration of course and/or speed to pass well clear of the other ship.

As soon as you discover there is a risk of a close-quarters situation. (Or any other answer showing that you realise early action must be taken.)

What must you do after you have taken action?

Continue to plot the echo until it is finally past and clear.

Always remember Rule 7 (b) and (c) which state:

'(b) Proper use shall be made of radar equipment if fitted and operational, including long-range scanning to obtain early warning of risk of collision and radar plotting or equivalent systematic observation of detected objects.

(c) Assumptions shall not be made on the basis of scanty information, especially scanty radar information.'

Test on Chapter 7

You must get 100% on all questions marked * before you go on to the next chapter.

*1. You see that the radar has detected the echo to the west.

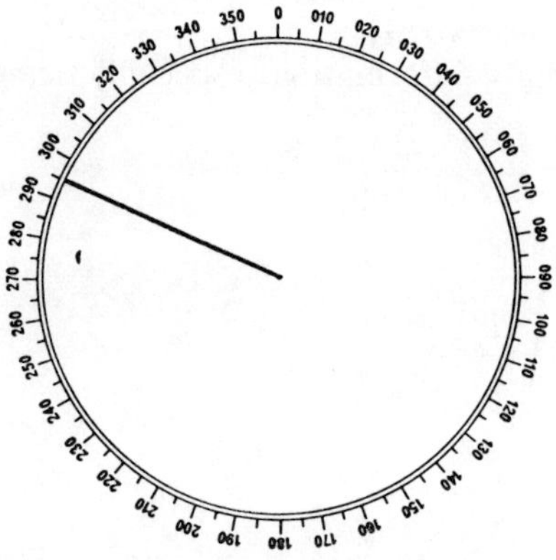

Range scale in use, 10 miles.

You must avoid a close-quarters situation. Before you decide on avoiding action what must you do?

*2. You sight this echo right ahead of you on the radar.

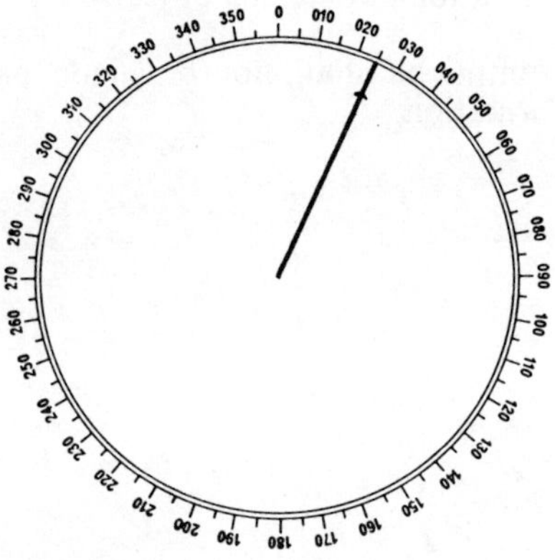

Range scale in use, 10 miles.

At the same time the look-out reports that he can see a ship ahead, showing masthead lights and both side lights. What must you do?

Test (continued)

*3. You see that the radar has detected this echo to the south. The visibility is 1 mile.

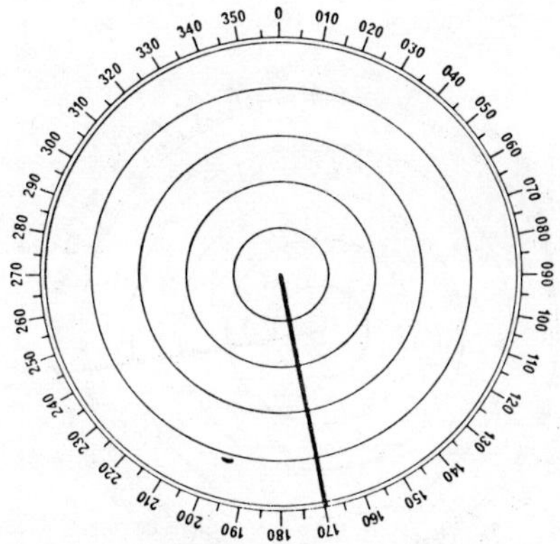

Range rings 2 miles apart.

You ascertain that a risk of a close-quarters situation exists. What action should you take, and when?

*4. You have just altered course and speed to avoid the ship shown on the radar to the north-west.

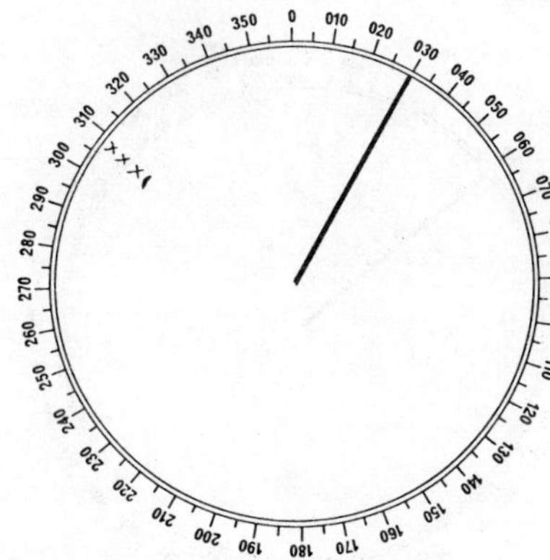

Range scale in use, 10 miles.

What should you do now?

Test (continued)

*5. This is your radar picture. It is a fine day with good visibility.

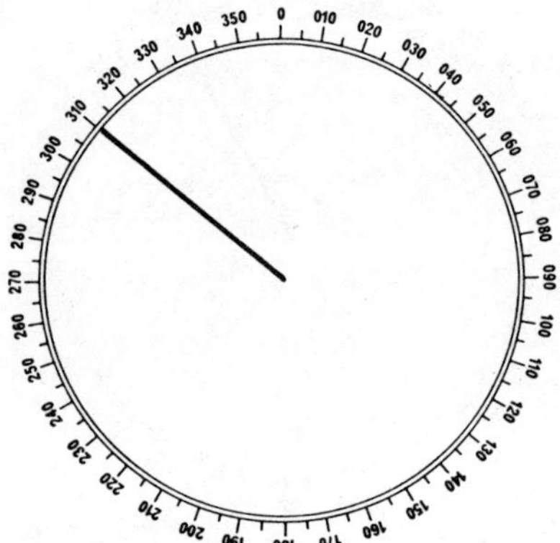

Range scale, 20 miles.

The visibility suddenly closes in. What should you do?

*6. This is your radar picture. You are doing 6 knots, and the visibility is very poor.

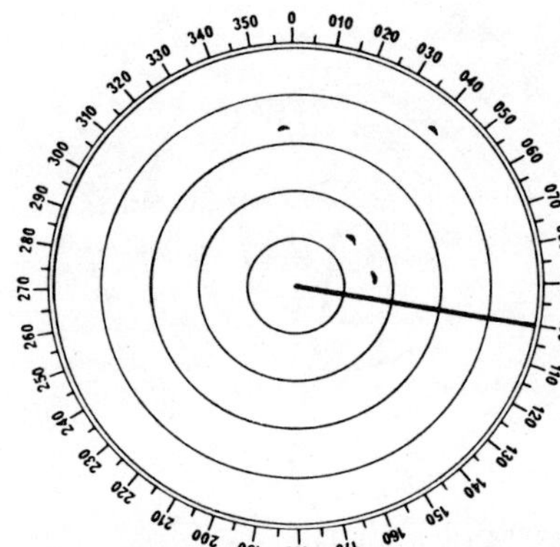

Range rings 2 miles apart.

You hear a fog signal, apparently on the port bow. What should you do?

Test (continued)

*7. In all weathers what should you bear in mind when your radar screen is apparently clear?

*8. What is the probable effect of fog, rain or snow upon the radar picture?

*9. If your radar set is working correctly, and an efficient watch is being kept on it, would you consider this to be a 'proper' look-out
  (a) in clear weather?
  (b) in restricted visibility?
  (If your answer to (a) or (b) is 'no', say what other look-out should be kept.)

Answers to Test

All questions must be answered 100% correctly. If you answer **any** question incorrectly, you must go back to page 306 and work through the chapter again. For question 1 pay special attention to the references given. For questions 2, 5 and 6 note that you will need to refer to earlier chapters in addition.

		Reference
*1.	Plot the echo, project the track onwards, and estimate the C.P.A.	pages 310–315
*2.	Sound one short blast (·), and alter course to starboard.	
*3.	You should make a substantial alteration of course and/or speed, bearing in mind that an alteration to starboard is generally preferable to an alteration to port. You should do this as soon as you see that risk of a close-quarters situation exists.	23–25
*4.	Continue to plot the echo until it is finally past and clear.	
*5.	Reduce to a safe speed adapted to the prevailing circumstances and conditions of restricted visibility. Sound fog signals. Place extra look-outs Have engines ready for immediate manoeuvre.	253–256

Answers to Test (continued)

		Reference
*6.	Take all way off the ship and navigate with caution until danger of collision is over.	pages 257–260
*7.	Small objects, wooden vessels or small icebergs may not be detected by your radar.	
*8.	They may reduce detection range and may obliterate some echoes.	
*9.	(a) No. A visual look-out. (b) No. An aural and a visual look-out.	

CHAPTER 8 REQUIREMENTS OF GOOD SEAMANSHIP AND SPECIAL CIRCUMSTANCES

No set of specific rules could be made that would cover all possible circumstances. When acting in accordance with the Rules you must show good seamanship and common sense.

Nevertheless, it is made quite clear in the Rules that you may only depart from the Rules when it is absolutely necessary, to avoid immediate danger. It is also made plain that you must be prepared for lights and signals not laid down in the Rules, but that these lights and signals must be properly authorised.

The Rules which cover exceptional cases are Rules 1 (b) and (c), 2, 7 (a), 17 (b), 24 (g), 31 and 36.

Read through those Rules once.

Rule 1 (c) states:

> 'Nothing in these Rules shall interfere with the operation of any special rules made by the Government of any State with respect to additional station or signal lights or whistle signals for ships of war and vessels proceeding under convoy, or with respect to additional station or signal lights for fishing vessels engaged in fishing as a fleet. These additional station or signal lights or whistle signals shall, so far as possible, be such that they cannot be mistaken for any light or signal authorized elsewhere under these Rules.'

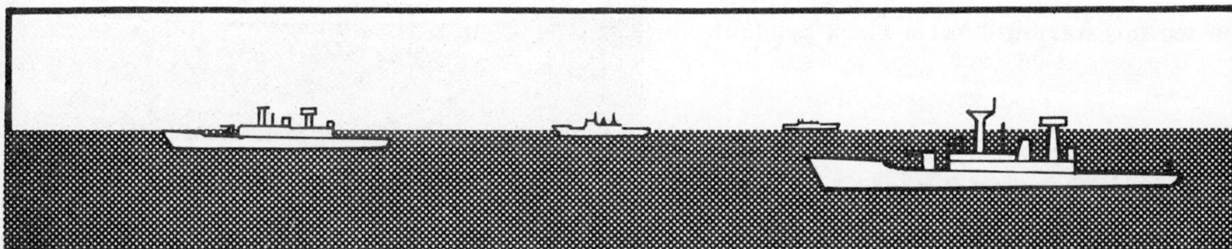

In the situation shown in the illustration, is it reasonable to expect special signals to be shown or sounded by the other vessels?

Yes. (They are ships of war.)

You are the Officer of the Watch of an ordinary power-driven vessel.

You see this warship hoist a black pennant.

Should you take special action upon sighting this signal? If so, what action?

No.

This group of lights shown below is evidently a fleet of vessels.

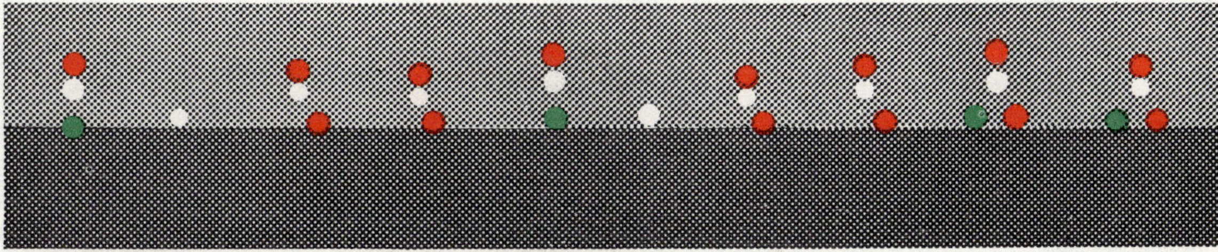

(a) What kind of vessels does the illustration show?
(b) Is it reasonable to expect special signals?

(a) Fishing vessels.
(b) Yes (they may be fishing as a fleet).

You are the Officer of the Watch of an ordinary power-driven vessel.

(a) What kind of vessels are shown in this illustration?
(b) What action should you take upon seeing these searchlight signals?

(a) Trawlers.
(b) No special action other than to keep out of the way of vessels engaged in fishing. Searchlights may be used for warning in accordance with Annex II of the Rules.

The Rules do not cover anywhere near all possible signals, so you must be prepared for unusual signals.

You must also be prepared for unusual circumstances as stated in Rule 2 (b):

> 'In construing and complying with these Rules due regard shall be had to all dangers of navigation and collision and to any special circumstances, including the limitations of the vessels involved, which may make a departure from these Rules necessary to avoid immediate danger.'

So, if any special circumstances make it dangerous to obey the Rules strictly you should act ____________ to avoid immediate danger.

as necessary

It may be that the other vessel is hampered, either by a navigation hazard or by another ship, and might find it difficult to act in accordance with the Rules.

Suppose these ships are about 2 miles away.

The bearing of the right-hand one is steady but she has the other one about $\frac{1}{2}$ mile on her beam. You have observed her making efforts to keep clear but these have not been effective. What should you consider doing?

You should consider sounding one short blast and making a bold alteration to starboard. (Whether you did so would depend upon whether you thought danger could be averted in any other way.)

You sight this convoy ahead, at a distance of 4 to 8 miles.

The bearing of the extreme left-hand vessel (the one right ahead of your ship) is steady.

What should you do in this situation?

Sound two short blasts and make a bold alteration to port.

Rule 2 (a) states:

> 'Nothing in these Rules shall exonerate any vessel, or the owner, master or crew thereof, from the consequences of any neglect to comply with these Rules or of the neglect of any precaution which may be required by the ordinary practice of seamen, or by the special circumstances of the case.'

In restricted visibility, it is the ordinary practice of seamen to keep silence on deck. If you were involved in a collision which was partly due to you not hearing a fog signal, owing to the noise of a radio played on the upper deck, would you be open to blame **under the Rules** for not ordering silence on deck?

Probably yes. (Under Rule 2.)

The sense of Rule 2 (quoted on the last page) is that, when neglect of any precaution not specified in the Rules might lead to collision, then you must take such a precaution.

Rule 5 states, 'Every vessel shall at all times maintain a proper look-out by sight and hearing as well as by all available means appropriate in the prevailing circumstances and conditions.....'

A proper look-out not only means a visual, aural and radar look-out, but special alertness required in any particular circumstances.

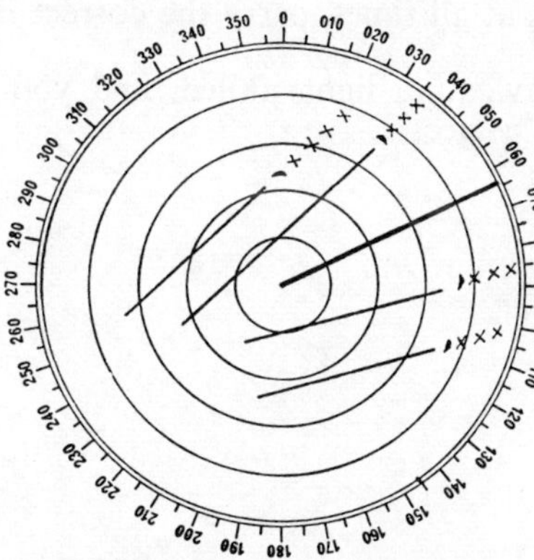

You are in a ship whose steering gear has failed twice in the last twenty-four hours. This is your radar picture.

Range rings are 1 mile apart.

The visibility is good. What duty should you consider including here, in keeping a proper look-out'?

The duty to be particularly alert when you are passing close to other ships, in case your steering gear fails again. (You are correct if your answer recognised the need for some special action because of the possibility of steering gear failure.)

Rule 2(a) refers to 'the consequences of any neglect.........'; Rule 5 states that 'Every vessel shall at all times maintain a proper look-out.........

Even a good look-out could be misled if a vessel does not display the lights and shapes appropriate to existing circumstances and conditions. (Rules 20 to 37.)

You **must,** at all times, carry the correct lights or signals.

If your navigation lights failed, and you were involved in a collision as a result, could this be construed as 'neglect'?

Probably yes. (Since you **must** always carry the lights, you should have foreseen possible failure, and had emergency lights ready for immediate use.)

You must not neglect **any** precaution which might avoid collision. If you do and a collision ensues, you would be in some degree to blame, whether or not this precaution is mentioned or implied in the Rules.

The Rules cannot legislate for every contingency, but their purpose is clear. It is that, by following them, you should ______ ________.

avoid collision

When in charge of a ship, whether you are the Captain or the Officer of the Watch, and whether it is a warship or a privately owned one, you must always interpret and apply these Rules in the way that will ______ ________ .

avoid collision

This is the end of the programme.

By itself, the study of this programme will not make you competent to avoid collision; you will also need to acquire the habits and skills of a good seaman by practice and observation on the bridge.

However, it is essential that you first have a good knowledge of the Regulations for Preventing Collisions at Sea. You now have this knowledge.

APPENDIX

The programmed text which you have just read was designed to give you a thorough knowledge of the Regulations for Preventing Collisions at Sea. It was written from the point of view of the Officer of the Watch or, in the case of a sailing vessel, the helmsman.

There are a few subjects covered by the Rules which were not mentioned, or were mentioned only briefly, either because they are concerned with situations which occur infrequently, or because they do not affect the situation materially as seen by the Officer of the Watch.

To complete your study of the Rule of the Road and for reference purposes you should now read this unprogrammed appendix in which the following subjects are covered:

Seaplanes.
'Non-displacement' craft.
Distress signals.
Specification of lights.
Signals to attract attention.
Screening of lights.
References relevant to lights.

Seaplanes

The word 'seaplane' is defined in Rule 3 (e) as 'any aircraft designed to manoeuvre on the water'.

Steering rules

Rule 3 (a) states: "For the purpose of these Rules, except where the context otherwise requires:

(a) The word 'vessel' includes every description of water craft, including non-displacement craft and seaplanes, used or capable of being used as a means of transportation on water."

Rule 18 (e) requires that a seaplane on the water shall, in general, keep clear of all vessels and avoid impeding their navigation. In circumstances, however, where risk of collision exists, she shall comply with the Rules for vessels in sight of one another.

Lights and shapes

The lights and shapes which a seaplane is required to carry are the same as those of a power-driven vessel of the same length. However, Rule 31 allows that when this is impracticable 'she shall exhibit lights and shapes as closely similar in characteristics and position as is possible'.

‘Non-displacement’ craft

Rule 3 (a) includes ‘non-displacement’ craft in the definition of the word ‘vessel’.

Steering rules

A non-displacement craft when operating in the non-displacement mode shall obey the Rules in the same way as a power-driven vessel of the same length.

Lights and shapes

The lights and shapes which must be displayed by a non-displacement craft are the same as for a power-driven vessel of the same length except that Rule 23 (b) lays down that, in addition, ‘. . . an air-cushion vessel when operating in the non-displacement mode . . . . . shall exhibit an all-round flashing yellow light’.

Distress signals

Annex IV details the signals which may be used or displayed by a vessel or seaplane on the water, in distress, and requiring assistance from other vessels or the shore. The signals may be used or displayed either together or separately.

It is important to note that none of the signals listed as distress signals, or any other signals which may be confused with distress signals, may be used for any other purpose than indicating that a vessel or seaplane on the water is in distress and requires assistance.

Specification of lights

Type of vessel and what it is doing	Masthead light(s)	Side lights	Stern light
Power-driven vessel 50 metres or more in length, under way.	(i) Forward light at least 6 metres above the hull and at a height not less than the breadth of the vessel. However, it need not be more than 12 metres. No more than one quarter of the length from the stem. Visibility, 6 miles.	Height not greater than three quarters of the height of the forward masthead light but not so low as to be interferred with by deck lights.	Visibility, 3 miles.
	(ii) After light at least 4·5 metres higher than forward light. Must not be less than half the length of the vessel between forward and after lights but need not exceed 100 metres. Visibility, 6 miles.	Shall not be placed in front of forward masthead light. Visibility, 3 miles.	

Type of vessel	Masthead light(s)	Side lights	Stern light
Power-driven vessel 12 metres or more but less than 50 metres in length.	The light in (i) on the previous page must be carried but light in (ii) optional. Visibility 5 miles if 20 metres or more in length. Height as in (i) on previous page. Visibility 3 miles if 12 metres or more but less than 20 metres in length. Height to be not less than 2·5 metres above gunwale.	As for (1) and (ii) on previous page except that they may be placed in front of forward masthead light in vessels under 20 metres. Visibility 2 miles.	Visibility, 2 miles.
Power-driven vessel when pushing other vessel(s) of any length. Power-driven vessel when towing—length of tow 200 metres or less. Power-driven vessel when alongside.	In place of forward masthead light, two white lights in a vertical line, not less than 2 metres apart, one of them in the same position as the masthead light. The lower of the two must be not less than 4 metres above the hull except when a towing light is required.	As in (i) on previous page.	As in (i) on previous page but, in addition, when towing astern, a yellow towing light of the same construction as—and above—the stern light.

Type of vessel	Masthead light(s)	Side lights	Stern light
Power-driven vessel when towing—tow exceeds 200 metres.	As for power-driven vessel towing where tow is 200 metres or less except that 3 vertical lights (equally spaced) instead of mast-head light must be carried. (Note.—If towing vessel 50 metres or more in length, after masthead light must be carried as in (ii) on p. 366.)	As in (i) on p. 366.	As for power-driven vessel towing where tow less than 200 metres.
A vessel or object being towed.	None.	As for vessel not under tow of the same length.	As for vessel not under tow of the same length.
A vessel being pushed ahead.	None.	As for a vessel of the same length not under tow, but at the forward end.	As for vessel of her length.
A vessel being towed alongside.	None.	As for a vessel of the same length not under tow, but at the forward end.	As for vessel of her length.

Type of vessel	Masthead light(s)	Side lights	Stern light
Vessel not under command.	Instead of masthead light, two all-round red lights. For vessels of 50 metres or more, visibility 3 miles. For vessels under 50 metres, visibility 2 miles. In vessels of 20 metres or more, lights to be 2 metres apart and lowest to be not less than 4 metres above hull. In vessels under 20 metres, lights to be 1 metre apart and the lower to be not less than 2 metres above gunwale.	Only when making way. For a vessel of the same length.	Only when making way. For a vessel of the same length.

Type of vessel	Masthead light(s)	Side lights	Stern light
A vessel of 50 metres or more but less than 100 metres in length, at anchor (not engaged in fishing).	No masthead light carried. An all-round white light near the stem and not less than 6 metres above the hull. A second all-round white light at or near the stern, not less than 4·5 metres below the forward masthead light. Visibility of both lights, 3 miles. **May** also use working lights.	None.	None.
A vessel of 100 metres or more, in length, at anchor.	As for a vessel of 50 metres or more but less than 100 metres except that working lights **shall** be used.	None.	None.
A vessel of less than 50 metres at anchor.	An all-round white light, visibility, 2 miles. A second white light as for a vessel over 50 metres, **may** be used.	None.	None.

Type of vessel	Masthead light(s)	Side lights	Stern light
Vessel restricted in her ability to manoeuvre, under way.	The masthead light for a vessel of her length, only when making way. Three all-round lights in a vertical line, equally spaced. If vessel 20 metres or more, lights to be 2 metres apart with the lowest 4 metres above the hull. If vessel under 20 metres, lights to be 1 metre apart with the lower 2 metres above the gunwale. Top light, red. Middle light, white. Bottom light, red. Visibility for vessel of 50 metres or more, 3 miles. Visibility for vessel under 50 metres, 2 miles.	Only when making way, as for a vessel of the same length.	Only when making way, as for a vessel of the same length.
Vessel restricted in her ability to manoeuvre, at anchor.	No light at masthead. Three all-round lights in a vertical line as for a vessel restricted in her ability to manoeuvre, under way. In addition, anchor lights for a vessel of the same length.	None.	None.

Type of vessel	Masthead light(s)	Side lights	Stern light
A vessel engaged in a towing operation, unable to deviate from her course.	As for a vessel engaged in a towing operation of the same length and length of tow. In addition, the lights for a vessel restricted in her ability to manoeuvre.	As for a vessel of the same length.	As for a vessel of the same length engaged in a towing operation.
A vessel engaged in dredging or underwater operations, restricted in her ability to manoeuvre, when under way or at anchor.	The masthead light for a vessel of her length, only when making way. In addition, the lights for a vessel restricted in her ability to manoeuvre, when under way or at anchor.	Only when making way, as for a vessel of her length.	Only when making way, as for a vessel of her length.

Type of vessel	Masthead light(s)	Side lights	Stern light
A vessel engaged in dredging or underwater operations, restricted in her ability to manoeuvre, when under way or at anchor, where an obstruction exists.	The masthead lights for a vessel of the same length only when making way and the lights for a vessel restricted in her ability to manoeuvre when under way or at anchor, as appropriate. In addition, in a vertical line on the side of the obstruction, two all-round red lights and on the side on which other vessels may pass, two all-round green lights. For a vessel of 20 metres or more, the vertical lines of red and green lights must be placed at the maximum practical horizontal distance from the lights for restricted in her ability to manoeuvre and in no case less than 2 metres. The upper of the red and green lights must not be higher than the lower of the lights for restricted in her ability to manoeuvre and the lowest not less than 4 metres above the hull. For a vessel of less than 20 metres the lights in vertical line must not be less than 1 metre apart and the lowest not less than 2 metres above the gunwale.	Only when making way, as for a vessel of the same length.	Only when making way, as for a vessel of the same length.

Type of vessel	Masthead light(s)	Side lights	Stern light
Vessel engaged in minesweeping, under way.	As for a vessel of the same length. In addition 3 all-round green lights, one at the foremast head and one at each end of the foreyard. Visibility for a vessel over 50 metres in length, 3 miles. Visibility for a vessel less than 50 metres but over 12 metres, 2 miles.	As for a vessel of the same length.	As for a vessel of the same length.
A vessel aground.	The lights for a vessel of her length, at anchor. In addition, 2 all-round red lights in a vertical line. If vessel 50 metres or more, visibility 3 miles. If vessel under 50 metres, visibility 2 miles. For a vessel of 20 metres or more, the lights in vertical line must be not less than 2 metres apart and the lowest not less than 4 metres above the hull. For a vessel under 20 metres, the lights in vertical line must be not less than 1 metre apart and the lowest at least 2 metres above the gunwale.	None.	None.

Type of vessel	Masthead light(s)	Side lights	Stern light
A vessel constrained by her draught.	As for a vessel of the same length. **May** also show 3 all-round red lights in a vertical line. Position of vertical lights as for a vessel aground.	As for a vessel of the same length.	As for a vessel of the same length.
Pilot vessel, on duty, under way.	Two all-round lights in a vertical line. The upper light, white. The lower light, red. To be positioned as for vessel aground.	As for a vessel of the same length.	As for a vessel of the same length.
Pilot vessel, on duty, at anchor.	The vertical line of lights for a pilot vessel, on duty, under way. The anchor lights for a vessel of her length.	None.	None.

Type of vessel	Masthead light(s)	Side lights	Stern light
Sailing vessel over 12 metres in length, under way.	No masthead light. **May** exhibit 2 all-round lights in a vertical line, the upper red, the lower green. Visibility 2 miles.	Visibility, 2 miles.	Visibility, 2 miles.
Vessels engaged in trawling, 50 metres or more in length, making way.	Two all-round lights carried in a vertical line. The upper light green. The lower light white. Visibility 3 miles. A masthead light abaft of and above the green light. Visibility 6 miles. The vertical lights to be positioned as previously described.	As for a vessel of her length.	As for a vessel of her length.

Type of vessel	Masthead light(s)	Side lights	Stern light
Vessel engaged in trawling, less than 50 metres in length, making way.	As for a vessel engaged in trawling, 50 metres or more in length, except visibility of vertical line of lights, 2 miles, and the masthead light abaft of and above the green light need not be carried.	As for a vessel of her length.	As for a vessel of her length.
Vessel engaged in trawling when not making way.	The same as when making way.	None.	None.

Type of vessel	Masthead light(s)	Side lights	Stern light
Vessels engaged in fishing with outlying gear extending less than 150 metres, making way.	Two all-round lights carried in a vertical line. The upper light, red. The lower light, white. On a vessel of 20 metres or more in length the lights shall be not less than 2 metres apart and on a vessel less than 20 metres, 1 metre apart. In either case the lower of the two lights shall be at a height above the sidelights of not less than twice the distance between the vertical lights. For a vessel of 50 metres or more, visibility 3 miles. For a vessel under 50 metres, visibility 2 miles.	As for a vessel of her length.	As for a vessel of her length.

Type of vessel	Masthead light(s)	Side lights	Stern light
Vessel engaged in fishing with outlying gear extending 150 metres or more, making way.	As for a fishing vessel with outlying gear extending less than 150 metres, making way. In addition, an all-round white light in the direction of the gear. This light to be not less than 2 metres or more than 6 metres away from the vertical line of red and white lights. It shall not be higher than the white light or lower than the side lights. If 50 metres or more in length, visibility 3 miles. If less than 50 metres in length, visibility 2 miles.	As for a vessel of her length.	As for a vessel of her length.
Vessel engaged in fishing, not making way.	As above.	None.	None.

Type of vessel	Masthead light(s)	Side lights	Stern light
Power-driven vessels of 12 metres or more but less than 20 metres in length.	Visibility 3 miles. **May** carry second masthead light abaft of and higher than the forward masthead light. Visibility 3 miles.	Visibility 2 miles. (May be combined in one lantern carried on the fore and aft line of the vessel.)	Visibility 2 miles.
Power-driven vessel of more than 7 metres but less than 12 metres in length.	Visibility 2 miles.	Visibility 1 mile. (May be combined in one lantern carried on the fore and aft line of the vessel.)	Visibility 2 miles.
Power-driven vessel of less than 7 metres in length whose maximum speed is 7 knots.	Visibility 2 miles.	As above.	Visibility 2 miles.
Power-driven vessel of less than 7 metres in length. Maximum speed does not exceed 7 knots.	Visibility 2 miles. (May, in lieu of masthead lights, side lights and stern light, exhibit an all-round white light of visibility 2 miles. However, wherever practicable, such a vessel shall carry side lights.)	As above.	Visibility 2 miles.

Type of vessel	Masthead light(s)	Side lights	Stern light
Sailing vessels, under way, less than 12 metres in length.	No masthead light.	Visibility 1 mile. (May carry side lights and stern light in one lantern at or near the masthead.)	Visibility 2 miles.
Sailing vessel less than 7 metres in length.	No masthead light.	As above. (If not practicable to carry side lights and stern light, she shall have available an electric torch or lighted lantern showing a white light which shall be exhibited in time to prevent collision.)	As above.
Vessels under oars.	As for sailing vessels less than 7 metres in length.		
Vessels engaged in fishing less than 50 metres in length.	As for vessels engaged in fishing of 50 metres or more in length, but they are not obliged to display a masthead light abaft of and higher than the all-round green light.		

Type of vessel	Masthead light(s)	Side lights	Stern light
Vessels of less than 7 metres in length. Not under Command, Restricted in their Ability to Manoeuvre—or—at Anchor or Aground (not in or near a narrow channel, fairway or anchorage or where other vessels normally navigate).	Not required to display the lights for larger vessels in these circumstances.		

Signals to attract attention

Rule 36 states:

> 'If necessary to attract the attention of another vessel any vessel may make light or sound signals that cannot be mistaken for any signal authorized elsewhere in these Rules, or may direct the beam of her searchlight in the direction of the danger, in such a way as not to embarrass any vessel.'

Screening of lights
Side lights must be fitted with inboard screens projecting forward from the light so as to prevent them being seen across the bows of the vessel. The screens shall be painted matt black.

References relevant to lights

Definition of Lights — Rule 21.
Visibility of Lights — Rule 22.
Positioning and Technical Details of Lights:

Vertical positioning and spacing —Annex I, Section 2.
Horizontal positioning and spacing—Annex I, Section 3.
Details of location of direction-indicating lights for fishing vessels, dredgers and vessels engaged in underwater operations—Annex I, Section 4.
Screens for sidelights —Annex I, Section 5.
Manoeuvring light —Annex I, Section 12.

The situations illustrated in this book have been compiled with the sole aim of assisting students to learn the International Regulations for Preventing Collisions at Sea, 1972. When deciding on a course of action in the face of a particular situation at sea a student must be guided only by Official Regulations and not by the contents of this book.

THE INTERNATIONAL REGULATIONS FOR PREVENTING COLLISIONS AT SEA, 1972

PART A. GENERAL

Rule 1

Application

(*a*) These Rules shall apply to all vessels upon the high seas and in all waters connected therewith navigable by seagoing vessels.

(*b*) Nothing in these Rules shall interfere with the operation of special rules made by an appropriate authority for roadsteads, harbours, rivers, lakes or inland waterways connected with the high seas and navigable by seagoing vessels. Such special rules shall conform as closely as possible to these Rules.

(*c*) Nothing in these Rules shall interfere with the operation of any special rules made by the Government of any State with respect to additional station or signal lights or whistle signals for ships of war and vessels proceeding under convoy, or with respect to additional station or signal lights for fishing vessels engaged in fishing as a fleet. These additional station or signal lights or whistle signals shall, so far as possible, be such that they cannot be mistaken for any light or signal authorized elsewhere under these Rules.

(*d*) Traffic separation schemes may be adopted by the Organization for the purpose of these Rules.

(*e*) Whenever the Government concerned shall have determined that a vessel of special construction or purpose cannot comply fully with the provisions of any of these Rules with respect to the number, position, range or arc of visibility of lights or shapes, as well as to the disposition and characteristics of sound-signalling appliances, without interfering with the special function of the vessel, such vessel shall comply with such other provisions in regard to the number, position, range or arc of visibility of lights or shapes, as well as to the disposition and characteristics of sound-signalling appliances, as her Government shall have determined to be the closest possible compliance with these Rules in respect to that vessel.

RULE 2

Responsibility

(*a*) Nothing in these Rules shall exonerate any vessel, or the owner, master or crew thereof, from the consequences of any neglect to comply with these Rules or of the neglect of any precaution which may be required by the ordinary practice of seamen, or by the special circumstances of the case.

(*b*) In construing and complying with these Rules due regard shall be had to all dangers of navigation and collision and to any special circumstances, including the limitations of the vessels involved, which may make a departure from these Rules necessary to avoid immediate danger.

RULE 3

General definitions

For the purpose of these Rules, except where the context otherwise requires:

(*a*) The word " vessel " includes every description of water craft, including non-displacement craft and seaplanes, used or capable of being used as a means of transportation on water.

(*b*) The term " power-driven vessel " means any vessel propelled by machinery.

(*c*) The term " sailing vessel " means any vessel under sail provided that propelling machinery, if fitted, is not being used.

(*d*) The term " vessel engaged in fishing " means any vessel fishing with nets, lines, trawls or other fishing apparatus which restrict manoeuvrability, but does not include a vessel fishing with trolling lines or other fishing apparatus which do not restrict manoeuvrability.

(*e*) The word " seaplane " includes any aircraft designed to manoeuvre on the water.

(*f*) The term " vessel not under command " means a vessel which through some exceptional circumstance is unable to manoeuvre as required by these Rules and is therefore unable to keep out of the way of another vessel.

(*g*) The term " vessel restricted in her ability to manoeuvre " means a vessel which from the nature of her work is restricted in her ability to manoeuvre as required by these Rules and is therefore unable to keep out of the way of another vessel.

The following vessels shall be regarded as vessels restricted in their ability to manoeuvre:

(i) a vessel engaged in laying, servicing or picking up a navigation mark, submarine cable or pipeline;

(ii) a vessel engaged in dredging, surveying or underwater operations;

(iii) a vessel engaged in replenishment or transferring persons, provisions or cargo while underway;

(iv) a vessel engaged in the launching or recovery of aircraft;

(v) a vessel engaged in minesweeping operations;

(vi) a vessel engaged in a towing operation such as severely restricts the towing vessel and her tow in their ability to deviate from their course.

(*h*) The term " vessel constrained by her draught " means a power-driven vessel which because of her draught in relation to the available depth of water is severely restricted in her ability to deviate from the course she is following.

(*i*) The word " underway " means that a vessel is not at anchor, or made fast to the shore, or aground.

(*j*) The words "length" and "breadth" of a vessel mean her length overall and greatest breadth.

(*k*) Vessels shall be deemed to be in sight of one another only when one can be observed visually from the other.

(*l*) The term "restricted visibility" means any condition in which visibility is restricted by fog, mist, falling snow, heavy rainstorms, sandstorms or any other similar causes.

PART B. STEERING AND SAILING RULES

Section I. Conduct of vessels in any condition of visibility

RULE 4

Application

Rules in this Section apply in any condition of visibility.

Rule 5

Look-out

Every vessel shall at all times maintain a proper look-out by sight and hearing as well as by all available means appropriate in the prevailing circumstances and conditions so as to make a full appraisal of the situation and of the risk of collision.

Rule 6

Safe speed

Every vessel shall at all times proceed at a safe speed so that she can take proper and effective action to avoid collision and be stopped within a distance appropriate to the prevailing circumstances and conditions.

In determining a safe speed the following factors shall be among those taken into account:

(*a*) By all vessels:

(i) the state of visibility;

(ii) the traffic density including concentrations of fishing vessels or any other vessels;

(iii) the manoeuvrability of the vessel with special reference to stopping distance and turning ability in the prevailing conditions;

(iv) at night the presence of background light such as from shore lights or from back scatter of her own lights;

(v) the state of wind, sea and current, and the proximity of navigational hazards;

(vi) the draught in relation to the available depth of water.

(*b*) Additionally, by vessels with operational radar:

(i) the characteristics, efficiency and limitations of the radar equipment;

(ii) any constraints imposed by the radar range scale in use;

(iii) the effect on radar detection of the sea state, weather and other sources of interference;

(iv) the possibility that small vessels, ice and other floating objects may not be detected by radar at an adequate range;

(v) the number, location and movement of vessels detected by radar;

(vi) the more exact assessment of the visibility that may be possible when radar is used to determine the range of vessels or other objects in the vicinity.

RULE 7

Risk of collision

(*a*) Every vessel shall use all available means appropriate to the prevailing circumstances and conditions to determine if risk of collision exists. If there is any doubt such risk shall be deemed to exist.

(*b*) Proper use shall be made of radar equipment if fitted and operational, including long-range scanning to obtain early warning of risk of collision and radar plotting or equivalent systematic observation of detected objects.

(*c*) Assumptions shall not be made on the basis of scanty information, especially scanty radar information.

(*d*) In determining if risk of collision exists the following considerations shall be among those taken into account:

(i) such risk shall be deemed to exist if the compass bearing of an approaching vessel does not appreciably change;

(ii) such risk may sometimes exist even when an appreciable bearing change is evident, particularly when approaching a very large vessel or a tow or when approaching a vessel at close range.

Rule 8

Action to avoid collision

(*a*) Any action taken to avoid collision shall, if the circumstances of the case admit, be positive, made in ample time and with due regard to the observance of good seamanship.

(*b*) Any alteration of course and/or speed to avoid collision shall, if the circumstances of the case admit, be large enough to be readily apparent to another vessel observing visually or by radar; a succession of small alterations of course and/or speed should be avoided.

(*c*) If there is sufficient sea room, alteration of course alone may be the most effective action to avoid a close-quarters situation provided that it is made in good time, is substantial and does not result in another close-quarters situation.

(*d*) Action taken to avoid collision with another vessel shall be such as to result in passing at a safe distance. The effectiveness of the action shall be carefully checked until the other vessel is finally past and clear.

(*e*) If necessary to avoid collision or allow more time to assess the situation, a vessel shall slacken her speed or take all way off by stopping or reversing her means of propulsion.

Rule 9

Narrow channels

(*a*) A vessel proceeding along the course of a narrow channel or fairway shall keep as near to the outer limit of the channel or fairway which lies on her starboard side as is safe and practicable.

(*b*) A vessel of less than 20 metres in length or a sailing vessel shall not impede the passage of a vessel which can safely navigate only within a narrow channel or fairway.

(*c*) A vessel engaged in fishing shall not impede the passage of any other vessel navigating within a narrow channel or fairway.

(*d*) A vessel shall not cross a narrow channel or fairway if such crossing impedes the passage of a vessel which can safely navigate only within such channel or fairway. The latter vessel may use the sound signal prescribed in Rule 34 (*d*) if in doubt as to the intention of the crossing vessel.

(*e*) (i) In a narrow channel or fairway when overtaking can take place only if the vessel to be overtaken has to take action to permit safe passing, the vessel intending to overtake shall indicate her intention by sounding the appropriate signal prescribed in Rule 34 (*c*) (i). The vessel to be overtaken shall, if in agreement, sound the appropriate signal prescribed in Rule 34 (*c*)(ii) and take steps to permit safe passing. If in doubt she may sound the signals prescribed in Rule 34 (*d*).

(ii) This Rule does not relieve the overtaking vessel of her obligation under Rule 13.

(*f*) A vessel nearing a bend or an area of a narrow channel or fairway where other vessels may be obscured by an intervening obstruction shall navigate with particular alertness and caution and shall sound the appropriate signal prescribed in Rule 34 (*e*).

(*g*) Any vessel shall, if the circumstances of the case admit, avoid anchoring in a narrow channel.

RULE 10

Traffic separation schemes

(*a*) This Rule applies to traffic separation schemes adopted by the Organization:

(*b*) A vessel using a traffic separation scheme shall:

(i) proceed in the appropriate traffic lane in the general direction of traffic flow for that lane;

(ii) so far as practicable keep clear of a traffic separation line or separation zone;

(iii) normally join or leave a traffic lane at the termination of the lane, but when joining or leaving from the side shall do so at as small an angle to the general direction of traffic flow as practicable.

(*c*) A vessel shall so far as practicable avoid crossing traffic lanes, but if obliged to do so shall cross as nearly as practicable at right angles to the general direction of traffic flow.

(*d*) Inshore traffic zones shall not normally be used by through traffic which can safely use the appropriate traffic lane within the adjacent traffic separation scheme.

(*e*) A vessel, other than a crossing vessel, shall not normally enter a separation zone or cross a separation line except:

(i) in cases of emergency to avoid immediate danger;

(ii) to engage in fishing within a separation zone.

(*f*) A vessel navigating in areas near the terminations of traffic separation schemes shall do so with particular caution.

(*g*) A vessel shall so far as practicable avoid anchoring in a traffic separation scheme or in areas near its terminations.

(*h*) A vessel not using a traffic separation scheme shall avoid it by as wide a margin as is practicable.

(*i*) A vessel engaged in fishing shall not impede the passage of any vessel following a traffic lane.

(*j*) A vessel of less than 20 metres in length or a sailing vessel shall not impede the safe passage of a power-driven vessel following a traffic lane.

Section II. Conduct of vessels in sight of one another

RULE 11

Application

Rules in this Section apply to vessels in sight of one another.

RULE 12

Sailing vessels

(*a*) When two sailing vessels are approaching one another, so as to involve risk of collision, one of them shall keep out of the way of the other as follows:

(i) when each has the wind on a different side, the vessel which has the wind on the port side shall keep out of the way of the other;

(ii) when both have the wind on the same side, the vessel which is to windward shall keep out of the way of the vessel which is to leeward;

(iii) if a vessel with the wind on the port side sees a vessel to windward and cannot determine with certainty whether the other vessel has the wind on the port or on the starboard side, she shall keep out of the way of the other.

(*b*) For the purposes of this Rule the windward side shall be deemed to be the side opposite to that on which the mainsail is carried or, in the case of a square-rigged vessel, the side opposite to that on which the largest fore-and-aft sail is carried.

RULE 13

Overtaking

(*a*) Notwithstanding anything contained in the Rules of this Section any vessel overtaking any other shall keep out of the way of the vessel being overtaken.

(*b*) A vessel shall be deemed to be overtaking when coming up with another vessel from a direction more than 22·5 degrees abaft her beam, that is, in such a position with reference to the vessel she is overtaking, that at night she would be able to see only the sternlight of that vessel but neither of her sidelights.

(*c*) When a vessel is in any doubt as to whether she is overtaking another, she shall assume that this is the case and act accordingly.

(*d*) Any subsequent alteration of the bearing between the two vessels shall not make the overtaking vessel a crossing vessel within the meaning of these Rules or relieve her of the duty of keeping clear of the overtaken vessel until she is finally past and clear.

RULE 14

Head-on situation

(*a*) When two power-driven vessels are meeting on reciprocal or nearly reciprocal courses so as to involve risk of collision each shall alter her course to starboard so that each shall pass on the port side of the other.

(*b*) Such a situation shall be deemed to exist when a vessel sees the other ahead or nearly ahead and by night she could see the masthead lights of the other in a line or nearly in a line and/or both sidelights and by day she observes the corresponding aspect of the other vessel.

(*c*) When a vessel is in any doubt as to whether such a situation exists she shall assume that it does exist and act accordingly.

Rule 15

Crossing situation

When two power-driven vessels are crossing so as to involve risk of collision, the vessel which has the other on her own starboard side shall keep out of the way and shall, if the circumstances of the case admit, avoid crossing ahead of the other vessel.

Rule 16

Action by give-way vessel

Every vessel which is directed to keep out of the way of another vessel shall, so far as possible, take early and substantial action to keep well clear.

Rule 17

Action by stand-on vessel

(*a*) (i) Where one of two vessels is to keep out of the way the other shall keep her course and speed.

(ii) The latter vessel may however take action to avoid collision by her manoeuvre alone, as soon as it becomes apparent to her that the vessel required to keep out of the way is not taking appropriate action in compliance with these Rules.

(*b*) When, from any cause, the vessel required to keep her course and speed finds herself so close that collision cannot be avoided by the action of the give-way vessel alone, she shall take such action as will best aid to avoid collision.

(*c*) A power-driven vessel which takes action in a crossing situation in accordance with sub-paragraph (*a*) (ii) of this Rule to avoid collision with another power-driven vessel shall, if the circumstances of the case admit, not alter course to port for a vessel on her own port side.

(*d*) This Rule does not relieve the give-way vessel of her obligation to keep out of the way.

RULE 18

Responsibilities between vessels

Except where Rules 9, 10 and 13 otherwise require:

(*a*) A power-driven vessel underway shall keep out of the way of:

(i) a vessel not under command;

(ii) a vessel restricted in her ability to manoeuvre;

(iii) a vessel engaged in fishing;

(iv) a sailing vessel.

(*b*) A sailing vessel underway shall keep out of the way of:

(i) a vessel not under command;

(ii) a vessel restricted in her ability to manoeuvre;

(iii) a vessel engaged in fishing.

(*c*) A vessel engaged in fishing when underway shall, so far as possible, keep out of the way of:

(i) a vessel not under command;

(ii) a vessel restricted in her ability to manoeuvre.

(*d*) (i) Any vessel other than a vessel not under command or a vessel restricted in her ability to manoeuvre shall, if the circumstances of the case admit, avoid impeding the safe passage of a vessel constrained by her draught, exhibiting the signals in Rule 28.

(ii) A vessel constrained by her draught shall navigate with particular caution having full regard to her special condition.

(*e*) A seaplane on the water shall, in general, keep well clear of all vessels and avoid impeding their navigation. In circumstances, however, where risk of collision exists, she shall comply with the Rules of this Part.

Section III. Conduct of vessels in restricted visibility

RULE 19

Conduct of vessels in restricted visibility

(*a*) This Rule applies to vessels not in sight of one another when navigating in or near an area of restricted visibility.

(*b*) Every vessel shall proceed at a safe speed adapted to the prevailing circumstances and conditions of restricted visibility. A power-driven vessel shall have her engines ready for immediate manoeuvre.

(*c*) Every vessel shall have due regard to the prevailing circumstances and conditions of restricted visibility when complying with the Rules of Section I of this Part.

(*d*) A vessel which detects by radar alone the presence of another vessel shall determine if a close-quarters situation is developing and/or risk of collision exists. If so, she shall take avoiding action in ample time, provided that when such action consists of an alteration of course, so far as possible the following shall be avoided:

(i) an alteration of course to port for a vessel forward of the beam, other than for a vessel being overtaken;

(ii) an alteration of course towards a vessel abeam or abaft the beam.

(*e*) Except where it has been determined that a risk of collision does not exist, every vessel which hears apparently forward of her beam the fog signal of another vessel, or which cannot avoid a close-quarters situation with another vessel forward of her beam, shall reduce her speed to the minimum at which she can be kept on her course. She shall if necessary take all her way off and in any event navigate with extreme caution until danger of collision is over.

PART C. LIGHTS AND SHAPES

RULE 20

Application

(*a*) Rules in this Part shall be complied with in all weathers.

(*b*) The Rules concerning lights shall be complied with from sunset to sunrise, and during such times no other lights shall be exhibited, except such lights as cannot be mistaken for the lights specified in these Rules or do not impair their visibility or distinctive character, or interfere with the keeping of a proper look-out.

(*c*) The lights prescribed by these Rules shall, if carried, also be exhibited from sunrise to sunset in restricted visibility and may be exhibited in all other circumstances when it is deemed necessary.

(*d*) The Rules concerning shapes shall be complied with by day.

(*e*) The lights and shapes specified in these Rules shall comply with the provisions of Annex I to these Regulations.

Rule 21

Definitions

(*a*) " Masthead light " means a white light placed over the fore and aft centreline of the vessel showing an unbroken light over an arc of the horizon of 225 degrees and so fixed as to show the light from right ahead to 22·5 degrees abaft the beam on either side of the vessel.

(*b*) " Sidelights " means a green light on the starboard side and a red light on the port side each showing an unbroken light over an arc of the horizon of 112·5 degrees and so fixed as to show the light from right ahead to 22·5 degrees abaft the beam on its respective side. In a vessel of less than 20 metres in length the sidelights may be combined in one lantern carried on the fore and aft centreline of the vessel.

(*c*) " Sternlight " means a white light placed as nearly as practicable at the stern showing an unbroken light over an arc of the horizon of 135 degrees and so fixed as to show the light 67·5 degrees from right aft on each side of the vessel.

(*d*) " Towing light " means a yellow light having the same characteristics as the " sternlight " defined in paragraph (*c*) of this Rule.

(*e*) " All round light " means a light showing an unbroken light over an arc of the horizon of 360 degrees.

(*f*) " Flashing light " means a light flashing at regular intervals at a frequency of 120 flashes or more per minute.

RULE 22

Visibility of lights

The lights prescribed in these Rules shall have an intensity as specified in Section 8 of Annex I to these Regulations so as to be visible at the following minimum ranges:

(*a*) In vessels of 50 metres or more in length:

—a masthead light, 6 miles;

—a sidelight, 3 miles;

—a sternlight, 3 miles;

—a towing light, 3 miles;

—a white, red, green or yellow all-round light, 3 miles.

(*b*) In vessels of 12 metres or more in length but less than 50 metres in length:

—a masthead light, 5 miles; except that where the length of the vessel is less than 20 metres, 3 miles;

—a sidelight, 2 miles;

—a sternlight, 2 miles;

—a towing light, 2 miles;

—a white, red, green or yellow all-round light, 2 miles.

(*c*) In vessels of less than 12 metres in length:

—a masthead light, 2 miles;

—a sidelight, 1 mile;

—a sternlight, 2 miles;

—a towing light, 2 miles;

—a white, red, green or yellow all-round light, 2 miles.

RULE 23

Power-driven vessels underway

(*a*) A power-driven vessel underway shall exhibit:

(i) a masthead light forward;

(ii) a second masthead light abaft of and higher than the forward one; except that a vessel of less than 50 metres in length shall not be obliged to exhibit such light but may do so;

(iii) sidelights;

(iv) a sternlight.

(*b*) An air-cushion vessel when operating in the non-displacement mode shall, in addition to the lights prescribed in paragraph (*a*) of this Rule, exhibit an all-round flashing yellow light.

(*c*) A power-driven vessel of less than 7 metres in length and whose maximum speed does not exceed 7 knots may, in lieu of the lights prescribed in paragraph (*a*) of this Rule, exhibit an all-round white light. Such vessel shall, if practicable, also exhibit sidelights.

RULE 24

Towing and pushing

(*a*) A power-driven vessel when towing shall exhibit:

(i) instead of the light prescribed in Rule 23 (*a*) (i), two masthead lights forward in a vertical line. When the length of the tow, measuring from the stern of the towing vessel to the after end of the tow exceeds 200 metres, three such lights in a vertical line;

(ii) sidelights;

(iii) a sternlight;

(iv) a towing light in a vertical line above the sternlight;

(v) when the length of the tow exceeds 200 metres, a diamond shape where it can best be seen.

(*b*) When a pushing vessel and a vessel being pushed ahead are rigidly connected in a composite unit they shall be regarded as a power-driven vessel and exhibit the lights prescribed in Rule 23.

(*c*) A power-driven vessel when pushing ahead or towing alongside, except in the case of a composite unit, shall exhibit:

(i) instead of the light prescribed in Rule 23 (*a*) (i), two masthead lights forward in a vertical line;

(ii) sidelights;

(iii) a sternlight.

(*d*) A power-driven vessel to which paragraphs (*a*) and (*c*) of this Rule apply shall also comply with Rule 23 (*a*) (ii).

(*e*) A vessel or object being towed shall exhibit:

(i) sidelights;

(ii) a sternlight;

(iii) when the length of the tow exceeds 200 metres, a diamond shape where it can best be seen.

(*f*) Provided that any number of vessels being towed alongside or pushed in a group shall be lighted as one vessel,

(i) a vessel being pushed ahead, not being part of a composite unit, shall exhibit at the forward end, sidelights;

(ii) a vessel being towed alongside shall exhibit a sternlight and at the forward end, sidelights.

(*g*) Where from any sufficient cause it is impracticable for a vessel or object being towed to exhibit the lights prescribed in paragraph (*e*) of this Rule, all possible measures shall be taken to light the vessel or object towed or at least to indicate the presence of the unlighted vessel or object.

RULE 25

Sailing vessels underway and vessels under oars

(*a*) A sailing vessel underway shall exhibit:

(i) sidelights;

(ii) a sternlight.

(*b*) In a sailing vessel of less than 12 metres in length the lights prescribed in paragraph (*a*) of this Rule may be combined in one lantern carried at or near the top of the mast where it can best be seen.

(*c*) A sailing vessel underway may, in addition to the lights prescribed in paragraph (*a*) of this Rule, exhibit at or near the top of the mast, where they can best be seen, two all-round lights in a vertical line, the upper being red and the lower green, but these lights shall not be exhibited in conjunction with the combined lantern permitted by paragraph (*b*) of this Rule.

(*d*) (i) A sailing vessel of less than 7 metres in length shall, if practicable, exhibit the lights prescribed in paragraph (*a*) or (*b*) of this Rule, but if she does not, she shall have ready at hand an electric torch or lighted lantern showing a white light which shall be exhibited in sufficient time to prevent collision.

(ii) A vessel under oars may exhibit the lights prescribed in this Rule for sailing vessels, but if she does not, she shall have ready at hand an electric torch or lighted lantern showing a white light which shall be exhibited in sufficient time to prevent collision.

(*e*) A vessel proceeding under sail when also being propelled by machinery shall exhibit forward where it can best be seen a conical shape, apex downwards.

Rule 26

Fishing vessels

(*a*) A vessel engaged in fishing, whether underway or at anchor, shall exhibit only the lights and shapes prescribed in this Rule.

(*b*) A vessel when engaged in trawling, by which is meant the dragging through the water of a dredge net or other apparatus used as a fishing appliance, shall exhibit:

(i) two all-round lights in a vertical line, the upper being green and the lower white, or a shape consisting of two cones with their apexes together in a vertical line one above the other; a vessel of less than 20 metres in length may instead of this shape exhibit a basket;

(ii) a masthead light abaft of and higher than the all-round green light; a vessel of less than 50 metres in length shall not be obliged to exhibit such a light but may do so;

(iii) when making way through the water, in addition to the lights prescribed in this paragraph, sidelights and a sternlight.

(*c*) A vessel engaged in fishing, other than trawling, shall exhibit:

(i) two all-round lights in a vertical line, the upper being red and the lower white, or a shape consisting of two cones with apexes together in a vertical line one above the other; a vessel of less than 20 metres in length may instead of this shape exhibit a basket;

(ii) when there is outlying gear extending more than 150 metres horizontally from the vessel, an all-round white light or a cone apex upwards in the direction of the gear;

(iii) when making way through the water, in addition to the lights prescribed in this paragraph, sidelights and a sternlight.

(*d*) A vessel engaged in fishing in close proximity to other vessels engaged in fishing may exhibit the additional signals described in Annex II to these Regulations.

(*e*) A vessel when not engaged in fishing shall not exhibit the lights or shapes prescribed in this Rule, but only those prescribed for a vessel of her length.

Rule 27

Vessels not under command or restricted in their ability to manoeuvre

(*a*) A vessel not under command shall exhibit:

(i) two all-round red lights in a vertical line where they can best be seen;

(ii) two balls or similar shapes in a vertical line where they can best be seen;

(iii) when making way through the water, in addition to the lights prescribed in this paragraph, sidelights and a sternlight.

(*b*) A vessel restricted in her ability to manoeuvre, except a vessel engaged in minesweeping operations, shall exhibit:

(i) three all-round lights in a vertical line where they can best be seen. The highest and lowest of these lights shall be red and the middle light shall be white;

(ii) three shapes in a vertical line where they can best be seen. The highest and lowest of these shapes shall be balls and the middle one a diamond;

(iii) when making way through the water, masthead lights, sidelights and a sternlight, in addition to the lights prescribed in sub-paragraph (i);

(iv) when at anchor, in addition to the lights or shapes prescribed in sub-paragraphs (i) and (ii), the light, lights or shape prescribed in Rule 30.

(*c*) A vessel engaged in a towing operation such as renders her unable to deviate from her course shall, in addition to the lights or shapes prescribed in sub-paragraph (*b*) (i) and (ii) of this Rule, exhibit the lights or shape prescribed in Rule 24 (*a*).

(*d*) A vessel engaged in dredging or underwater operations, when restricted in her ability to manoeuvre, shall exhibit the lights and shapes prescribed in paragraph (*b*) of this Rule and shall in addition, when an obstruction exists, exhibit:

(i) two all-round red lights or two balls in a vertical line to indicate the side on which the obstruction exists;

(ii) two all-round green lights or two diamonds in a vertical line to indicate the side on which another vessel may pass;

(iii) when making way through the water, in addition to the lights prescribed in this paragraph, masthead lights, sidelights and a sternlight;

(iv) a vessel to which this paragraph applies when at anchor shall exhibit the lights or shapes prescribed in sub-paragraphs (i) and (ii) instead of the lights or shape prescribed in Rule 30.

(*e*) Whenever the size of a vessel engaged in diving operations makes it impracticable to exhibit the shapes prescribed in paragraph (*d*) of this Rule, a rigid replica of the International Code flag " A " not less than 1 metre in height shall be exhibited. Measures shall be taken to ensure all-round visibility.

(*f*) A vessel engaged in minesweeping operations shall, in addition to the lights prescribed for a power-driven vessel in Rule 23, exhibit three all-round green lights or three balls. One of these lights or shapes shall be exhibited at or near the foremast head and one at each end of the fore yard. These lights or shapes indicate that it is dangerous for another vessel to approach closer than 1,000 metres astern or 500 metres on either side of the minesweeper.

(*g*) Vessels of less than 7 metres in length shall not be required to exhibit the lights prescribed in this Rule.

(*h*) The signals prescribed in this Rule are not signals of vessels in distress and requiring assistance. Such signals are contained in Annex IV to these Regulations.

Rule 28

Vessels constrained by their draught

A vessel constrained by her draught may, in addition to the lights prescribed for power-driven vessels in Rule 23, exhibit where they can best be seen three all-round red lights in a vertical line, or a cylinder.

Rule 29

Pilot vessels

(*a*) A vessel engaged on pilotage duty shall exhibit:

(i) at or near the masthead, two all-round lights in a vertical line, the upper being white and the lower red;

(ii) when underway, in addition, sidelights and a sternlight;

(iii) when at anchor, in addition to the lights prescribed in sub-paragraph (i), the anchor light, lights or shape.

(*b*) A pilot vessel when not engaged on pilotage duty shall exhibit the lights or shapes prescribed for a similar vessel of her length.

RULE 30

Anchored vessels and vessels aground

(*a*) A vessel at anchor shall exhibit where it can best be seen:

(i) in the fore part, an all-round white light or one ball;

(ii) at or near the stern and at a lower level than the light prescribed in sub-paragraph (i), an all-round white light.

(*b*) A vessel of less than 50 metres in length may exhibit an all-round white light where it can best be seen instead of the lights prescribed in paragraph (*a*) of this Rule.

(*c*) A vessel at anchor may, and a vessel of 100 metres and more in length shall, also use the available working or equivalent lights to illuminate her decks.

(*d*) A vessel aground shall exhibit the lights prescribed in paragraph (*a*) or (*b*) of this Rule and in addition, where they can best be seen:

(i) two all-round red lights in a vertical line;

(ii) three balls in a vertical line.

(*e*) A vessel of less than 7 metres in length, when at anchor or aground, not in or near a narrow channel, fairway or anchorage, or where other vessels normally navigate, shall not be required to exhibit the lights or shapes prescribed in paragraphs (*a*), (*b*) or (*d*) of this Rule.

Rule 31

Seaplanes

Where it is impracticable for a seaplane to exhibit lights and shapes of the characteristics or in the positions prescribed in the Rules of this Part she shall exhibit lights and shapes as closely similar in characteristics and position as is possible.

PART D. SOUND AND LIGHT SIGNALS

Rule 32

Definitions

(*a*) The word " whistle " means any sound signalling appliance capable of producing the prescribed blasts and which complies with the specifications in Annex III to these Regulations.

(*b*) The term " short blast " means a blast of about one second's duration.

(*c*) The term " prolonged blast " means a blast of from four to six seconds' duration.

Rule 33

Equipment for sound signals

(*a*) A vessel of 12 metres or more in length shall be provided with a whistle and a bell and a vessel of 100 metres or more in length shall, in addition, be provided with a gong, the tone and sound of which cannot be confused with that of the bell. The whistle, bell and gong shall comply with the specifications in Annex III to these Regulations. The bell or gong or both may be replaced by other equipment having the same respective sound characteristics, provided that manual sounding of the required signals shall always be possible.

(*b*) A vessel of less than 12 metres in length shall not be obliged to carry the sound signalling appliances prescribed in paragraph (*a*) of this Rule but if she does not, she shall be provided with some other means of making an efficient sound signal.

Rule 34

Manoeuvring and warning signals

(*a*) When vessels are in sight of one another, a power-driven vessel underway, when manoeuvring as authorized or required by these Rules, shall indicate that manoeuvre by the following signals on her whistle:

—one short blast to mean " I am altering my course to starboard ";

—two short blasts to mean " I am altering my course to port ";

—three short blasts to mean " I am operating astern propulsion ".

(*b*) Any vessel may supplement the whistle signals prescribed in paragraph (*a*) of this Rule by light signals, repeated as appropriate, whilst the manoeuvre is being carried out:

(i) these light signals shall have the following significance:

—one flash to mean " I am altering my course to starboard ";

—two flashes to mean " I am altering my course to port ";

—three flashes to mean " I am operating astern propulsion ";

(ii) the duration of each flash shall be about one second, the interval between flashes shall be about one second, and the interval between successive signals shall be not less than ten seconds;

(iii) the light used for this signal shall, if fitted, be an all-round white light, visible at a minimum range of 5 miles, and shall comply with the provisions of Annex I.

(*c*) When in sight of one another in a narrow channel or fairway:

(i) a vessel intending to overtake another shall in compliance with Rule 9 (*e*) (i) indicate her intention by the following signals on her whistle:

—two prolonged blasts followed by one short blast to mean " I intend to overtake you on your starboard side ";

—two prolonged blasts followed by two short blasts to mean " I intend to overtake you on your port side ".

(ii) the vessel about to be overtaken when acting in accordance with Rule 9 (*e*) (i) shall indicate her agreement by the following signal on her whistle:

one prolonged, one short, one prolonged and one short blast, in that order.

(*d*) When vessels in sight of one another are approaching each other and from any cause either vessel fails to understand the intentions or actions of the other, or is in doubt whether sufficient action is being taken by the other to avoid collision, the vessel in doubt shall immediately indicate such doubt by giving at least five short and rapid blasts on the whistle. Such signal may be supplemented by a light signal of at least five short and rapid flashes.

(*e*) A vessel nearing a bend or an area of a channel or fairway where other vessels may be obscured by an intervening obstruction shall sound one prolonged blast. Such signal shall be answered with a prolonged blast by any approaching vessel that may be within hearing around the bend or behind the intervening obstruction.

(*f*) If whistles are fitted on a vessel at a distance apart of more than 100 metres, one whistle only shall be used for giving manoeuvring and warning signals.

RULE 35

Sound signals in restricted visibility

In or near an area of restricted visibility, whether by day or night, the signals prescribed in this Rule shall be used as follows:

(*a*) A power-driven vessel making way through the water shall sound at intervals of not more than 2 minutes one prolonged blast.

(*b*) A power-driven vessel underway but stopped and making no way through the water shall sound at intervals of not more than 2 minutes two prolonged blasts in succession with an interval of about 2 seconds between them.

(*c*) A vessel not under command, a vessel restricted in her ability to manoeuvre, a vessel constrained by her draught, a sailing vessel, a vessel engaged in fishing and a vessel engaged in towing or pushing another vessel shall, instead of the signals prescribed in paragraphs (*a*) or (*b*) of this Rule, sound at intervals of not more than 2 minutes three blasts in succession, namely one prolonged followed by two short blasts.

(*d*) A vessel towed or if more than one vessel is towed the last vessel of the tow, if manned, shall at intervals of not more than 2 minutes sound four blasts in succession, namely one prolonged followed by three short blasts. When practicable, this signal shall be made immediately after the signal made by the towing vessel.

(*e*) When a pushing vessel and a vessel being pushed ahead are rigidly connected in a composite unit they shall be regarded as a power-driven vessel and shall give the signals prescribed in paragraphs (*a*) or (*b*) of this Rule.

(*f*) A vessel at anchor shall at intervals of not more than one minute ring the bell rapidly for about 5 seconds. In a vessel of 100 metres or more in length the bell shall be sounded in the forepart of the vessel and immediately after the ringing of the bell the gong shall be sounded rapidly for about 5 seconds in the after part of the vessel. A vessel at anchor may in addition sound three blasts in succession, namely one short, one prolonged and one short blast, to give warning of her position and of the possibility of collision to an approaching vessel.

(*g*) A vessel aground shall give the bell signal and if required the gong signal prescribed in paragraph (*f*) of this Rule and shall, in addition, give three separate and distinct strokes on the bell immediately before and after the rapid ringing of the bell. A vessel aground may in addition sound an appropriate whistle signal.

(*h*) A vessel of less than 12 metres in length shall not be obliged to give the above-mentioned signals but, if she does not, shall make some other efficient sound signal at intervals of not more than 2 minutes.

(*i*) A pilot vessel when engaged on pilotage duty may in addition to the signals prescribed in paragraphs (*a*), (*b*) or (*f*) of this Rule sound an identity signal consisting of four short blasts.

Rule 36

Signals to attract attention

If necessary to attract the attention of another vessel any vessel may make light or sound signals that cannot be mistaken for any signal authorized elsewhere in these Rules, or may direct the beam of her searchlight in the direction of the danger, in such a way as not to embarrass any vessel.

Rule 37

Distress signals

When a vessel is in distress and requires assistance she shall use or exhibit the signals prescribed in Annex IV to these Regulations.

PART E. EXEMPTIONS

Rule 38

Exemptions

Any vessel (or class of vessels) provided that she complies with the requirements of the International Regulations for Preventing Collisions at Sea, 1960, the keel of which is laid or which is at a corresponding stage of construction before the entry into force of these Regulations may be exempted from compliance therewith as follows:

(*a*) The installation of lights with ranges prescribed in Rule 22, until four years after the date of entry into force of these Regulations.

(*b*) The installation of lights with colour specifications as prescribed in Section 7 of Annex I to these Regulations, until four years after the date of entry into force of these Regulations.

(*c*) The repositioning of lights as a result of conversion from Imperial to metric units and rounding off measurement figures, permanent exemption.

(*d*) (i) The repositioning of masthead lights on vessels of less than 150 metres in length, resulting from the prescriptions of Section 3 (*a*) of Annex I, permanent exemption.

(ii) The repositioning of masthead lights on vessels of 150 metres or more in length, resulting from the prescriptions of Section 3 (*a*) of Annex I to these Regulations, until nine years after the date of entry into force of these Regulations.

(*e*) The repositioning of masthead lights resulting from the prescriptions of Section 2 (*b*) of Annex I, until nine years after the date of entry into force of these Regulations.

(*f*) The repositioning of sidelights resulting from the prescriptions of Sections 2 (*g*) and 3 (*b*) of Annex I, until nine years after the date of entry into force of these Regulations.

(*g*) The requirements for sound signal appliances prescribed in Annex III, until nine years after the date of entry into force of these Regulations.

ANNEX I

Positioning and technical details of lights and shapes

1. *Definition*

The term " height above the hull " means height above the uppermost continuous deck.

2. *Vertical positioning and spacing of lights*

(*a*) On a power-driven vessel of 20 metres or more in length the masthead lights shall be placed as follows:

(i) the forward masthead light, or if only one masthead light is carried, then that light, at a height above the hull of not less than 6 metres, and, if the breadth of the vessel exceeds 6 metres, then at a height above the hull not less than such breadth, so however that the light need not be placed at a greater height above the hull than 12 metres;

(ii) when two masthead lights are carried the after one shall be at least 4·5 metres vertically higher than the forward one.

(*b*) The vertical separation of masthead lights of power-driven vessels shall be such that in all normal conditions of trim the after light will be seen over and separate from the forward light at a distance of 1,000 metres from the stem when viewed from sea level.

(*c*) The masthead light of a power-driven vessel of 12 metres but less than 20 metres in length shall be placed at a height above the gunwale of not less than 2·5 metres.

(*d*) A power-driven vessel of less than 12 metres in length may carry the uppermost light at a height of less than 2·5 metres above the gunwale. When however a masthead light is carried in addition to sidelights and a sternlight, then such masthead light shall be carried at least 1 metre higher than the sidelights.

(*e*) One of the two or three masthead lights prescribed for a power-driven vessel when engaged in towing or pushing another vessel shall be placed in the same position as the forward masthead light of a power-driven vessel.

(*f*) In all circumstances the masthead light or lights shall be so placed as to be above and clear of all other lights and obstructions.

(*g*) The sidelights of a power-driven vessel shall be placed at a height above the hull not greater than three-quarters of that of the forward masthead light. They shall not be so low as to be interfered with by deck lights.

(*h*) The sidelights, if in a combined lantern and carried on a power-driven vessel of less than 20 metres in length, shall be placed not less than 1 metre below the masthead light.

(*i*) When the Rules prescribe two or three lights to be carried in a vertical line, they shall be spaced as follows:

(i) on a vessel of 20 metres in length or more such lights shall be spaced not less than 2 metres apart, and the lowest of these lights shall, except where a towing light is required, not be less than 4 metres above the hull;

(ii) on a vessel of less than 20 metres in length such lights shall be spaced not less than 1 metre apart and the lowest of these lights shall, except where a towing light is required, not be less than 2 metres above the gunwale;

(iii) when three lights are carried they shall be equally spaced.

(*j*) The lower of the two all-round lights prescribed for a fishing vessel when engaged in fishing shall be at a height above the sidelights not less than twice the distance between the two vertical lights.

(*k*) The forward anchor light, when two are carried, shall not be less than 4·5 metres above the after one. On a vessel of 50 metres or more in length this forward anchor light shall not be less than 6 metres above the hull.

3. *Horizontal positioning and spacing of lights*

(*a*) When two masthead lights are prescribed for a power-driven vessel, the horizontal distance between them shall not be less than one-half of the length of the vessel but need not be more than 100 metres. The forward light shall be placed not more than one-quarter of the length of the vessel from the stem.

(*b*) On a vessel of 20 metres or more in length the sidelights shall not be placed in front of the forward masthead lights. They shall be placed at or near the side of the vessel.

4. *Details of location of direction-indicating lights for fishing vessels, dredgers and vessels engaged in underwater operations*

(*a*) The light indicating the direction of the outlying gear from a vessel engaged in fishing as prescribed in Rule 26 (*c*) (ii) shall be placed at a horizontal distance of not less than 2 metres and not more than 6 metres away from the two all-round red and white lights. This light shall be placed not higher than the all-round white light prescribed in Rule 26 (*c*) (i) and not lower than the sidelights.

(*b*) The lights and shapes on a vessel engaged in dredging or underwater operations to indicate the obstructed side and/or the side on which it is safe to pass, as prescribed in Rule 27 (*d*) (i) and (ii), shall be placed at the maximum practical horizontal distance, but in no case less than 2 metres, from the lights or shapes prescribed in Rule 27 (*b*) (i) and (ii). In no case shall the upper of these lights or shapes be at a greater height than the lower of the three lights or shapes prescribed in Rule 27 (*b*) (i) and (ii).

5. *Screens for sidelights*

The sidelights shall be fitted with inboard screens painted matt black, and meeting the requirements of Section 9 of this Annex. With a combined lantern, using a single vertical filament and a very narrow division between the green and red sections, external screens need not be fitted.

6. *Shapes*

(*a*) Shapes shall be black and of the following sizes:

(i) a ball shall have a diameter of not less than 0·6 metre;

(ii) a cone shall have a base diameter of not less than 0·6 metre and a height equal to its diameter;

(iii) a cylinder shall have a diameter of at least 0·6 metre and a height of twice its diameter;

(iv) a diamond shape shall consist of two cones as defined in (ii) above having a common base.

(*b*) The vertical distance between shapes shall be at least 1·5 metre.

(*c*) In a vessel of less than 20 metres in length shapes of lesser dimensions but commensurate with the size of the vessel may be used and the distance apart may be correspondingly reduced.

7. *Colour specification of lights*

The chromaticity of all navigation lights shall conform to the following standards, which lie within the boundaries of the area of the diagram specified for each colour by the International Commission on Illumination (CIE).

The boundaries of the area for each colour are given by indicating the corner co-ordinates, which are as follows:

(i) *White*

x	0·525	0·525	0·452	0·310	0·310	0·443
y	0·382	0·440	0·440	0·348	0·283	0·382

(ii) *Green*

x	0·028	0·009	0·300	0·203
y	0·385	0·723	0·511	0·356

(iii) *Red*

x	0·680	0·660	0·735	0·721
y	0·320	0·320	0·265	0·259

(iv) *Yellow*

x	0·612	0·618	0·575	0·575
y	0·382	0·382	0·425	0·406

8. *Intensity of lights*

(*a*) The minimum luminous intensity of lights shall be calculated by using the formula:

$$I = 3{\cdot}43 \times 10^6 \times T \times D^2 \times K^{-D}$$

where I is luminous intensity in candelas under service conditions,

T is threshold factor 2×10^{-7} lux,

D is range of visibility (luminous range) of the light in nautical miles,

K is atmospheric transmissivity.

For prescribed lights the value of K shall be 0·8, corresponding to a meteorological visibility of approximately 13 nautical miles.

(*b*) A selection of figures derived from the formula is given in the following table:

Range of visibility (luminous range) of light in nautical miles *D*	*Luminous intensity of light in candelas for* $K = 0{\cdot}8$ *I*
1	0·9
2	4·3
3	12
4	27
5	52
6	94

Note: The maximum luminous intensity of navigation lights should be limited to avoid undue glare.

9. *Horizontal sectors*

(*a*) (i) In the forward direction, sidelights as fitted on the vessel must show the minimum required intensities. The intensities must decrease to reach practical cut-off between 1 degree and 3 degrees outside the prescribed sectors.

(ii) For sternlights and masthead lights and at 22·5 degrees abaft the beam for sidelights, the minimum required intensities shall be maintained over the arc of the horizon up to 5 degrees within the limits of the sectors prescribed in Rule 21. From 5 degrees within the prescribed sectors the intensity may decrease by 50 per cent up to the prescribed limits; it shall decrease steadily to reach practical cut-off at not more than 5 degrees outside the prescribed limits.

(*b*) All-round lights shall be so located as not to be obscured by masts, topmasts or structures within angular sectors of more than 6 degrees, except anchor lights, which need not be placed at an impracticable height above the hull.

10. *Vertical sectors*

(*a*) The vertical sectors of electric lights, with the exception of lights on sailing vessels shall ensure that:

(i) at least the required minimum intensity is maintained at all angles from 5 degrees above to 5 degrees below the horizontal;

(ii) at least 60 per cent of the required minimum intensity is maintained from 7·5 degrees above to 7·5 degrees below the horizontal.

(*b*) In the case of sailing vessels the vertical sectors of electric lights shall ensure that:

(i) at least the required minimum intensity is maintained at all angles from 5 degrees above to 5 degrees below the horizontal;

(ii) at least 50 per cent of the required minimum intensity is maintained from 25 degrees above to 25 degrees below the horizontal.

(*c*) In the case of lights other than electric these specifications shall be met as closely as possible.

11. *Intensity of non-electric lights*

Non-electric lights shall so far as practicable comply with the minimum intensities, as specified in the Table given in Section 8 of this Annex.

12. *Manoeuvring light*

Notwithstanding the provisions of paragraph 2 (*f*) of this Annex the manoeuvring light described in Rule 34 (*b*) shall be placed in the same fore and aft vertical plane as the masthead light or lights and, where practicable, at a minimum height of 2 metres vertically above the forward masthead light, provided that it shall be carried not less than 2 metres vertically above or below the after masthead light. On a vessel where only one masthead light is carried the manoeuvring light, if fitted, shall be carried where it can best be seen, not less than 2 metres vertically apart from the masthead light.

13. *Approval*

The construction of lanterns and shapes and the installation of lanterns on board the vessel shall be to the satisfaction of the appropriate authority of the State where the vessel is registered.

ANNEX II

Additional signals for fishing vessels fishing in close proximity

1. *General*

The lights mentioned herein shall, if exhibited in pursuance of Rule 26 (*d*), be placed where they can best be seen. They shall be at least 0·9 metre apart but at a lower level than lights prescribed in Rule 26 (*b*) (i) and (*c*) (i). The lights shall be visible all round the horizon at a distance of at least 1 mile but at a lesser distance than the lights prescribed by these Rules for fishing vessels.

2. *Signals for trawlers*

(*a*) Vessels when engaged in trawling, whether using demersal or pelagic gear, may exhibit:

(i) when shooting their nets:
two white lights in a vertical line;

(ii) when hauling their nets:
one white light over one red light in a vertical line;

(iii) when the net has come fast upon an obstruction:
two red lights in a vertical line.

(*b*) Each vessel engaged in pair trawling may exhibit:

(i) by night, a searchlight directed forward and in the direction of the other vessel of the pair;

(ii) when shooting or hauling their nets or when their nets have come fast upon an obstruction, the lights prescribed in 2 (*a*) above.

3. *Signals for purse seiners*

Vessels engaged in fishing with purse seine gear may exhibit two yellow lights in a vertical line. These lights shall flash alternately every second and with equal light and occultation duration. These lights may be exhibited only when the vessel is hampered by its fishing gear.

ANNEX III

Technical details of sound signal appliances

1. *Whistles*

(*a*) *Frequencies and range of audibility*

The fundamental frequency of the signal shall lie within the range 70–700 Hz.

The range of audibility of the signal from a whistle shall be determined by those frequencies, which may include the fundamental and/or one or more higher frequencies, which lie within the range 180–700 Hz (± 1 per cent) and which provide the sound pressure levels specified in paragraph 1 (*c*) below.

(*b*) *Limits of fundamental frequencies*

To ensure a wide variety of whistle characteristics, the fundamental frequency of a whistle shall be between the following limits:

(i) 70–200 Hz, for a vessel 200 metres or more in length;

(ii) 130–350 Hz, for a vessel 75 metres but less than 200 metres in length;

(iii) 250–700 Hz, for a vessel less than 75 metres in length.

(*c*) *Sound signal intensity and range of audibility*

A whistle fitted in a vessel shall provide, in the direction of maximum intensity of the whistle and at a distance of 1 metre from it, a sound pressure level in at least one 1/3rd-octave band within the range of frequencies 180–700 Hz (± 1 per cent) of not less than the appropriate figure given in the table below.

Length of vessel in metres	*1/3rd-octave band level at 1 metre in dB referred to 2×10^{-5} N/m²*	*Audibility range in nautical miles*
200 or more	143	2
75 but less than 200 ...	138	1·5
20 but less than 75 ...	130	1
Less than 20	120	0·5

The range of audibility in the table above is for information and is approximately the range at which a whistle may be heard on its forward axis with 90 per cent probability in conditions of still air on board a vessel having average background noise level at the listening posts (taken to be 68 dB in the octave band centred on 250 Hz and 63 dB in the octave band centred on 500 Hz).

In practice the range at which a whistle may be heard is extremely variable and depends critically on weather conditions; the values given can be regarded as typical but under conditions of strong wind or high ambient noise level at the listening post the range may be much reduced.

(*d*) *Directional properties*

The sound pressure level of a directional whistle shall be not more than 4 dB below the sound pressure level on the axis at any direction in the horizontal plane within $\pm$ 45 degrees of the axis. The sound pressure level at any other direction in the horizontal plane shall be not more than 10 dB below the sound pressure level on the axis, so that the range in any direction will be at least half the range on the forward axis. The sound pressure level shall be measured in that 1/3rd-octave band which determines the audibility range.

(*e*) *Positioning of whistles*

When a directional whistle is to be used as the only whistle on a vessel, it shall be installed with its maximum intensity directed straight ahead.

A whistle shall be placed as high as practicable on a vessel, in order to reduce interception of the emitted sound by obstructions and also to minimize hearing damage risk to personnel. The sound pressure level of the vessel's own signal at listening posts shall not exceed 110 dB (A) and so far as practicable should not exceed 100 dB (A).

(f) Fitting of more than one whistle

If whistles are fitted at a distance apart of more than 100 metres, it shall be so arranged that they are not sounded simultaneously.

(g) Combined whistle systems

If due to the presence of obstructions the sound field of a single whistle or of one of the whistles referred to in paragraph 1 (*f*) above is likely to have a zone of greatly reduced signal level, it is recommended that a combined whistle system be fitted so as to overcome this reduction. For the purposes of the Rules a combined whistle system is to be regarded as a single whistle. The whistles of a combined system shall be located at a distance apart of not more than 100 metres and arranged to be sounded simultaneously. The frequency of any one whistle shall differ from those of the others by at least 10 Hz.

2. *Bell or gong*

(a) Intensity of signal

A bell or gong, or other device having similar sound characteristics shall produce a sound pressure level of not less than 110 dB at 1 metre.

(*b*) *Construction*

Bells and gongs shall be made of corrosion-resistant material and designed to give a clear tone. The diameter of the mouth of the bell shall be not less than 300 mm. for vessels of more than 20 metres in length, and shall be not less than 200 mm. for vessels of 12 to 20 metres in length. Where practicable, a power-driven bell striker is recommended to ensure constant force but manual operation shall be possible. The mass of the striker shall be not less than 3 per cent of the mass of the bell.

3. *Approval*

The construction of sound signal appliances, their performance and their installation on board the vessel shall be to the satisfaction of the appropriate authority of the State where the vessel is registered.

ANNEX IV

Distress signals

1. The following signals, used or exhibited either together or separately, indicate distress and need of assistance:

(*a*) a gun or other explosive signal fired at intervals of about a minute;

(*b*) a continuous sounding with any fog-signalling apparatus;

(*c*) rockets or shells, throwing red stars fired one at a time at short intervals;

(*d*) a signal made by radiotelegraphy or by any other signalling method consisting of the group · · · – – – · · · (SOS) in the Morse Code;

(*e*) a signal sent by radiotelephony consisting of the spoken word "Mayday";

(*f*) the International Code Signal of distress indicated by N.C.;

(*g*) a signal consisting of a square flag having above or below it a ball or anything resembling a ball;

(*h*) flames on the vessel (as from a burning tar barrel, oil barrel, etc.);

(*i*) a rocket parachute flare or a hand flare showing a red light;

(*j*) a smoke signal giving off orange-coloured smoke;

(*k*) slowly and repeatedly raising and lowering arms outstretched to each side;

(*l*) the radiotelegraph alarm signal;

(*m*) the radiotelephone alarm signal;

(*n*) signals transmitted by emergency position-indicating radio beacons.

2. The use or exhibition of any of the foregoing signals except for the purpose of indicating distress and need of assistance and the use of other signals which may be confused with any of the above signals is prohibited.

3. Attention is drawn to the relevant sections of the International Code of Signals, the Merchant Ship Search and Rescue Manual and the following signals:

(*a*) a piece of orange-coloured canvas with either a black square and circle or other appropriate symbol (for identification from the air);

(*b*) a dye marker.

Notes

Notes